Constructing China

Constructing China

Clashing Views of
the People's Republic

Mobo Gao

PLUTO  PRESS

First published 2018 by Pluto Press
345 Archway Road, London N6 5AA

www.plutobooks.com

British Library Cataloguing in Publication Data
A catalogue record for this book is available from the British Library

ISBN   978 0 7453 9982 9   Hardback
ISBN   978 0 7453 9981 2   Paperback
ISBN   978 1 7868 0242 2   PDF eBook
ISBN   978 1 7868 0244 6   Kindle eBook
ISBN   978 1 7868 0243 9   EPUB eBook

This book is printed on paper suitable for recycling and made from fully
managed and sustained forest sources. Logging, pulping and manufacturing
processes are expected to conform to the environmental standards of the
country of origin.

Typeset by Stanford DTP Services, Northampton, England

Simultaneously printed in the United Kingdom and United States of America

Contents

List of Abbreviations

CCP	Communist Party of China
CR	Cultural Revolution
EEZ	exclusive economic zone
GDP	gross domestic product
GLF	Great Leap Forward
PLA	People's Liberation Army
PRC	People's Republic of China
ROC	Republic of China
SCS	South China Sea
SEM	Socialist Education Movement
SFPC	State Family Planning Commission

Acknowledgements

This book has been in the making for over a decade and in a way it is a sequel to *The Battle for China's Past: Mao and Cultural Revolution* published in 2008 by Pluto. I have since then been receiving emails that either comment on or ask questions about that book, or contents and arguments in that book, many from high school students. I therefore, first of all, thank David Castle of Pluto for the publication of my first book with the publisher and for David's unfailing support from the beginning to the end during the long process of my working on this book, with valuable suggestions and patience.

A scholarly book product of this kind cannot be accomplished without assistance and support of colleagues in the field. I would especially like to mention Kerry Brown, David Goodman, Michael Dutton, Lin Chun, Daniel Vukovich, Joel Andreas, Dorothy Solinger, and Yan Hairong who have made various valuable comments at one time or another. They of course don't necessarily agree with all, or indeed any, of what I say in the book. Any and all mistakes and errors are mine.

A special acknowledgement of thanks has to be made for Professor Xu Youyu of Shanghai University. Many times I had to request Professor Xu to check publication details of some citation of Chinese references in this book. With his enormous network of expertise in China Professor Xu never fails in obtaining the right answers or solutions.

I am also grateful to the five anonymous reviewers of the book proposal, although one of the five would not make any specific comments because, as stated by the reviewer, he or she could not agree with me whatsoever to start with. Or something like that.

I would like to take this opportunity to thank my colleagues and friends, Dr Xie Baohui of the University of Adelaide for his assistance in the technicality of some charts and numbers, Professor Gregory McCarthy of Peking University and Dr Lian Jia of Shandong University for their comments.

Finally, let me thank the Pluto team, who have worked with professional diligence on the book, especially Neda Tehrani, Robert Webb, and Dan Harding.

Introduction

THE RIGHT TO KNOWLEDGE

In June 2016, at a news conference, when a Canadian journalist put a human rights question to Wang Yi, the Chinese foreign minister, who was visiting Canada (Buckley 2017), Mr. Wang lost his cool and was visibly angry. While most would agree that the Chinese authorities should learn how to handle tough questions from the media in general and Western media in particular, what Mr. Wang interpreted as lecturing is a good starting point for discussing the relationship between the production of knowledge and rights. In the West it appears to be taken for granted that a journalist should be asking politicians tough questions, so as to hold them accountable. In his reply, Mr. Wang, however, suggests that the journalist has no right to ask such questions if she does not know China. While Mr. Wang accuses the Canadian journalist of being arrogant, the Western media and social media responses generally take Mr. Wang to be arrogant. Why the difference in response? And why was Mr. Wang so upset?

This has something to do not only with the production of knowledge but also the right to knowledge, which is related to history as the people in China see it. From one perspective, China not only was invaded, semi-colonized, exploited and plundered but also, and because of that experience, does not have the right to knowledge. The Chinese don't have what is called *huanyu quan* (discursive right) on the international stage. What is right and wrong, what is good or bad, what should be valued and what is legitimate are dictated to the Chinese by the West. Ultimately, the West has the right to knowledge and has the power and resources to produce knowledge about China—to construct China.

This sense of frustration and powerlessness is demonstrated by current discussions among some Chinese thinkers who use a set phrase to capture the phenomenon. The Mandarin-speaking Chinese tend to use set phrases that are neat and succinct to refer to a situation or event, like 9/11 is used in the US. For instance, the Chinese would use a set phrase "June the Fourth" (*liu si*) to refer to the Tiananmen events of 1989, or "people mountain people sea" (*ren shan ren hai*) to refer to a packed crowd.

In the past decade or so, there has been a six-syllable phrase floating around the intellectual discussion circle—*ai da, ai e, ai ma* (挨打，挨饿，挨骂)—the first two syllables mean "to endure defeats in wars" or "to endure aggression," the second two mean "to endure hunger" and the last two "to endure being lectured." These Chinese people understand modern Chinese history as a history of China bearing the consequences of being defeated in wars ever since the first Sino-British Opium War in 1839–42, the so-called history of a "Hundred Years of Humiliation." The Chinese had endured hunger even since one could remember. To the majority of the Chinese, the China led by Mao, especially since the Korean War in 1950, no longer suffered defeat at the hands of foreign aggression. So *ai da* is gone.

The post-Mao reform is understood to have bidden goodbye to hunger. So *ai e* is gone. With the two enduring and sufferable situations gone, China now endures being lectured, *ai ma*, by the West, for moral inferiority, for its lack of democracy and its abuse of human rights, or indeed for anything they can think of: currency manipulation, taking millions of jobs from the West, stealing Western technology, etc.

In other words, the Chinese government is not legitimate. Hence Wang Yi's indignation: China has lifted 600 million of people out of poverty; China has managed to become the second largest world economy in a short period of time. "Do you know China?"—Wang asked the journalist whether she had ever been to China. For Wang, if you have not been to China, how do you have the knowledge to talk about China? Wang did not have in mind the individual human right of freedom of speech: of course he knew that a journalist in Canada at a press conference had the right to ask him any question. To Wang it was not an issue of political or civil rights but that of whether you are qualified to talk about something you have no knowledge of. Therefore, his term the "right to speak about" was not about a political right but an epistemological right: the right to knowledge.

The incident demonstrates not only the complex issue of rights but also the complex issue of knowledge: an epistemological right which in many ways is a political right, raising questions over categories of knowledge and how knowledge is produced.

EPISTEMOLOGICAL RIGHT

This epistemological right has two traditions in China: one traditional and one Maoist. The contemporary Maoist tradition was coined by Mao himself, in the form of "you have no right to speak about something if you have not done any research on it" (*meiyou diaocha yanjiu jiu meiyou fayan quan*). Mao's own credentials as a leader of the peasant revolution was based partly on one of his earliest influential writings titled *The Hunan Peasant Movement Report*. In fact, some of the Cultural Revolution (CR) violence was inspired by the proclaimed violence during the peasants' anti-landlord movement described in this report; evidence that knowledge produced in such a revolutionary discourse guides human behaviors several generations later.

"You have no right to speak about something if you have not done any research on it" had become one of the Communist Party of China's (CCP) governance technologies. Following the rationale that knowledge can be gained from experience and from participation and observation, Mao sent his most beloved son, Mao Anying, to work and live in the countryside as soon as the latter returned from the Soviet Union to Yan'an. Mao also sent one of his daughters to rural farms during the CR. The movements of "up to the mountains and down to the country-side" (*shangshan xiaxiang*), and "May the Seventh Cadres Schools" (*wuqi ganxiao*),* were also associated with this epistemological right.

By the same token, upon the serious consequences of the Great Leap Forward (GLF), Mao sent all of his bodyguards to their own hometowns, and some office personnel, to various places to gather information about the real situation at the grassroots level. During the beginning of the CR, Mao and his radicals sent hundreds of army officers all over the country to gather information (Qi Benyu 2016). This contemporary tradition of epistemological right is still held in high esteem as governance technology. Thus, the Chinese government still carry out a lot of experi-mentation before a policy is implemented. The most celebrated example is the special economic zone of a small fishing village, Shenzhen, where the policy of attracting foreign investment was experimented with before it unfolded all over China. Mr. Wang Yi's undiplomatic outburst is another example of this epistemological belief.

---

* On May 7, 1966, a letter to Lin Biao Mao advocates the idea that army soldiers should not just be trained to fight but also need to participate in studies, in political discussions and in material production. During the mid-period of the CR party officials and government bureaucrats were sent to grassroots units, like the factory floor, farms or rural China to participate in production labor. Hence it is called the May Seventh School.

The traditional strand of the tradition of this epistemological right to knowledge is the Confucian foundation of meritocratic legitimacy of ruling and governance. In the *Book of Rites: The Great Learning*, the Master says that to maintain peace under heaven the country has to be governed. To govern the country the family has to be put in order. To have the family in order, one has to cultivate oneself. To cultivate oneself one has to put one's mind in the right place. To have one's mind in the right place one has to be sincere. To be sincere one has to investigate. After this investigation, one will have the knowledge. Once you have the knowledge you will be honest. From honesty to the right mind, from the right mind to personal cultivation and from personal cultivation one is able to have order in the family: then one can govern the country so as to achieve peace under heaven.* According to this line of reasoning, knowledge consists of facts or truth in existence to be found by an honest person who has the sincerity to govern for the peace of the world. Apart from the fact that there is a questionable assumption that a ruler would be honest and sincere, what the Master takes for granted is also the questionable reductionist conceptualization of knowledge—an issue that I will come back to later—very different from the postmodern conceptualization that knowledge does not exist innocently for one to find: it has to be produced.

ANTI-ORIENTALISM IN POST-DENG CHINA

Edward Said's groundbreaking conceptualization of Orientalism (Said 1978) was very much inspired by Foucault's powerful argument for the relationship between power and the production of knowledge. According to this Foucauldian take on imperial discourse by Said, the cultural construct of the knowledge of Orientalism was, by design or necessity, a strategy of constructing a positive image of the Western Self while casting the "East" as its negative alter ego Other. "The Orient has helped to define Europe (or the West) as its contrasting image, idea, personality, experience." Orientalist knowledge has been so pervasive that "Orientals are seen to be perpetrating Orientalism no less than

---

* The full Chinese version is reproduced here; the English is my own interpreted translation: "古人欲明德于天下者，先治其国；欲治其国者，先齐其家；欲齐其家者，先修其身；欲修其身者，先正其心；欲正其心者，先诚其意；欲诚其意者，先致其知。致知在格物。格物而后知至，知至而后意诚，意诚而后心正，心正而后身修，身修而后家齐，家齐而后国治，国治而后天下平."

'non-Orientals'" (Lau 2009). There is a non-Oriental Orientalism in which knowledge producers with Eastern affiliations not only accept the Orientalist knowledge but also comply with perceived expectations of Western readers, as shown in Zhang Yimou's film *Raise the Lanterns*, in which the so-called Chinese tradition of family life and sexual ploys are reinvented for exoticism. In order to combat this new Orientalism in the twenty-first century, some scholars call for what are re-Orientalist discursive practices and rhetorical strategies as sites of subversion to expose the power of Orientalist discourse among the non-Oriental, so as to provide avenues for questioning the endurance of Orientalist practices today (Lau and Mendes 2011).

Along similar lines, some Chinese writers argue that some Chinese people themselves reproduce Orientalist knowledge about China. By twisting the term "reverse racism"* for their own purported use, these writers argue that the elation of this kind of knowledge produced by some Chinese—from the celebrated May Fourth Movement activist Dr. Hu Shi to the much-revered Qian Zhongshu, from contemporary popular essay writers such as Yu Shicun and Wang Xiaobo and fiction writer Wang Shuo to propagandist politicians like Ma Licheng—demonstrates reverse racism in the sense that anything Chinese is denigrated and condemned. These Chinese *fenqing* (angry young men) argue that China should fight against this kind of reverse racism which advocates self-hatred, and self-dwarfing (*ziwo aihua*). One prominent writer of this group of post-Deng writers, Wang Xiaodong, calls this kind of reverse racism the slavery of the Western master (*yangnu*). According to him and other *fenqing*, China should express its unhappiness with the current state of affairs (Song et al. 2009), and should be able to say no to the West (Song Qiang et al. 1996).

CHINESE NATIONALISM?

The reaction of the angry young Chinese men against the epistemological rights of the West is typically interpreted as Chinese nationalism. Barack Obama, an eloquent speaker who charmed both the Right and Left in the West, for instance, took this line of discourse and warned in an

---

* "Reverse racism" as a concept and as a set of political activities arose from the struggle of black people against racism at the hands of white people. Nelson Mandela both condemned "reverse racism" (MacGregor 1995) and was accused of being a reverse racist (Gumoisai 1993 and Dunn 1998).

interview with *The Atlantic* of a China that would "resort to nationalism as an organising principle" (quoted in Eric Li 2017).* The interpretation of this strong Chinese tide against Orientalism as Chinese nationalism in some ways makes sense, as China's economic take-off paved a path for the Chinese to recover some confidence in their own culture and the dignity of China as a nation. However, this kind of approachable and easiest popular conceptualization of Chinese nationalism leaves us with more problems than answers. For instance, is China a nation state? Which nations of the Chinese state are Chinese nationalist?

In countries like Australia and the US, the indigenous nations are either wiped out or uprooted. The white settlers formed their nation states. Gradually people of other national backgrounds migrated to these states as citizens. These new migrants don't form their own distinct culture, language and economic national identity even though the first generation of them may cling on to similar ethnic communities. They are all called Australians or Americans. In contrast, the Chinese state has not wiped out or uprooted the indigenous peoples, 56 of them are officially recognized, though some of them could arguably be said to have been pushed aside by migrants of other national groups, mostly by what is called the Han nationality. Most of these people have stayed and lived where they originally belonged and their populations increased dramatically (Sautman 2001, 2006). It is very hard to say therefore what the nation, or nations, of the Chinese state are. What is Chinese nationalism? Is it nationalism of the Chinese state, or nationalism of the Han Chinese, who are the majority? If the latter, who are the Han Chinese?

HEGEMONY OVER THE RIGHT TO KNOWLEDGE
AND CONCEPTUAL PARADIGM

Apart from addressing the questions raised above, this book aims to explore some more conceptually challenging issues of the relationship between rights and knowledge. Why do the Chinese (the term Chinese being very ambiguous, an issue that is dealt with later on in the book) either exercise self-denial or self-hatred, like the May Fourth Movement radicals who wanted to disown the Chinese tradition and the post-Mao

---

* Obama's famous remarks during his visit to Australia—that if the Chinese were to live like us we would need five or six planets—infuriated some angry young Chinese men, as it implied that only Western people are allowed to live a life of comfort and luxury.

self-claimed liberals who wanted to disown not only the Mao era but also the very idea of revolution? The underlying reason is that they have no right to knowledge. They either reproduce, by translation or reinterpreting, the kind of knowledge that is fed to them from the West, often without proper digestion, or else they could not produce anything.

The response to this state of affairs from the Chinese state machine has been different and changing. In the era of Deng, the state response from the lack of Chinese knowledge of China was to shelve political discussion so as to develop the economy, a strategy diagnosed by the prominent scholar Wang Hui as "depoliticized politics" (Wang Hui 2003). This strategy is neatly expressed in Deng's two dictums of "no debates" and "development [of the economy] is main principle." When Jiang Zemin came to hold power, the so-called "three representatives" were propagated as theoretically innovative, which basically was an attempt to answer the question of what the CCP was for in China at that time. The answer was: the CCP represented (1) advanced productive forces, (2) advanced culture and (3) the fundamental interest of the broad masses of people. This dictum therefore justified the enrolment into the CCP of well-known elites engaged in either material or cultural production, such as capitalist entrepreneurs and popular media stars. During the leadership of Hu Jintao, the idea of "harmonious development" was advocated so as to shift emphasis from development at all costs—as the grave consequences of such a policy were too obvious—to attention to environmental issues and societal cohesion that had been cracked by disparity. Finally, with Xi Jinping in power, there is a drive toward a balanced knowledge of China among the three traditions: the Chinese traditional tradition, the Maoist revolutionary tradition and the tradition of learning from the West (Gan Yang 2007). To achieve such a balance Xi wants to de-emphasize the West slightly and to recover some value from both the Chinese tradition and the Mao era. In his attempt at such a balancing act, Xi is seen to be the most repressive leader since the 1989 Tiananmen events (Ringen 2016b) and is predicted to fail in his attempt (Shambaugh 2015).

It is far from clear whether Xi can succeed in building up his narrative of China in what he calls "China's Dream," since he has just finished his first term as the number one leader in China. What is clear is that there is not yet knowledge of China that is accepted by both the Chinese and the West. The ideas of "the Beijing Consensus" (Cooper 2004) and the "China Model" (Dirlik 2016) floated around for a while as tantalizing conceptualizations of Chinese knowledge, but they did not stay long enough to sustain intellectual attention. This attempted knowledge of China is not taken seriously, because the West fundamentally has hegemony over the right to knowledge. This kind of hegemony does not have much to do with restriction of freedom or even overt power of imposition. I am practicing my freedom now by questioning Western hegemony. This is precisely the power of Western hegemony as it does not have to impose overt restrictions. The Chinese impose restrictions on academic freedom precisely because they don't have the hegemonic right to knowledge. Their restriction and repression on freedom further delegitimizes their discursive qualifications. This is a vicious circle for the Chinese while it is a virtual circle for Western hegemony. Therefore it is in the national interest of Western scholars to promote this virtuous circle for the West and vicious circle for China. The powerful and stronger produce knowledge which in turn serves the interests of the powerful and the stronger while weakening the weak.

The book argues that because Western hegemony on epistemological rights was formulated during the long process of imperialism and colonialism that was global and transnational, the national interests of Western nations and transnational interests very often overlap.

By pointing out the connection between knowledge production/knowledge consumption and national interest I am not arguing that all of the seekers of knowledge and producers of knowledge, either consciously or even unconsciously, produce knowledge exclusively for their own national interests. The fact that there are what Wang Xiaodong calls "reverse racists" and Orientals in China who practice Orientalism suggests that there are those who pursue knowledge from what they think is right versus wrong and good versus bad. This is why Chinese Orientals justify their position by arguing that it is in China's national interest to adopt Western knowledge.

In other words, there are academics, scholars, think tank specialists and journalists who pursue their individual interests and knowledge based on their belief in some particular conceptualization of the world they live in, such as the conceptualization of democracy and human rights. The hard science scientific community and the social science and humanities community work very much within conceptual and intellectual paradigms (Kuhn 1962) in any particular time and space. The paradigm within which most work since the collapse of the former Soviet Union, or the "end of history," which is used to lecture the Chinese, is that of human rights and democracy. This intellectual paradigm serves the geopolitical interest of the West, irrespective of whether any particular individual producer or consumer of the knowledge of truth realizes it.

There are some who try to break the straitjacket of this intellectual paradigm. The recent effort to give the Chinese some legitimacy to access a right to knowledge is very articulate (Bell 2015) but again, predictably, met with strong critiques (Nathan 2015 and Fish 2015). Although scholars like Ryan Mitchell have presented a nuanced understanding of what Bell is trying to say, such as what is democracy and whether democracy has merits depending on contexts and on how ideals are transformed in actual situations (Mitchell 2015), the argument that China is not a democracy is enough to put any "panda hugger" on the defensive. Only democracy can render a government legitimate, and only democracy can balance power and hold those in power accountable. Such a paradigm of what I call the democracy thesis is so hegemonic that any attempt to dismount its right to knowledge is almost impossible.

THE POVERTY OF THE EPISTEMOLOGICAL RIGHT TO KNOWLEDGE

The epistemological root to Chinese Foreign Minister Wang Yi's diplomatic outburst that those who do not know about China have no right to talk about it has too many romantic but naïve assumptions: that knowledge can be gained by study, that knowledge gained from study is the truth of nature and that there is a two-way relationship between knowledge and goodwill—if you have goodwill you can reach knowledge and knowledge will lead you to goodwill. That is why some Chinese believe that by assisting people outside China to study the Chinese language and culture through, say, the Confucius Institute, the people of the world will know the truth about China, and will be friendly or less hostile to it. This naïve or reductionist epistemology does not embrace the complexity of knowledge and its context: that knowledge is constructed and that there are no independent facts or theory. Even the truth of physics is found by postulates and then has to be proved or falsified by practice. Those like Wang Yi who believe the reductionist epistemology have yet to understand that social phenomena can be evaluated from different perspectives and therefore different knowledge can be produced for the same phenomenon. Perspectives on China and the Chinese always involve politics, and perspectives on international affairs always involves geopolitics. We need to come round to the conceptual understanding that anyone can have different knowledge about China, that China is never completely knowable, that whether one is friendly with China has less to do with knowledge and more to do with attitude; whether one has a friendly attitude toward China is political.

The rise of China, a phenomenon that is arguably the single most significant event of our time, causes a lot of anxiety all over the world. One expression of this anxiety is the increasing media and scholarly coverage of China's internal and international policies and actions. There is also profound anxiety from grassroots communities in the West. They are anxious to know what life will be like if the Chinese come to dominate the world. Knowledge of China is thus in huge demand. There is therefore a need to inquire about how knowledge of China comes about. Who formulates knowledge of China and on what basis? This book addresses the issue of what we know about China and what kind of knowledge of China is produced for what consumption.

The book aims to show that the production of knowledge of China is a construction which is the result of a combination of national and transnational interest, as well as the result of a conceptual paradigm. National interest may underline much of the research into and about China. And many of the individual scholars and researchers may not be able to produce knowledge about China outside the national interest box. Transnational interest includes class interest, ideological orientation and religious and political values and beliefs.

The overall aim of this book is to show that knowledge of China should not be taken as given. Instead, it should be examined within the context of production and consumption. This is more or less a common-sense wisdom accepted in most other fields of humanities and social sciences, but not in the field of Sinology, especially contemporary Chinese studies. The reason for this state of the field is that the production and consumption of knowledge of contemporary China is far too political both inside and outside China.

The book will demonstrate that there are no theory- or framework-independent facts to be discovered about China. There are statistics, but statistics can be structured for specific consumption, and even solid empirical statistics need to be interpreted so as to be considered as knowledge. For instance, statistics show that during both the GLF and the CR, two periods generally accepted both inside and outside China as disastrous, there was a mushroom of local industrial and entrepreneurial initiatives. Those who are theoretically oriented toward anti-communism and who consider the Chinese Communist regime under Mao Zedong as evil would use these statistics to argue that those local initiatives were grassroots resistance against the oppressive regime, defying China's Stalinist planned economy. However, those who are sympathetic with China's efforts toward building socialism will use these statistics to argue for the opposite: it was during these two periods that Mao and the Chinese government launched policies to encourage local initiative so as to break down the straitjacket of the Soviet model of a planned economy.

It is not just a matter of using the same dataset to produce different kinds of knowledge for specific consumption. This book will also show that different producers of knowledge select different datasets while ignoring other data about the same event or same personality. Thus the post-Mao authorities allow the publication of data that show the bad aspects of the CR but not the positive side, and allow the publications that show Deng Xiaoping in a good light but not publications that show him in a bad light. Written by a high-profile American academic, Vogel's (2011) biography of Deng Xiaoping, published in English outside China, translated in Chinese subsequently, has only 30 or so pages covering Deng Xiaoping's life up to 1979. In his selected biographies of key people of the People's Republic of China (PRC) in the book, Mao is not even included. Vogel intends to produce the knowledge that the transformation of China did not take place until Deng became the paramount leader after the Third Plenum of Eleventh CCP Congress in 1978.

Furthermore, this book will demonstrate that some "facts" or data about China are conjectures to prove a point of certain knowledge for consumption by a Western audience. For instance, even though there is some kind of consensus that there was a famine following the radical policies of the GLF, the death toll of this disputed famine is anybody's guess, ranging from several million to 55 million. What is interesting is that those who are anti-Communist want to stretch the number as high as possible while those who are sympathetic to the Chinese Revolution would like to see the numbers as low as possible. What is also interesting is that the higher the numbers one proposes the more attention one gets in the West, as the reception of an English academic Frank Dikötter and the Chinese ex-journalist Yang Jisheng shows, in contrast to the work of Yang Songlin and Sun Jingxian.

By addressing the issue of how knowledge of China is produced with a specific purpose for particular consumers, the book intends to argue that in a world system that embeds inherent injustice and unfairness toward developing countries, those who want to challenge the established order have to bring the state in. Chinese nationalism, especially Chinese nationalism in the Mao era, in this context, is not Chinese ethnic or racial chauvinism, but a political project to counter the existing world order of Western dominance. It is not nationalism per se but political and economic independence.

The book also intends to demonstrate that some elements of China's revolutionary legacy have to be brought back in any discussion of Chinese internal politics and China's relationship with the outside world. Furthermore, the book aims to show that for transnational interest the neoliberals in China who want to join the existing world order and who are critical of the Chinese state from a human rights and democratic perspective may not want to place China's domestic politics, class interest and the West's transnational interest in historical contexts.

Finally, for the Left in the West who are critical of China, the book aims to argue that democracy versus authoritarianism is neither a useful research topic, nor fruitful political agenda. If the Left in the West is really serious about finding a new narrative for the human race on this planet, a whole range of conceptual paradigms in the context of the West should be deconstructed or unpackaged in seeking knowledge of China, as each of the chapters aims to argue.

The issue of who the Chinese are is very much related to the production and consumption of knowledge of China because it is about whom knowledge is produced for. In Chapters 2 and 3, the issues of race, ethnicity and nationality, as well as that of the so-called overseas Chinese, will be addressed. The chapters aim to argue that Western concepts of race, ethnicity and nationality are inadequate in addressing the issue of who the Chinese are. The term Chinese is undefinable in that it is not an ethnic term, nor is it a definite term referring to the citizens of China. The Republic Revolutionary Sun Yat-sen even called for the exclusion of Manchus as non-Chinese for his idea of a nation state of the Republic. The Nationalist Kuo Ming Tang (KMT) leader Chiang Kai-shek (Jiang Jieshi) claimed that the Chinese consisted of a lineage of five groups, the Han, the Mongols, the Manchus, the Tibetans and Hui (Muslims). When the PRC was established, Beijing called for applications for nationality status, and over time more than 200 applications were received. After many years of scholarly studies and debates 56 nationalities have officially been recognized. If the Tibetans and Uyghurs are not Chinese, why are the Manchu, Mongolians, Koreans, Zhuang, Naxi and so on called Chinese? On the other hand, if the English settlers in Australia and their descendants are not called overseas English why are the settlers, whose origin of migration was China and their descendants, called overseas Chinese? These issues are not only historical but also political, involving national and transnational interest, as well as a conceptual and intellectual paradigm of knowledge.

The issue of what China is very much relates to the production and consumption of knowledge of China because the unpacking of different contexts of China will lead to a different knowledge of China. China was not and has never been a nation state in a contemporary sense. There might have been an imagined civilization of China but there was not an imagined nation state of China until the beginning of the twentieth century. This does not mean there has been no concept of a "country home" (*guojia*) in pre-modern China. I will argue that neither the conceptualization of nation state nor that of "civilization state" is adequate in addressing the issue of what China is. In terms of territory, China became bigger and bigger over time, not because there was an ethnic Chinese who invaded and expanded its empire, like the Romans, but because it was invaded and conquered by its surrounding neighbors. Such was the case of the Yuan Dynasty as a result of the invasion from the Mongols, and the Qing Dynasty established by the invading Manchus. In fact this mutation and fusion as a consequence of conquest by invaders from the north and north-west went back as early as Nanbei Chao (*c.*420–589 AD), Wudai Shiguo (*c.*907–60), and Bei Song (960–1127). Until the modern ages when there was imperial and colonial invasion from the Western nation states, China had been a nationless state, or a state of nations. All those concepts from the Western conceptual paradigm such as empire, union, commonwealth don't fit in with a China that has come out of these historical circumstances. The Chinese concept of *tianxia* not only fails to capture the historical developments of China but also fails to represent contemporary China as it is Sino-centric, taking a cultural value position of the Chinese civilized versus the barbarians. Modern China is the reverse: since the end of the nineteenth century landmarked by the May Fourth Movement in 1919, the consensus among the Chinese political and intellectual elite has been and still is that Western cultural and political values are more civilized. Those in the West who claim that the Chinese want Western politicians to kowtow to China and that the Chinese are nationalist and arrogant and Sino-centric are actually not only barking up the wrong tree but also demonstrating a sense of entitlement, be it a government, state or the so-called Chinese.

In any community within a national boundary there are different groups of class interest. These different classes may have some national interest in common. For instance, when Britain was under the threat of Nazi German invasion even the working class was willing to submit themselves to the leadership of Winston Churchill, but voted him out soon after victory in World War II. Equally, the Chinese Nationalists and the Communists formed a united front, however fragile it was, to fight the Japanese invasion. Very often however, different classes of people are led by the ruling elite to believe that they have a common interest in nationalism. This kind of "false consciousness" germinated by a dominant intellectual paradigm at any given time is in total contrast to the self-consciousness of the ruling elite who always, if not all the time, have in mind transnational interest, defined as the capitalist interest that is built on the free flow of transnational capital to exploit labor in the most profitable locations regardless of nationality, and to change regimes in the name of human rights and democracy. Those who have the master mind of transnational interest include not only the transnational companies and financial institutions but also the political and intellectual elite. If the proposition that the "working class of the world unite for they have nothing to lose but chains" is not entirely an intellectual fiction, that the political and intellectual elite in China have the common transnational interest with their counterpart of the rest of the world is certainly a reality.

The Chinese government spokespeople are fond of repeating the cliché that the US, the most developed country, and China, the most populous developing country, should cooperate and complement each other to achieve a win-win situation. What will happen if and when the national interests of the two countries in particular, and the West in general, clash? Chapter 10 on national interest and transnational interest related to the intellectual elite in the West presents evidence of and analyzes how the Western intellectual elite produces knowledge of China for the consumption of either their perceived national interest, or for transnational interest. Because of the financial, military and technological dominance of the West, and their dominance of the production of knowledge, the national interest and transnational interest of most Western countries are often one and the same.

I argue that even in a genuine pursuit of the knowledge of China, there is no innocent single China to be discovered. As soon as one uses personal experience and/or abstracts from documented information to formulate knowledge one is taking a position. For example, even the seemingly innocent linguistic description of simplified Chinese characters versus traditional forms can easily be and is very often used as evidence of truth for anti-communism: the simplification of Chinese characters is viewed as the Communist barbarianism of destroying traditional Chinese culture.

For the political and intellectual elite in the West, national and transnational interest can be and very often are one and the same. For their Chinese counterparts, the situation is much more frustrating. During the Mao era they were coerced into the conceptual paradigm that their national interest was often in contradiction with the dominant capitalist transnational interest. But the post-Mao mainstream Chinese political and intellectual elite have become increasingly transnational. However, because of Western dominance, Chinese national interest and transnational interest are not always one and the same either in imagination or in reality. For example, independent Taiwan or Tibet would be good for transnational interest but not for Chinese national interest. Sometimes the Chinese intellectual and the political elite may find themselves in a dilemma when their national interest clashes with the transnational interest of the West.

Chapter 5 is not only a critique of the Chinese political and intellectual elite guided by the conceptual paradigm of *qimeng* (enlightenment), but also a dissection of the split personality of the Chinese political and intellectual elite. The *qimeng* paradigm, prominent during the 1980s and lingering a little longer during the 1990s, underlines what Chow calls the King Kong syndrome: China as a spectacular primitive monster whose despotism necessitates the salvation of its people by outsiders (Chow 1998). The battle cry of this *qimeng* was that a Western-style civilization of democracy and science was urgently required to enlighten the backward and uncivilized Chinese. For a brief period, roughly during the first 30 years of the PRC, the socialism-to-communism conceptual paradigm looked like an answer to the question of *qimeng*. Although being dangerously challenged in a few months in 1957, the leftist revolutionary paradigm remained dominant in the Mao era until toward the end of the CR. The increasing critique and condemnation of the Mao era started as soon as Mao was dead in 1976, and by the 1980s the *qimeng* paradigm was reignited and was renamed *xin qimeng* (neo-enlightenment). *Xin qimeng* argues that the 1949 Revolution kidnapped *qimeng* and that following the track of enlightenment had to be reassumed. After nearly a century of development through which dramatic changes rendered China unrecognizable by any standards, the Chinese political and intellectual elite still repeats the themes of the May Fourth Movement of bringing Western humanist enlightenment to dispel the Chinese darkness. While the *qimeng* paradigm toward the end of the twentieth century was liberating, to regurgitate the same paradigm in the 1980s is no more than somniloquism.

With the increasing development of China's economic power on the international stage, the *qimeng* or *xin qimeng* paradigm has faded from the Chinese intellectual scene in rhetoric but remains mainstream in content. The Chinese political and intellectual elite are now engaged in the fight over whether democracy and human rights, mainly political and civil rights, but not socio-economic rights, should be held as universal. They now have a split personality because they are caught in the contradiction between perceived Chinese national interest (such as the sovereignty issue over Taiwan) and transnational interest (the independence of Taiwan or even other parts of China), and the contradiction between not only traditional Chinese human values and modern Western values but also between different class interests.

What happened during the GLF as history is one battleground on which those who are sympathetic with the Chinese Revolution paradigm fight against those who hold firm to the intellectual paradigm of anti-communism and anti-Mao transnationalism. Chapter 9 on the GLF gives concrete examples of how knowledge of China is produced by selecting or even fabricating data. The representative work in China by Yang Jisheng and in the West by Frank Dikötter will also be dissected in this chapter.

Chapters 7 and 8 on the CR is another case study of how data are selected to produce knowledge of China for specific consumption. The interpretation and the remembering of the CR demonstrates class interest against Maoism and transnational ideology against communism. There is an enormous amount of work on this topic, both in Chinese and English. Alongside a critique of the mainstream literature on the issue Chapters 7 and 8 will present alternative knowledge on the CR from the perspectives of the working class and rural Chinese and with the hindsight of the socio-economic consequences of the post-Mao era reforms.

China's foreign policy is driven by China's political and intellectual elite's combined desire for and understanding of national interest and transnational interest. On the one hand, leaders of the Mao era and post-Mao era wanted to preserve and defend what they considered was the national interest. On the other hand, they also took into consideration and were in many ways constrained by transnational interests. However, Mao and the post-Mao leaders, especially Deng Xiaoping, had different transnational interests in mind. The Sino-Japanese relationship will be addressed as an example to support the above argument. For Mao, China's national interest and the class interest of the laboring people are one and the same. Therefore, the crime of Japan's invasion of China was the responsibility of the capitalist ruling class while the laboring people of Japan were also the victims. However, when the class paradigm was thrown out of the window by the post-Mao regime, Japan as a whole, and indeed the Japanese as an ethnic group, were to be held responsible for the atrocities. Hence the resurgence of Chinese nationalism regarding Japan, with or without explicit or implicit elite encouragement. Chapters 11 and 12 on China's foreign policy will not only discuss various issues of China's border disputes and the South China Sea (SCS) but also the underlying political and international rationale.

Given the dominance of Western powers in all spheres, including political, military, technological and conceptual paradigms in humanities and the social sciences, the production of knowledge of China is predominantly Western both inside and outside China. While an understanding of China derived from this mainstream Western dominance has its own insight and value, this book aims to show that an understanding of China can be gained from a different conceptual framework and from alternative perspectives. By critiquing the current understanding of China based on the predominant Western production of knowledge (either from the Left or the Right), this book provides arguments for such an alternative.

By demonstrating how complex historical China is and how diverse the Chinese are, the book argues that an understanding of China derived from the Western conceptualization of ethnicity, nation states, race and nationalism is inadequate. By analyzing the examples of the two most controversial events in the Mao era, the GLF and the CR, the book deconstructs how Western production of knowledge of China is based on political positions or a specific intellectual paradigm. The book argues that the Western Left needs to be critical of not only Western transnational interests which they benefit from, but also their privileged position of dictating intellectual agenda and political correctness, especially in relation to developing countries, including China. They should be reminded that their intellectual paradigm of human rights and democracy promotes the political agenda for the existing transnational structure, which in many ways is not only identical with their own national interest, but also identical with the interests of the ruling elite. At the center of the book is an examination of the relationship between national and transnational interest and how this relationship is related to the production and consumption of knowledge of China.

At least four conclusions can be drawn from this discussion of the complex relationship between them: (1) in any nation state there may be some interest that is common to all, e.g. against foreign invasion; (2) national interest and transnational interest may overlap, and can be identical for people of all classes in the leading Western nations due to the history of colonialism and imperialism; (3) national and transnational can be, but not always, one and the same for the ruling elite in developing countries; and (4) a position by the Chinese neoliberal intelligentsia of advocating the conceptual paradigm of universalism of human rights and democracy in fact works in favor of the existing transnational order, but against the interests of the working class in their own countries.

THE LITERATURE IN THE FIELD

The task of taking on the issue of understanding China from the point of view of Orientalism developed by Said has been done by China scholars such as Dirlik (1996), Hägerdal (1997), Martínez-Robles (2008), and Hung (2003). Two related books, again inspired by the approach of Orientalism, *Western Images of China* by Colin Mackerras (1989) and its Chinese counterpart by Zhou Ning, aim at a general historical survey of how China was viewed from the West. The edited volume *Sinographies: Writing China* by Eric Hayot, Haun Saussy and Steven G. Yao (2008), though not exactly an Orientalism approach, sets out to demonstrate different Chinas written in different texts, covering different time frames and genres of representation.

The closest publication to this book is the insightful *China and Orientalism: Western Knowledge Production and the PRC* (2013), in which Daniel Vukovich argues that there is a new Sinological form of Orientalism at work in the world that has shifted from a logic of "essential difference" to one of "sameness" or general equivalence. This book has one aim in common with Vukovich which is to dispel the myth of objective knowledge of China. However, this book adopts the approach of political economy. It aims to show not only that there is no apolitical scholarship but also that politics is not just race, ethnicity or the East versus the West. Regarding this book's examination of the complex relationship between national interests and transnational interests, Zak Cope's (2012) work on "Western working-class aristocracy" in its relation to the working class in developing countries is relevant.

By adopting a political economy perspective over a cultural studies perspective, this book is a critique of not only the Left and the Right in the West, but also the Chinese New Left's critique of the post-Mao Chinese Right. In this regard, Wang Hui's monumental work *The Rise of Modern Chinese Thought* (2015b) on modernity is relevant. The West, both Left and Right, either in the field of journalism, think tank, NGOs or academia, tend to employ "the Chinese themselves say so" logic, especially when the "say so" is to condemn the Chinese Revolution and the Mao era. However, there is a need to pay attention to the fact that the Chinese themselves are of different classes with different interests, and that the Chinese themselves can and do pick and choose facts and information for the production and consumption of knowledge. They follow fashionable conceptual paradigms. Even if we cannot claim that production of knowledge for particular class interests is wrong or right, correct or incorrect, we should be sophisticated enough to know and to show that there can be possible production of knowledge for other class interests, and we should be aware which class interest is dominating and why. In this sense this book is a critique of the field.

I

Scholarship, National Interest and Conceptual Paradigm

INTRODUCTION

Scholarship is not only historically complex but also contingent upon national interest, geopolitics and, no less significantly, upon a conceptual and intellectual paradigm at any specific time and space. The conceptual paradigm that frames CCP-led China as a totalitarian or dictatorial regime (Ringen 2016b) is still prevalent today. The Chang and Halliday claim (2005) that Mao was an evil monster who killed 70 million Chinese with pleasure is just one extreme example.

Not surprisingly, many serious scholars on China don't take Chang and Halliday seriously (Benton and Lin Chun 2009), but the "true" knowledge produced by Chang and Halliday has spread far and wide, and has been taken seriously not only, reportedly, by US President George W. Bush but also the last Governor of Hong Kong Chris Patten, who was later to be honored as the chancellor of Oxford University. One of the most credible media outlets, the BBC, applauded the book; the broadsheet paper *The Australian* listed Chang and Halliday's book as a 2005 Book of the Year; and journalist Nicolas Rothwell declared that "reading the book about the twentieth century's most bloodstained dictator was a litmus event" and that he "cannot recall finishing a book that inspired in me such sharp feeling of nausea, horror and despair" (Rothwell 2005: R5). One of the book's reviewers calls it "a work of unanswerable authority" and claims that Mao "is comprehensively discredited from beginning to end in small ways and large, a murderer, a torturer, an untalented orator, a lecher, a destroyer of culture, an opium profiteer, a liar" (Hensher 2005). "China's Monster, Second to None" is the title of a reviewer of Chang and Halliday in the authoritative *New York Times* (Kakutani 2005). Another authoritative Western media outlet, the German *Der Spiegel*, endorsed Chang and Halliday, as did the influential British political commentator William Hutton (Hutton

2005) and the veteran London School of Economics scholar Michael Yahuda (2005).

The book by Chang and Halliday as a history or biography of Mao is a fraud (Gao 2008). But why do so many intelligent and clever people endorse such a blatantly flawed book? The answer lies not only in national interests, transnational interests and the leftovers of Cold War discourse, but also in the "truths" of the social sciences and humanities that are in fact constructed narratives. Those who position themselves for certain national and transnational interests tend to believe in certain kinds of stories. It is the interaction of cerebral inclination with certain stories that formulates a conceptual paradigm that frames scholarship.

HARARI, TRUMP, NATIONALISM AND GLOBALISM

In his TED Talk, Yuval Noah Harari (2017) declares that twentieth-century Left versus Right politics is outdated and that now it is globalism versus nationalism. Harari argues, I think rightly, that all the major problems today are global, such as climate change, genetic engineering and unemployment—not due to Chinese migrant workers, but due to robots. Therefore nationalism will not work. Referring to the phenomenon of the current US President Donald Trump's constant utterances of "untruth," Harari argues that there is no such thing as post-truth in the era of Trump, because there have never been truths that are not constructed and there have never been truths that are not confined to human understanding at any specific time and space. As evidence Harari refers to the Bible. The only difference now as opposed to the past, is that the truth, or untruth in the Trump era, is not told by the established elite who think they naturally have the epistemological right to knowledge, but by a vulgar and unintellectual buffoon who can do this against all global gravity because of modern technology. Not very much unlike Mao during the CR, Trump avoided the normal taken-for-granted intellectual and media hierarchy by going straight to address "the masses" via Twitter.

However, it appears that the very clever buffoon is not a globalist but a nationalist, at least according to his utterances. This is the problem: while the solutions to all of the major issues require a globalist approach, especially in the powerful and domineering knowledge-producing West, issues seem to be more nationalist. It is an irony, not expected by many even a couple of years ago, that China under the leadership of Xi Jinping is even called upon to lead the world globally on climate change. Hasn't the Chinese government been accused of using nationalism to boost its legitimacy by almost all of the commentators almost all of the time?

US SCHOLARS AND US NATIONAL INTEREST

The most recent US think tank cum academic report on how to deal with China is a good case study of how scholarship is intertwined with national interest (Schell and Shirk 2017). The report was a result of a large undertaking involving many prominent US scholars including Orville Schell, Susan Shirk, Thomas J. Christensen, Elizabeth C. Economy, Andrew J. Nathan, David Shambaugh as well as Jeffrey A. Bader, David M. Lampton, Douglas H. Paal., J. Stapleton Roy and Michael D. Swaine, though the latter group were not listed as authors of the report. On top of that there are a number of think tank specialists who used to be in important US government positions such as Charlene Barshefsky, the former US trade representative, and the chief trade negotiator and principal trade policymaker for the US, Kurt M. Campbell, a former assistant secretary of state for East Asian and Pacific affairs, and Winston Lord, a former US ambassador to China.

The project also involved many prominent external experts including Joseph S. Nye Jr. and Roderick MacFarquhar of Harvard University; Henry M. Paulson from the Paulson Institute; Mickey Kantor of Mayer Brown, Barry Naughton and Peter Cowhey from the University of California, San Diego; Wendy Cutler from the Asia Society Policy Institute; Jeffrey I. Kessler of WilmerHale; Dennis Blair of the Sasakawa Peace Foundation, USA; Graham Webster of Yale University Law School; Harold J. Newman, Asia Society trustee; Kenneth Jarrett at the US Chamber of Commerce in Shanghai; and Alan Beebe of AmCham China.

Of the long-term issues—energy and climate change, global governance, Asia Pacific regional security, North Korean nuclear threat, maritime disputes, Taiwan and Hong Kong, human rights, defense and military relations, trade and investment relations—considered by the Task Force project, the report makes six major recommendations as priorities for the Trump administration:

1. North Korea: give up nuclear capabilities or face sanctions.
2. Prioritize US commitment to its allies, Japan and South Korea, and revival of the Trans-Pacific Partnership (TPP).

3. Trade with China: focus on job losses because of China, unfair trading and the need to "level the playing field."
4. South and East China Seas: China is assertive, the US should remain territorially neutral but maintain freedom of navigation plus an active US presence in the area, and should ratify the UN Convention on the Law of the Sea.
5. "Respond to Chinese Civil Society Policies that Harm US Organizations, Companies, Individuals, and the Broader Relationship," such as severely restricting (and in some cases block) US think tanks, non-governmental organizations, media outlets, and Internet companies from operating freely in China.
6. Take over leadership of the climate change issue.

In the context of what I aim to do in this chapter, there are a number of interesting points about the report's recommendations. To start with, let us look at the North Korean issue. Surely, North Korea will not launch a nuclear war with either South Korea, Japan or the US. The only rationale that one can think of is that North Korea wants to have nuclear weapons and launching facilities as a deterrent. It is North Korea that is afraid of aggression. Therefore, all the US and its allies need to do to maintain peace is to make a firm commitment that they would not invade North Korea unless and until North Korea makes the first move in aggression. It is very much in the media of the "international community" to support the US policy on North Korea by portraying its leader as a mad person, a crazy lunatic who certainly does not know what North Korea's national interest is.

When the Task Force project was in progress there was no envisioning of another mad man who would oppose the TPP in the name of the US national interest. Trump actually got elected on the promise of getting rid of the TPP. So does that mean Trump and his supporters do not know what the US national interest is? In fact the then seemingly more promising presidential candidate, Hillary Clinton, also disowned TPP, at least orally in her election campaign. To blame US unemployment on China is one of the most attractive slogans of the Trump team. One wonders why the elite in this group, the elite for which Trump and his supporters are supposed to have contempt for, share this sentiment with the latter. For most Chinese, and probably most people in developing countries, there has never been "a level playing field" for them. If and when they can gain a point or two in the law of the jungle it is the result of their sheer hard work and possibly avenging determination. The rules have been made by the developed countries in global organizations like the World Trade Organization (WTO), the International Monetary Fund and the World Bank, and it took China more than ten years to negotiate with the US to enter the WTO; one major member of this report was the chief US representative in these long and hard negotiations. One of the most stringent conditions for a developing country have been imposed on China's entrance to the WTO. Now the report claims that the field is not level. One should be reminded of what happened in the late nineteenth century in the "new continent": the Chinese gold diggers could manage to dig out some gold in the mines that had been mined and abandoned by the white miners. The white miners were very upset and screamed "the Chinks steal our gold." Clearly the truth can be framed differently and knowledge can be produced according to one's interests.

Equally interesting is how the rise of China pushed the US to change the rules of the game, when one reads recommendation four: it was of US national interest to ignore the UN Convention on the Law and Sea until China asserted its claim of sovereignty over the SCS. Finally, there is an urge for the US to take over the leadership on climate change. It does take some leadership globally to solve the issue of climate change, as argued by Harari in his TED Talk. However, China has not claimed to hold the leadership position on this or on any other issue. Most of the time since Deng Xiaoping has been in power, China has been trying to figure out what the Big Brother wants. Surely, a recommendation of a multilateral and more collaborative approach to climate change would have been better.

Another point is the question of who funded the project and why. The Task Force that produced this report involved a number of institutions, including the Center on US–China Relations founded in 2006 based in New York; the 21st Century China Center established in 2011 at the University of California, San Diego; the Annenberg Retreat at Sunnylands, also known as the "Camp David of the West," a non-profit foundation which convenes leaders in southern California and other locations for high-level meetings to address serious issues facing the nation and the world, including the 2013 summit between President Obama and President Xi of the PRC and the 2016 US-ASEAN leaders summit; the Carnegie Corporation of New York; the Henry Luce Foundation; the Janet and Arthur Ross Foundation; and Harold and

Ruth Newman. The institutions involved, and the individual contributors, are a mixture of academic and think tank centers, an indication of how the production of knowledge is not something concerning the ivory towers of scholarship anymore, if it was ever the case.

What also has to be noticed is the acknowledgment of the hospitality shown by "our friends at Oxford University, in particular Rana Mitter at the China Centre and Timothy Garton Ash at St. Antony's College." Appreciation of "the Japanese and South Korean consulates in New York City and their respective embassies in Washington, DC for … fact-finding missions to Tokyo and Seoul" is also acknowledged. The absence of any "Chinese" academic or Chinese involvement in the project is understandable on the basis that this is not a task force that provides recommendations on how to engage with China but how to deal with China. The preface of the report states that one assumption is "inherent in this report—that it is in the national interest of the US to strive, if possible, for stable and mutually beneficial relations with China, and to maintain an active presence in the Asia-Pacific region." How do you have mutually beneficial relations with China to maintain peace and stability in the region if you don't engage with China? This question is perhaps answered by the wording "if possible." In other words, if China doesn't contravene US national interest then there will be peace and stability. The authors of this report are already making concessions for the sake of peace if you compare them with Robert Kagan (Kagan 2017), whose *Foreign Policy* article headline is "Backing Into World War III: America Must Check the Assertive, Rising Powers of Russia and China Before It's Too Late."

This Task Force project and its recommendations are worthy of study for two main reasons. The first reason is that there is a tangible shift in conceptualization of how to deal with China. In other words, new knowledge needs to be and is being produced. The second reason is that it reveals how closely scholarship is related to what is perceived and conceived to be the national interest. Only the naïve Chinese anti-Maoist and anti-Communist "liberals" still hang on to the story of universal truth beyond national interest, as will be demonstrated in later chapters.

NATIONAL INTEREST AND MEARSHEIMER

It has either been taken for granted or specifically argued that US national interest in particular and Western interest in general serves the interest of the international community. Western hegemony is interpreted as maintaining international rule-based order and providing a public good. This is biblical knowledge of the post-World War II world. In the words of Pei Minxin, a US scholar of Chinese background, popular among the Western media because of his neoliberal critique of China, the West has the capacity to maintain the international rule-based order and provide global public goods (Pei 2017). Globalism is Americanism, which is good for everyone, as this shrewd metaphor exemplifies: Freedom's McDonald Golden Arch Gate flattens the globe. This epistemological truth is articulated strongly by Mearsheimer, the US realist international relations scholar:

> It is often said that the international relations (IR) scholarly community is too American-centric and needs to broaden its horizons. I disagree. In the mid-1970s, Stanley Hoffmann called IR an "American social science." That label was appropriate then, and it is still appropriate today especially with regard to all the important ideas and theories that dominate discourse in our discipline. This situation is not likely to change significantly anytime soon and for entirely legitimate and defensible reasons. Indeed, students inside and outside of the United States seem to read the same articles and books and for the most part employ the same concepts and arguments … I feel intellectually more at home in Beijing than Washington … So, when I speak in China— where there is a deep fascination with American IR theories—I sometimes start my talks by saying, "It is good to be back among my people." And I do not speak one word of Chinese, although I do speak the same language as my Chinese interlocutors when we talk about the basic realities of international politics. (Mearsheimer 2016)

These fascinating and candid remarks provide enough information for three important points: there is an almost innate assumption that globalism is Americanism; the US dominates the production and consumption of knowledge and is the key to truth; and finally, the Chinese scholarship community is not immune to it.

THE SOAS INCIDENT AND KNOWLEDGE PRODUCTION

The School of Oriental and African Studies (SOAS) of London University hit the headlines in early 2017 when journalists discovered that students, backed by many of their lecturers, had set up a campaign to "Decolonise Our Minds" by transforming the curriculum. The gist of this campaign is that students of Oriental and African studies should study the philosophies and literary cannons of Oriental and African countries as well as that of Western European countries. The event made news headlines because the students dared to suggest decentering the works of Kant, Locke and Smith. That would be the end of the world as we know it.

"They Kant Be Serious!" spluttered the Daily Mail headline in its most McEnroe-ish tone. "PC students demand white philosophers including Plato and Descartes be dropped from university syllabus." "Great thinkers too male and pale, students declare," trumpeted the *Times*. The *Telegraph*, too, was outraged: "They are said to be the founding fathers of Western philosophy, whose ideas underpin civilized society. But students at a prestigious London university are demanding that figures such as Plato, Descartes and Immanuel Kant should be largely dropped from the curriculum because they are white" (Malik 2017).

What SOAS academics and students in fact argued was that Enlightenment thinkers had a highly restricted notion of freedom; freedom as "the property of propertied white men." John Locke, for instance, "widely regarded as having provided the philosophical foundations of modern liberal conceptions of tolerance," was "a shareholder in a slaving company." Immanuel Kant, "often seen as the greatest of Enlightenment philosophers," held a "belief in a racial hierarchy, insisting that 'Humanity is at its greatest perfection in the race of the whites' and that 'the African and the Hindu appear to be incapable of moral maturity'" (Malik 2017). In other words, Enlightenment arguments about freedom and liberty were only for the superior, and it was this very philosophy that justified the colonial enterprises and the slave trade that were expanding precisely at the time when Enlightenment knowledge was produced and spread.

This debate on the Enlightenment is very much relevant to the theoretical underpinning of this book: Who constructs China, how is it constructed and for what purpose? Who produces what knowledge for who to consume? The SOAS campaigners argue that Enlightenment thinkers such as Kant were racist and that the Eurocentric knowledge produced by them served the purpose of European colonialization and imperialism.

If we just focus on Europe in and of itself at that time it is hard to repudiate the conclusion that the Enlightenment was transformative and liberating in Europe, in that fundamental tradition, faith and authority were questioned. But the point is that one cannot focus on Europe in and of itself because the world was already global, and Europe was transformed in the process of transforming the Other: the Orientals and Africans. Therefore the knowledge of Enlightenment was constructed in the process of civilizing the Other while affirming Europe itself. There was an internal dynamic in Europe, but the dynamic process had an external dimension.

This dynamic is expressed by the two streams of Enlightenment as discussed by Johnathon Israel (2001, 2006, 2011). The conservative stream, characterized by Eurocentrism and represented by Locke, Smith, Kant, Voltaire, Montesquieu and Hume, became the mainstream and serves the West's national and even racial interest, whereas the radical stream, according to Israel, is all-embracing, the heart and soul of the Enlightenment from which the colonized and developing countries should draw their theoretical and philosophical inspiration. One could argue that the Enlightenment conceptual paradigm not only inspired the French Revolution and the American Revolution, but also Marxism, the May Fourth Movement in China and the rise of the Communist Party at the beginning of the twentieth century. However, it is the con-servative thinkers that have been held high, especially in China (as I will demonstrate in later chapters), whereas the radical thinkers who provided the heart and soul of the Enlightenment, such as d'Holbach, Diderot, Condorcet and the Dutch philosopher Baruch Spinoza, are hardly known. Israel further argues that many radical enlighteners believed in anti-Christian naturalism, which had powerful roots in medieval Islamic philosophy and even had strong affinities with Chinese Confucianism. It was the radicals who were free of the Eurocentrism that marked the mainstream Enlightenment. According to this inter-pretation, Marxism is somewhat in the middle between the conservative and radical Enlightenment: radical in its critique of imperialism and colonialism but conservative in assuming that Western capitalism was progress, even though it had left a trace of destruction on "mummy" societies like China (Lin Chun 2013).

SOME CONSTRUCTED TRUTHS ABOUT CHINA

I have pointed to an apparent paradox or irony: the habitual, powerful and domineering knowledge produced in the West has been universalist, for example in the truth of the Bible, and the universal value of human rights and globalism, such as free trade and the global flow of capital, now tends to be more nationalist, while the accused offender of nationalist China is seen to be a defender of globalism. Why has there been such a change in a matter of years? The transformation has in fact been taking place for years, but it takes hindsight to realize what has been happening in one's life, as is always the case for mortal human beings. When wars to invade Iraq and Libya were launched, the West did not expect one of the consequences to be refugees flooding toward Europe. When neoliberalism triumphantly dominated the globe and when the Communist camp headed by the Soviet Union collapsed, it was not expected that the combination of global capital with competent cheap labor in China would compete with the West to the extent that the West would feel threatened.

Such a transformation demands conceptual examination. The transformation stops being paradoxical and ironic if we acknowledge that the knowledge produced by the domineering West is inherently incapable of explaining the process. The knowledge produced is ahistorical and historicist but not historical: the historicist and ahistorical truth is that history has to be the way that the West understands it: the Chinese government is illegitimate because the Chinese have been brainwashed and are without agency.

There are several constructed "truths" in the prevalent knowledge of China, some related to political structure and some to economic development. These constructed truths are stumbling blocks to a more nuanced understanding of China. One truth, propagated recently by Ringen, emeritus professor at Oxford University, is that China is authoritarian at best and dictatorial at worst. Ringen is proud to be a non-China expert, because for him the conceptualization of dictatorship is not only necessary but sufficient to describe current China. Confident that he can get the knowledge of China right, Ringen, in the words of William H. Overholt (2017: 126), "chooses every number that makes China look bad and systematically excludes more important numbers that would provide a balanced perspective." As pointed out by Overholt, Ringen merely picks a number but doesn't relate it to other numbers. For instance, he claims that the housing price is very high in China, which is true, but he does not add that 80 to 90 percent of Chinese families own their homes—probably the highest percentage in the world (interestingly some own more than one house largely because of the legacy left from the Mao era). Ringen argues that education costs are high, which is again true, but he does not add that China is now almost totally literate, from a point of total illiteracy in 1949. He does not mention the United Nation statistics which shows that the status of women in China is far superior to most Asian countries, including India and Japan.

Another truth is that there cannot be proper or healthy economic development in a planned economy controlled by the government. It is worse when the economy is not helped by the West. According to this truth, the post-Mao economic take-off is a miracle. Otherwise how can one explain the fact that China, a country so poor and so unfree, can have developed its economy to such a scale in a matter of three decades?

To say that economic development in post-Mao China is a miracle may just be a metaphor or a figure of speech, but to take this as it is and without further explanation in relation to the preceding years, i.e. economic development in the Mao era, is a biblical approach to history which is not only ahistorical but also historicist. If and when this historicist and ahistorical knowledge of economic development is unpacked, criticism of Chinese nationalism is not only outdated but is nationalist and may even be racist. If and when the historicist and ahistorical knowledge of political structure is unpacked, criticism of China's human rights, undoubtedly in existence, is still the leftover from the Cold War for its deliberate negligence of the issues of socio-economic rights.

In this connection, however, it is important to bear in mind the revealing insights developed in recent work by political economist Sean Starrs, quoted by Chomsky. By exploring some significant consequences of the neoliberal globalization of the world economy over the past generation, Starrs argues that corporate ownership of the world's wealth is becoming a more realistic measure of global power than national wealth, as the world departs more than before from the model of nationally discrete political economies. The results of his investigations are quite striking. It turns out that in virtually every economic sector—manufacturing, finance, services, retail and others—US corporations are well in the lead in ownership of the global economy. Overall, their ownership is close to 50 percent of the total, roughly the same maximum figure of estimated US national wealth in 1945 (Chomsky 2017).

Of all the truths about China the most fundamental theorem is the democracy thesis: welfare states are democratic states, whereas China is a power state that does not care about the people. Because India is declared the world's largest democracy it is hard for the democracy thesis believers to compare China with India. According to the UN Human Development Report 2015, quoted in Overholt (2017), infant mortality per 1,000 live births in China is 10.9 versus India at 41.4; child mortality per 1,000 in China is 12.7 versus India at 52.7; child malnutrition as a percentage of the population in China is 9.40 versus India at 22.7; and public expenditure as a percentage of gross domestic product (GDP) in China is 5.60 versus India at 4. But in the words of Overholt, "Ringen caricatures assumptions common in the Western literature on China: if only China would hold elections like India and the Philippines, its corruption would diminish, its growth would increase, its environmental problems would be minimal, and its people would obtain the welfare benefits they are denied by the extractive dictatorship" (Overholt 2017: 128).

Another axiom of truth is that the Chinese are nationalists (Gries 2004; Snelder 2014; Zhao Suisheng 2004; Callahan 2005; Wang Zheng 2014). The Chinese Communists were nationalist fanatics against the West, or the Chinese government uses nationalism to sustain their power and to cover their illegitimacy and to divert domestic anger externally. A non-democratic government that is not elected by the Western model of one person one vote can only be nationalist, and is nationalist whatever it does to defend China's national interest. In any case, there cannot be national interest for the Chinese people since they don't own the state. Very few bother to look at findings that the Chinese young are actually becoming less nationalistic (Schrader 2017).

An important and often taken-for-granted spin-off theorem of the democracies thesis is that a lack of democratic accountability breeds corruption (Pei Minxin 2016). The assumption is that only democratic institutions such as an independent judiciary and a free press can control corruption. As for the phenomenon of the revolving door channeling the in and out of politicians, intellectual elites, commercial companies and the industrial-military complex, corruptions in the so-called democracies in countries like India and the Philippines, or corruption in the newly developed democracies in South Korea and Taiwan, and lack of prevalent corruptions in non-democracies such as Hong Kong and Singapore, are just inconvenient details that cannot be allowed to disturb the conceptual integrity of the democracy thesis.

Finally, another truth often taken for granted about China is regarding personal struggles for power. Although it is fair to say that it is very hard and maybe too early to gauge what the Xi Jinping leadership is, there are attempts to jump to the conclusion of personal power struggle regarding whatever Xi does (Lam 2015; Li Cheng 2016). Veteran China-watcher Andrew Nathan (2017), in his review of Li and Pei, states that:

> Li is right, however, along with other analysts like David Shambaugh, to point out that Xi is challenging the fragile norms of the system by arrogating so much power to himself. He has violated the principle of collective leadership by taking control of most of the leading small groups—such as those on foreign affairs, domestic security, finance and economics, and promoting reform—and by creating a personality cult around himself under which he has been designated as the "core" of leadership. His anticorruption campaign has destroyed the networks of rivals like Bo Xilai, the former high-flying Party secretary of Chongqing, and Zhou Yongkang, the former security chief.

It is true that all politics involves power; but interpretations of Chinese politics based on personal power struggles fails to take into consideration not only specific policies, but also historical contexts. For instance, one of the historical contexts is that the Chinese model of development of environmental destruction and increasing disparity has come to the point where it is no longer sustainable. There is a need for authority to tackle the issue. As an example of specific policies, the anti-corruption campaign has to claim victims in order to deter further deterioration. To implement such an anti-corruption campaign in such a historical context Xi has to have the authority, unless he, similarly to Gorbachev, allows the system to collapse.

CONCLUSION: THE IMPORTANCE OF CONCEPTUAL FRAMEWORKS

The above discussion indicates that apart from national and transnational interest, research agendas and the production of knowledge—and therefore the construction of China—can also be framed by time- and space-specific conceptualizations of ourselves and of the world. In the process of constructing China, conceptual frameworks orientate one's selection not only of research agendas but also of empirical data.

The rise and fall of a rebel group in the US, the Concerned Asian Scholars, represents the importance of conceptual frameworks. A group of American scholars in the late 1960s and early 1970s, inspired by the revolutions in China including the CR, and disgusted by the consequences of the Vietnam War, organized themselves into what were the Concerned Asian Scholars. As Fabio Lanza (2016) demonstrates, these rebel scholars took the Chinese to be subjects—not as objects of study to be civilized, but subjects not only of their own destiny but with ideas as human beings. The Concerned Asian Scholars argue that academics are also political beings and that no scholarship is neutral. It is their belief that all research ultimately reflects a political standpoint. The very fact of accepting neutrality is making a position of acknowledging the status quo of Western dominance.

However, these rebels as a group did not have a conceptual framework to sustain themselves. They did not associate their critique of their teachers with a theory or with Marxism, which is the most likely candidate to frame their resistance against US imperialism. Even Noam Chomsky, one of the most articulate living intellectuals, who participated with the Concerned Asian Scholars, has no theoretical orientation except anarchism. Once the Vietnam War ended, and especially once the Chinese CR collapsed, with overwhelming evidence of victimization of the political and intellectual elite during the period, the American rebel group was disintegrated. Compassion becomes hatred for some, and any sympathy with China has become that of dissidents and human rights activists.

2

China, What China?

INTRODUCTION

The historical entity with the referent "China" before the Republic of Revolution in 1911, was, like previous dynasties in China's long history, not a nation state in the typical sense. The collapse of the Qing Dynasty in 1911 left the Republic of China (ROC) with a vast multinational territory, the government of which was weak amid warlordism, civil wars, Western and Russian colonial ambitions, and Japan's brutal aggression and territorial occupation. More than a century later the Chinese are still struggling to come to terms with this historical baggage. As Esherick (2006: 229) points out, it is remarkable that of all the empires China is the only one that kept its territory intact, when the Qing Dynasty was transformed into the ROC in 1911, and with Mongolia and Taiwan excepted, with only 14 percent loss of territories (mostly Mongolian steppe) and 2 percent loss of population. One of the ironies, as observed by Escherick is that it was the foreign power's ambition—like the Russian on Mongolia, the Japanese on Manchuria and the British on Tibet—that helped the Chinese keep the Qing Dynasty territory intact. As a result the Chinese were motivated not to have their own nation state but to have a multinational state.

That is why there is an issue of what China is. What China is, is of course closely related to the issue of Chinese nationalism. This chapter attempts to unpack this historical baggage, in the process deconstructing the production of knowledge of what China is.

The issue of what China is is very much related to the production and consumption of knowledge because different definitions lead to different knowledge of China. There might have been an imagined "civilization community" of China but there was not an imagined "nation state community" of China until the beginning of the twentieth century. This chapter will argue that neither the conceptualization of the nation state nor that of the civilization state is adequate in addressing the issue of what China is. China in terms of territory became bigger and bigger over time, not because there were ethnic Chinese who invaded and expanded its empire, like the Romans or the Russians, but because it was invaded and conquered by its neighbors. Such was the case of the Yuan Dynasty as a result of the invasion from the Mongols, and the Qing Dynasty that was established by the invading Manchus.

In Chapter 3, I will discuss historical evidence that the so-called "Chinese," the Han Chinese, are a product of mutation and fusion of different tribes and ethnic peoples, even as early as *xia shang zhou*, the supposed early stages of the Hua Xia Chinese (people with elegant clothing and elaborate rituals). Just as there is no essentialist bloodline "Chinese" Chinese, there is no essentialist nationalist China. There had been invasions and conquests among and between the contiguous tribes throughout the formation of what is called China from the earliest recorded time, through the South-North Dynasties (Nanbei Chao *c.*420–589 AD), Five Dynasties and Ten Countries (Wudai Shiguo *c.*907–60), and the Northern Song (Bei Song 960–1127) to the Qing Dynasty. As Zhao Tingyang (2016) argues, China was a vortex that moved from the areas around the Yellow River of Henan, Shaanxi, Shanxi, Shandong and Hebei to areas around the Yangtze River of Jiangsu, Zhejiang, Hubei, Hunan, Anhui and Jiangxi, a vortex that drew in cultures and ethnic groups on its edge. Since the modern age, when there was imperial and colonial invasion from the Western nation states, China has been in a state of flux. Concepts from the Western discourse such as empire, union and commonwealth don't fit in with a China that has come out of these historical circumstances. The Chinese concept of *tianxia* (Zhao Tingyang 2011) does not fit today's China either, as *tianxia* takes the cultural value position of the civilized Chinese versus the barbarians. Modern China is the reverse: since the end of the nineteenth century, landmarked by the May Fourth Movement in 1919, the consensus among the Chinese political and intellectual elite has been and still is that Western cultural and political values are more civilized.

CHINESE NATIONALISM

A survey study on Chinese nationalism issues by Jackson S. Woods and Bruce J. Dickson (2017) shows that

1. Nationalism does not boost government legitimacy: "key components of regime legitimacy are not correlated with the victimization

narrative. Those who have prospered from the CCP's economic reforms in the past and expect to continue to prosper in the future are no more likely to accept the CCP's victimization narrative than those who have not prospered."

2. Patriotism education does not make the Chinese more nationalist: "younger people in urban China are less nationalistic than their elders." Their research data indicate that it is not necessarily the case that the Han Chinese and the less educated are more nationalistic. All else being equal, Han males are no more likely to be either victims of nationalism or patriots than females, ethnic minorities or highly educated individuals.

3. The Han Chinese are no more nationalistic than other Chinese citizens.

4. The victimization narrative does not make the Chinese more anti-foreign, with the exception of Japan.

As discussed in Chapter 3, the Chinese conceptualization of civilization versus barbarianism has never been ethnic or racist, nor religious. Nor is the Chinese conceptualization of what China is ethnic, racial or religious. Here lies the root of the problem of defining what Chinese nationalism is. How do you define Chinese nationalism when the entity referred to as China is not a nation state? The Nationalist leader Chiang Kai-shek attempted to solve this dilemma by claiming that the five then-recognized ethnic groups—Han, Hui, Mongolian, Manchu and Tibetan—were blood-related branches of the same lineage. The PRC, on the other hand, has been trying to build up a multinational state of 56 nationalities, an attempt that has proved to be difficult.

If Chinese nationalism is defined such that the Han Chinese want to have their own nation, then Chinese nationalism is a logical and self-evident definition. But this is not what appears to be happening. What seems to be happening and what is condemned or denounced as Chinese nationalism (Gries 2004; Leibold 2006) is that the supposedly Han Chinese want to claim all the other nationalities as part of China. Logically, there may be Tibetan nationalism, Manchu nationalism, Mongolian nationalism or Uyghur nationalism, or Taiwan or even Hong Kong nationalism, which may want to break away from what is called China. But the opposite is hard to define. If anything, there is Chinese multinationalism: the Han Chinese (accepting the current official categorization) want a multinational and multicultural China; they want Taiwan, Hong Kong, Tibet and Xinjiang to be included.

The dilemma of how to define and discuss Chinese nationalism is expressed by Cole's assertion that Chinese nationalism is "civilizational" in that it relies on "bloodlines" and Confucian traditions. It has no borders, but it does have "a deep sense of victimhood that has in turn infused [its] nationalism with paranoia and xenophobia" (Cole 2017: 126), a standard accusation of Chinese nationalism. This assertion is full of contradictions and confusions. First of all, if Chinese nationalism is civilizational and therefore Confucian then it cannot consist of bloodlines. Secondly, if one supports democratic thesis like Taiwan independence, as Cole apparently does, then one cannot state at the same time that the Chinese are xenophobic, since the Chinese not only don't want to exclude the Taiwanese but they would love them to be part of the same country.

A Chinese nationalism of paranoia and xenophobia out of a sense of victimhood makes sense only if that is defined as Chinese sentiments about what the Western powers and the Japanese had done to China in recent modern history. Are these sentiments reasonable or just paranoid? Anybody's answer to this question depends not only on his or her geopolitical position but also on one's knowledge of what China is.

ORIENTALISM AND GEOPOLITICS

For Fairbank, who is considered the Chinese studies doyen in the US, China was an empire, and it had only cultural nationalism but not political nationalism. Wang Hui, considered a leading scholar of the Chinese Left, questions such a characterization. Inspired by what is called the Japanese Kyoto School of historians such as Naito Conan and Miyazaki Ichisada, Wang Hui (2016) argues that the Chinese state was "quasi-modern" in pre-modern times because a bureaucratic state that functioned like a modern state was formed as early as the Qin and further developed in about the tenth century, long before the initial progress of nation states in the West in the thirteenth and fourteenth centuries. Providing huge amounts of detail in his monumental four-volume *Origin of Chinese Modern Thought*, Wang argues that the early traditional Chinese state was "modern" in that there was effective governance of international trade, market economy and currency. It was already a "multinational state," in which all those who were within the boundary were its "nationals." For the Kyoto School scholars the Japanese term for nationalism is 国民主義 (state's national ism or citizen ism), instead of the current term used in China which is 民族主义 (ethnicity ism). In other words, typical of Wang Hui, he argues that in understanding China we should transcend the Western dichotomy of empire and nation state. Traditional China should not be judged in Western terms to be either an empire (Anand 2009) or a nation state. China was neither. But China did build a state machine in what can be considered ancient times. With the hindsight of US administrative failure during the "end of history," inventive scholar Francis Fukuyama (2014) has come to the same view and argues that the Chinese built "the first modern state" as far back as the third century BC.

Along these lines of argument, the Chinese terms of *tianxia* (all under heaven) and *chaogong* (paying tribute), were actually manufactured knowledge by the Chinese political and intellectual elite to validate the legitimacy of their rule. The tributary system was in practice a trade system (Kang 2010) and conceptualization of *tianxia* (Zhao Tingyang 2011, 2016) was to justify the authority of the emperors, the sons of heaven. The Hua (people of elegant clothing and elaborate rituals) did think that they were civilized as opposed to the Yi (the people who did not wear elegant clothing and did not observe rituals). But the Hua and Yi referents could shift, and the Hua category could refer to any ethnic group who wore elegant clothing and observed rituals. Therefore who was civilized or barbarian was not ethnic or national. This can be seen in *chuqiu fanlu*—the *Luxuriant Dew of Chunqiu*—written by Dong Zhongshu.

"The imagined community" (Anderson 1991) is in many ways a dialog between the anthropological research and the Western concept of nation states, reflecting the Western colonialist creation of modern states in South Asia. But this Orientalist conceptualization cannot be applied to China, since China had strong multinational bureaucratic states in pre-modern times, with the plural "states" to indicate a long history of evolution. Wang Hui (2011a) further argues that modern Chinese nationalism was a form of Chinese resistance and struggle against Western imperialism and colonialism, including the resistance of the Tibetan people. European criteria that a nation state has to be a single ethnic group (Gellner 1983) and that the political and ethnic unit has to be one and the same cannot apply to China, since in China different ethnic groups have mixed and lived together side by side for a long time.

From this perspective one could argue that to accuse China of Chinese nationalism over Tibet is using Tibet as an object of European Orientalism that fits the US aim of geopolitics, just like the Nazi German Orientalism that considered Tibet as lost Christianity, or the origin of the Aryan race. This kind of construction of Tibet in relation to China is for geopolitical purposes and it is selective in its evidence. For instance, the Tibetan claim to Greater Tibet includes the Amdo and Kham areas, but the claimers do not point out that these areas have been under non-Tibetan administration for more than 700 years. On the one hand, the Tibetan exile government wants to include these Amdo and Kham areas as part of its Greater Tibet and therefore not part of China. On the other hand, it does not claim areas that now belong to Bhutan and Sikkim but were part of Tibet in the past (Wang Hui 2011b: 93). This kind of double standard is an indication that the Tibetan exile government has been used as a ploy in the knowledge of Orientalism and the chess game of contemporary geopolitics.

A MULTINATIONAL CHINA IN ANCIENT TIMES

As Johnson (2016) points out, in the West, the classics such as Homer's epic and the Bible are considered as stories passed on orally where the written versions appeared only many years later. In other words, these classics cannot be viewed as literal records of history. In contrast, due to the uninterrupted and continuous use of characters as a written script, as evidenced in oracle bones, the Chinese seem to have written records about their history and culture from much earlier on. It is true that there have always been debates and questions about whether what had been written in Chinese classics were authentic records of history. During the early twentieth century, when forward-looking Chinese thinkers and intellectuals started to take up ideas from the West, they began to question traditional Chinese views of their history as recorded in these classics. Gu Jiegang is one of the revisionist Chinese historians who argues that the way in which the Chinese classics were passed on is the same as the way classics in the West were passed orally (Gu Jiegang 1982). Therefore the Chinese classics may not be an authentic record of history. As Johnson points out, Gu Jiegang's highly acclaimed position on Chinese historiography confirms the views of skeptical Western commentators who doubt that classic Chinese texts are authentic records of ancient China. They tend to think that Chinese efforts to prove their long and continuous history and culture is just Chinese cultural chauvinism (Johnson 2016).

By the same token, there has been suspicion over the claim of the extent of ancient Chinese civilization. In mainstream Chinese historiography, China as an entity had a vast territory from early on, from Beijing in the north to Guangdong in the south, and from coastal east to today's Sichuan Province. Again, as Johnson points out, some Western scholars argue that the concept of China was meaningless pre-Qin. This is an argument I tend to agree with. However, my argument is not against the claim of classic Chinese records of cultural civilization but to deconstruct an ethnicity-based China. When the traditional Chinese historians claim the vast territories of China they are not talking about ethnicities, races or nationalities. Instead, they are talking about a Chinese cultural sphere. If we don't have this specific point in mind, then the debate regarding Chinese historiography is at cross-purposes. The real debate is whether those different kingdoms had different cultures pre-Qin. Did the Kingdom of Chu, for instance, have its own culture that was not only unique but very different from the so-called Chinese culture?

As narrated by Johnson (2016), during the Beijing Olympics in 2008, some antique smugglers got some bamboo slip manuscripts that had been stolen from ancient grave sites to Hong Kong. Nobody wanted to buy them, because something from the black market could not be openly validated to be authentic, until a former graduate from Tsinghua University (Beijing) bought them and then donated them to his Alma Mater. The 75-year-old Li Xueqin was appointed by Tsinghua University to lead a team to examine those bamboo slips. Carbon-14 tests confirmed that these slips were books written in about 300 BC (Johnson 2016). Bamboo slip books of this kind, and the Tsinghua bamboo slip manuscripts, are just the latest discovery, and are not the most ancient written records in China. The earliest written record appeared on oracle bones, most from the Shang Dynasty (c.1600–1050 BC). Writings on oracle bones provide evidence of significant understanding of ancient China, but these oracle bone writings do not represent systematic record keeping and they are hard to find. On the other hand, the bamboo slips threaded together by ropes to form volumes were already books that recorded Chinese history, legends and philosophical ideas.

Liu Guozhong (2016) is one of the scholars who studied these bamboo slips: the findings confirm, at least partially, traditional Chinese historiography. These texts confirm that what we know of Chinese culture and civilization includes the territory of Chu, and that all thinkers of those kingdoms participated in their contribution to what is called Chinese civilization. So there was a large Chinese cultural sphere even when different kingdoms were in existence.

These bamboo slip manuscripts should put an end to the debate over whether or not Chinese historical records were later reconstructions of oral histories. According to Allan (2015), those texts were written at the very beginning to record oral history, while works like *Daodejing* (the ancient book on Taoism) were written long before skeptics have suggested and were in fact very close to what traditional Chinese historiography claims.

Those different kingdoms or different tribes might be of different ethnicities, but we don't know because it was not the conceptual framework of Chinese historiography to look at the world in terms of ethnicity. The bamboo slip manuscripts provide evidence for the existence of an ancient multinational state, for which a series of serious concepts of how to run the state were proposed and debated. There were theories of meritocracies (Bell 2015) advocated by the Mo School and the ideas of *chan rang* (to abdicate and to hand the crown to someone else) and *rang xian* (to give up one's official position in favor of someone more worthy) were seriously debated and considered by various schools of philosophers for a form of state (Allan 2015), like the Confucian school of Mencius. Clearly in China then, there was a state: the conceptualization of which is beyond the dichotomy of empire and nation state.

THE TAIWAN ISSUE

The Taiwan issue is a typical and classical example of how the construction of China is on the one hand based on a fashionable theoretical paradigm and on the other motivated or/and supported by international geopolitics. Scholars, academics and think tank specialists approach the issue based on the assumptions of their national interests, but at the same time place themselves on the moral high ground, consolidated by a theoretical paradigm that appears to be universal, objective and even caring for the Other. In the case of Taiwan the theoretical paradigm is the now well-versed democracy thesis. This is a thesis that is used to justify aggression against what are sometimes called "failed states" and other times "rogue states" by "the international community," which mostly produces knowledge and largely consumes knowledge.

THE DEMOCRACY THESIS AND WHAT CHINA IS

The democracy thesis is skillfully used by Lee Teng-hui, who is often referred to as the "father of Taiwan's democracy" (Kastner 2011) and actually identifies himself as Japanese more than Chinese or Taiwanese (*South China Morning Post* 2015). In one of his books, originally published in 2014 in Japanese, Lee declares that the Diaoyutai Islands do not belong to Taiwan and that this is an unquestionable fact. Then in 2016, when the Democratic Progress Party leader Tsai Ing-wen was elected president, this book (Lee Teng-hui 2016) was released in a Chinese edition to make sure that Tsai understood the message given by the father of democracy, whose legacy Tsai benefits from. In responding to the assertion made by Lee in this publication the ROC government office issued a statement which declared that the ROC government had consistently asserted that the Diaoyutai Islands are an island group appertaining to Taiwan and "It is an indisputable fact that from the perspective of geography, geology, history and international law, the Diaoyutais are an inalienable part of ROC territory," and that "no person or country can deny our nation's sovereignty over the islands" (ROC Central News Agency 2016).

This statement was made in February 2016 when the government was still under Nationalist control and the "president-elect" Tsai Ing-wen was not yet in power. Still, after the Japanese Prime Minister Shinzō Abe met with US President Donald Trump at the White House on February 11, 2017, and after Trump had agreed, in his telephone conversation with the Chinese leader Xi Jinping, to hold "the one China policy," Tsai's office issued an official statement that "The Diaoyutai Islands are part of our territory. This is the long-standing stance of the government and our position has not changed" (ROC Central News Agency 2017).

It is worth pointing out a subtle difference between the two official statements by the ROC Central News Agency in the space of a year: the words "Diaoyutais are an inalienable part of ROC territory" are noticeably absent in the 2017 statement, which only says that "The Diaoyutai Islands are part of our territory." But what is "our" if not the ROC, and why do the Taiwanese authorities want to avoid the use of ROC? The underlying message conveyed by the avoidance of "China" can be seen from the Chinese title of the translation of Lee Teng-hui's Japanese book mentioned above: 余生：我的生命之旅与台湾民主之路 (*Remaining*

Life: My Life Journey and the Road of Taiwan's Democracy). The message is: Taiwan is a democracy and China is not. Taiwan is not China.

Even though the ROC is different from the PRC, the mention of China is an admittance of Taiwan being China. To accept even two Chinas would imply a final reunification, like East and West Germany, or North and South Korea. How does one make a Taiwanese identity that is different from China? Democracy. Taiwan is a vibrant democracy while China is a dictatorship. Moral support of a democratic Taiwan against an evil dictatorship is such a simple and beautiful theoretical and intellectual paradigm. The case of Taiwan shows that, after all, nation state is not about ethnicity or nation but about politics.

The question "what is China?" gets more interesting if we consider another thorny issue of territorial dispute in the SCS. Even under Lee Teng-hui, the Taiwan authorities repeatedly stated that legally, historically, geographically or in reality, all of the SCS and Spratly Islands were Taiwan's territory and under Taiwanese sovereignty. The claims made by the ROC and the PRC overlap and are more or less the same. In fact the PRC just inherited the claims made by the Nationalist government under Chiang Kai-shek who took the ROC to Taiwan after the defeat of his fight with the Communists in 1949. The Taiwan issue has too much to do with what China is.

TAIWAN AND WHAT CHINA IS

A very brief outline of the history of Taiwan is required here before I proceed. Taiwanese aborigines inhabited the island of Taiwan, previously known by Europeans as Formosa, as it was named by the Portuguese in the sixteenth century. Though there had been mainland Chinese fishing in surrounding areas like Penghu for centuries, it was only when the Dutch and Spanish colonized the island that it opened to mainland Chinese migrations. The island was then taken over by the Qing Dynasty, but was ceded to Japan in 1895 after the Chinese suffered a defeat in the Sino-Japanese War. After the collapse of the Qing government in 1911, the ROC was established on the mainland in 1912. Following the Japanese surrender in 1945 at the end of World War II, the ROC took control of Taiwan. But the Chinese Civil War between the Nationalist ROC under Chiang Kai-shek and Communists under Mao Zedong led to ROC's loss of the mainland and the flight of the ROC government to Taiwan in 1949. While in Taiwan, the ROC was protected by the US in the context of the Cold War; it continued to claim to be the legitimate government of all of China. Again with the support of the US and its allies, the ROC continued to represent China at the United Nations until 1971, when the PRC assumed China's seat, causing the ROC to lose its UN membership, one of the consequences of US President Nixon's change of policy on China. From then on the PRC has consistently claimed sovereignty over Taiwan, and refused diplomatic relations with any country that recognizes the ROC as a state. Most international organizations either refuse Taiwanese membership or allow it to participate only as a non-state actor. The most crucial party in the Taiwan issue is of course the US government, which has maintained an ambiguous "one China policy." On the one hand, it officially acknowledges the fact that both sides of the Taiwan Straits hold that there is only one China and that Taiwan is part of China. On the other hand, it commits itself to the defense of Taiwan if the unification of the two sides is not peaceful.

Hence the Taiwan issue: it is not a country recognized unambiguously by the international community, nor a territory run by the PRC. You could say there are two Chinas. But the PRC does not even want to accept that: there is only one China and Taiwan is just a province of China left "unliberated" because of the US intervention in the context of the Cold War. But PRC strategies on Taiwan have evolved: from the strategy of "liberation" in the Mao era, to peaceful unification under the formula of "one country two systems" (the Hong Kong model) under the leadership of Jiang Zemin, to the strategy of winning over Taiwan through economic development and trade between the two sides during the leadership of Hu Jintao. The PRC has changed from its position of the PRC as the government of "one China" to that of "one country two systems—virtually two governments." All in all the PRC has shifted from its strategy of being offensive to that of being defensive and preventing Taiwan from becoming independent. For the PRC government and many people in mainland China, the Taiwan issue is still the unfinished business of a civil war, the progress of which was interrupted by the US. The starting point of the interruption was when the US moved its Fifth Fleet to the Taiwan Straits when the Korean War broke out in 1950, only one year after the PRC was established. Therefore, the PRC has threatened the use of military force in response to any formal declaration of independence by Taiwan or if peaceful unification is no longer possible (NIDS 2017).

On the other hand, strategies taken by Taiwan have also evolved from the civil war, in rhetoric if not in reality, from the position of retaking the mainland and defeating the Communists under the leadership of Chiang Kai-shek, to that of maintaining and defending its own existence, to that of carving out a distinctive Taiwanese identity through the democracy thesis. However, even today Taiwan has not renounced its official position that there is one China and that Taiwan is the government of China which includes the mainland. With increasing domestic political division between the aspirations of eventual Chinese unification and Taiwanese independence, Taiwan has changed its strategy of being defensive to that of being offensive and aiming to win independence.

This shows not only how complicated the Taiwan issue is, but also that what China is remains unsettled. Is mainland China part of the ROC, as the Nationalist government continues to claim, as the former president Ma Ying-jeou (2017) of the KMT background did? Should the solution be, as some suggest, to let the mainland be part of the ROC to solve the reunification problem? Or should there be a China that is neither PRC nor ROC, but unified under a different name?

THE US NATIONAL INTEREST REGARDING TAIWAN

The elephant in the room regarding the Taiwan issue is of course the US. When the PRC and the US started to talk about the establishment of a diplomatic relationship in 1972, the main stumbling block was the Taiwan issue. The final solution was the US's acknowledgment of the status quo that both sides of the Taiwan Strait insisted that there was only one China and that Taiwan was part of China, and that the US would not challenge this status quo, with the condition that unification of the two sides had to be peaceful. China has been insisting from then on that any country that wants to establish a diplomatic relationship with China has to accept that there is only one China, that Taiwan is part of China and that only the PRC represents China.

Though many scholars in the US play with the universally acknowl-edged knowledge of democracy thesis, a prestigious thesis with potential rewards for publication and grants, the potential damage to the US national interest by abandoning the one China policy (*de facto* if not *de jure*) is hard to fathom: so hard that many in the US political and intellectual elite call for caution, as demonstrated by the most recent recommendation for a newly elected US president by a group of prominent US thinkers, discussed in Chapter 1:

> In addressing these new challenges, the incoming administration should be mindful of lessons from the past. This is especially true of the sensitive question of Taiwan, where it would be exceedingly dangerous to unilaterally abandon our long-standing "One China policy"—an understanding that has served as the basis for the US relationship with China, helped protect Taiwan's security, prosperity, and democracy, and preserve peace and stability in Asia for almost four decades. No national interest is furthered by abandoning or conditioning this policy on other issues. To do so would very likely end up increasing Taiwan's vulnerabilities destabilizing the Asia-Pacific region, and jeopardizing broad US interests. (Schell and Shirk et al. 2017: executive summary, p. 1)

Quite likely some of the participants and writers of the group that produced this recommendation would accept or even advocate the democracy thesis. But the geopolitical reality is such that the perceived US national interest takes priority, at least for now in the case of the Taiwan issue.

THE HONG KONG ISSUE

In the final section of this chapter I am not going to do a rundown of the history of Hong Kong, as many readers will know about it or can look it up online. Instead, I want to discuss three issues in relation to the theme of this chapter regarding what China is. The first is why the Communist government did not just take over Hong Kong in 1949 when it had the chance. The second is how the democracy thesis was pushed in Hong Kong. The third is how the idea of Hong Kong localization has come about.

The PRC's Letting of Hong Kong Be

Toward the end of the civil war between the People's Liberation Army (PLA) under Mao and the Nationalist army, the PLA could have taken over Hong Kong easily, though not without a fight if the British decided to defend its colony. Indeed, in subsequent years the PRC could have taken over Hong Kong if it had wanted to, as it would have been very hard for the UK to defend Hong Kong under the circumstances. After all, post-Qing Dynasty Chinese governments never accepted the treaties by which Hong Kong was ceded to Britain, as they were considered "unequal," signed under duress as a result of the infamous Opium Wars. At the very beginning, when the Communists started to establish the PRC, they were very uncertain themselves about what was in store for them internationally. They knew the main "enemy" was the US, and they wanted to ensure that they didn't antagonize Britain in an attempt to neutralize, if not support, another important international player. As time went by—with the Cold War concretizing due to the Korean War, and China facing economic and technological sanctions from Western powers—the PRC found that Hong Kong was a good window for China to have some access to the West, in terms of trade, technology and even foreign currency exchange. It was by no means an accident that the first and most successful special economic zone developed in post-Mao China was the fishing village of Shenzhen, Hong Kong's neighbor.

On top of that, by not taking over Hong Kong by force, China won a reputation for observing international treaties, one of which is that the 99 years of the lease of what is called the New Territories would run out in 1997. When the British and the Chinese were discussing the handover of Hong Kong they were first talking about the New Territories. The Chinese needed only to state that even by the treaty the Chinese didn't officially accept that the New Territories should be returned to China, and the British didn't have a leg to stand on because without the New Territories the Hong Kong Island itself, which was ceded to Britain permanently according to the first Opium War treaty, could not function.

The Democracy Thesis Played Out in Hong Kong

The British, and the West in general, seemed to have suddenly realized that Hong Kong was not a democracy after about 200 years of colonial rule. Impacted by the brutal 1989 Tiananmen crackdown, the issue of democracy in Hong Kong became a common call not just among the elite but also among many in the street. One has to remember that it was also around the time that the Berlin Wall fell, that the end of the Cold War was in sight, and that Francis Fukuyama was about to claim the "end of history." Therefore the democracy thesis was highly fashionable and believable at that time. The Chinese and the British had reached an agreement by which Hong Kong would formally be part of China but would keep its autonomy as a special region in which the governing system and way of life would remain the same. The Chinese central government would not even tax Hong Kong, and what it required was to keep the defense of Hong Kong under its wing, the arrangement of which included the stationing of the PLA in Hong Kong. In conclusion, the British would hand over Hong Kong to China and China promised to let Hong Kong keep its status quo in virtually everything.

It was at this point that the last governor of Hong Kong, the charismatic and powerful Chris Patten, rode high on the democracy thesis and started to change the status quo by introducing something like democratic elections (Maxwell 2014). Hence the see-saw games between the PRC and the British during the term of the last governor. Although the tension between China and the UK over Hong Kong faded after the departure of the last governor, the issue of colonial legacy has never been dealt with. Due to the constraints of the one country two system agreement, there was never a decolonization process in Hong Kong after the handover. A good example is the Hong Kong judicial system, in which most of the judges are British or foreign citizens (Yi Guoming 2017). However, as Cheung (Alvin Y. H. Cheung 2017, personal communication) points out, the current situation in Hong Kong is so unique that foreign citizens who have permanent residence status may be considered Hong Kong "nationals." This is unusual because in theory the judges of a nation state should be citizens of that state. This is one of the reasons why it was raised as an issue in 2017 when a Hong Kong judge of British citizenship, David Dufton, sentenced seven Hong Kong policemen to two years in jail after they were convicted of being violent to democracy demonstrator Ken Tsang, the beating of whom was filmed by a local broadcaster TVB.

One could argue that the sentence demonstrates Hong Kong's judicial independence and the rule of law. But others would argue that the sentence was not only a double standard (Yi Guoming 2017) but deliberately political: Ken Tsang was also convicted of violence against the police, but the sentencing was very light. As pointed out by Gu Minkang, associate dean of the Law School at the Hong Kong City University, democracy activists like Huang Zhifeng (Josh Wong) were also given very light sentencing on the basis that they had the well-intentioned motivation of pursuing freedom and democracy (Gu Minkang 2017). As Zheng Yongnian (2017) points out, even though Occupy Central (referring to the 2014 occupation of central Hong Kong for 79 days led by democracy activists—all three cases mentioned here are related to Occupy Central) was declared illegal by the Hong Kong government at that time, the activists still occupied the moral high ground by claiming to strive for democracy. According to this democracy thesis, police responsibility of maintaining law and order is interpreted as suppressing democracy and therefore their heavy-handedness was morally wrong.

Localization (Independence) of Hong Kong

After several years of peaceful coexistence between Hong Kong and the mainland, unexpected developments started to unravel all kinds of assumptions and accepted wisdom. One unexpected development is that China has moved quickly in economic growth, so much so that it has cast a shadow over Hong Kong's past glory. For example, Hong Kong's neighboring city, Shenzhen, was a fishing village a mere 40 years ago but has developed into a modern city, and by 1997 already had about 2 percent of China's share of GDP. Hong Kong, on the other hand, went downhill, from 1997 when its GDP was roughly 20 percent of China's total GDP to a mere 2 percent by 2015. Another unexpected development is that in 2008 the Global Financial Crisis started to hit Hong Kong, and as a consequence inequality went up and living standards went down. Finally, the neoliberal expansion into China had an additional consequence in Hong Kong: the multimillionaires and multibillionaires, mostly the princelings, started to penetrate Hong Kong's finance and real estate property, the latter development of which further pushed prices out of reach of local Hong Kongers. Under these circumstances, some angry Hong Kong young took up the conceptual paradigm of democracy against tyranny and unfreedom. Some even aroused anti-mainland Chinese sentiments by calling mainland Chinese tourists locusts. Lately some of these even call for independence or to get back to being British. One can hardly blame the Hong Kong *fenqing* (the angry young) given the fact that all the Chinese rich want is to get in bed with Hong Kong capitalists who do not have the slightest desire to deal with social issues. Even though those Hong Kongers who have anti-mainland Chinese sentiments are most likely the minority, the very fact that some of them started to take up the issue of different ethnicity is startling. The irony is that while the Chinese government, in order to honor the commitment of one country two systems has done hardly anything to decolonize British rule, the democratic activists use the argument of "decolonization" to advocate democracy from China.

CONCLUSION

In this chapter I have discussed the complex issues of why what China is remains a problem. What China is is not only an ethnic issue but a cultural issue. It is not only a national issue but a multinational issue; it is not only a nation state issue but a historical issue; it is not only a geopolitical issue but a conceptual paradigm issue. What China is depends not only on historical circumstances but also on current economic and political reality. Finally, what China is depends on how the production and consumption of knowledge are played out by "the international community," that is, the dominant West. Knowledge of what is the truth or what is the right value by the Western knowledge manufacturer can help create new realities almost out of thin air. What China is regarding Tibet, Xinjiang, Taiwan and even Hong Kong is very much reliant on what kind of knowledge is produced and consumed inside and outside China.

The democracy thesis, as applied to Taiwan and Hong Kong, is generally accepted and promoted by both the Left and the Right in the West which has discursive power. But there are dissenting voices. As Amin (2013) points out, it is a challenge for the Western Left when the democracy thesis is employed by global capitalism to lecture developing countries for being nationalist. A blanket condemnation of nationalism on the part of China runs the risk of not only neglecting historical territorial imperialism, but also the current economic global imperialism.

3
Chinese? Who are the Chinese?

INTRODUCTION

A student who comes from the officially and internationally recognized territory of the PRC to Australia introduces himself as Chinese. When asked where in China he is from the student replies with the word "Tibet." His newly acquainted Australian friends immediately correct him by saying "No, you are NOT Chinese! You are Tibetan." After some further persuasion the student starts to introduce himself as Tibetan.

This real story told by a colleague of mine illustrates the power of racial discourse. An average Westerner would be most likely to think that the student had been brainwashed by the Chinese.

The issue of who the Chinese are is very much related to the production and consumption of knowledge of China because it is about whom knowledge is constructed for. In this chapter, the issues of race, ethnicity and nationality as well as that of the so-called overseas Chinese will be addressed. The chapter aims to argue that Western concepts of race, ethnicity and nationality are inadequate in addressing the issue of who the Chinese are. The term Chinese is undefinable in that it is not an ethnic term, nor is it a definite term referring to the citizens of China.

WHO ARE THE CHINESE?

The term Chinese is at best ambiguous and at worst confusing. If the term Chinese refers to citizens or those who hold passports of the state of the PRC, then peoples of all ethnicities within this political boundary of the PRC should be referred to as "Chinese," just as the peoples who have Australian citizenship or even permanent residence status, irrespective of ethnic or cultural backgrounds, are referred to as "Australians." This is how the Chinese state would like to define the term Chinese: citizens of China, or in a less official term, *zhongguo ren* (China person).

In this political definition of Chinese, the Tibetans, Mongolians and all the officially recognized 56 ethnic groups are Chinese.

However, under this broad umbrella term of Chinese, further ethnic labels can be and usually are applied to identify oneself or to differentiate each other. A person of Tibetan ethnic background is labeled as a Tibetan person (*xizang ren*), a person of Manchurian background is called a Manzhou person (*manzhou ren*) and a person who is of Islamic background may be called Hui person (*hui ren* or *huizu ren*). For most readers in the West, and specifically those who are speakers of English, all these persons are Chinese, except the ones they don't think they should be Chinese, like the Tibetans.

The Tibetan case is special for many reasons. Apart from the fact that Tibetans have their own distinctive culture and religious tradition, Tibet is located on the south-west border of China. To some extent, the Mongolians and the Uyghurs are the same. "In English, we can write Han Chinese, but it is impossible to hyphenate other nationalities with Chinese. Mongol Chinese and Tibetan Chinese are impossibilities" (Bulag 2002: 17, 18). Bulag seems to think that there is a natural property of Chineseness and that non-Han cannot be linked to the proper Chinese.

What complicates the situation—and this is one of the reasons why who the Chinese are and what China is are such complex issues—is Tibet's relationship with a multifaceted China. There has been a long history of interaction between the Tibetans and other ethnic groups, either in peace or in wars, with migrations from all sides to different locations, for hundreds, if not thousands, of years. Invasions and wars have been constant features in human history, leading not only to murder and plunder but also to integration, followed by occupations and conquests. For instance, Tibet is often portrayed as culturally and linguistically homogenous, but according to Roche (2017), this is a myth. There are more than 60 minority languages currently spoken in Tibet. And they are neither Tibetan nor Chinese.

The back and forth aggressions and conquests between and among contiguous tribes or ethnic groups complicated the issues of ethnicity and national boundaries. For instance, the Mongols who invaded China also invaded Tibet in 1240. Tibet was incorporated into the Mongol Empire until 1354, as China was until 1368. The Mongol conquest of Tibet and China meant that both Tibet and China were parts of one country under what was called the Yuan Dynasty. When the Yuan Dynasty collapsed, the Ming Dynasty (1368–1644) restored order in China, and what the relationship was between the Ming court and Tibet and whether or not Ming China had sovereignty over Tibet are issues that are still being debated by historians. Van Praag (1987) argues that even Chinese court historians viewed Tibet as an independent foreign tributary. However, Wang Jiawei and Nyima Gyaincain (Wang and Nyima 1997) argue that the assertions by van Praag are "fallacies." Wang and Nyima argue that the Ming emperor sent edicts to Tibet twice in the second year of the Ming Dynasty and that Tibet was viewed as a significant region to pacify various Tibetan tribes. "Analysis of the relationship is further complicated by modern political conflicts and the application of West-phalian sovereignty to a time when the concept did not exist."

In any case, history repeated itself: the Manchus from the north of China proper invaded China, and Tibet. Tibet was under Qing administrative rule (1720–1912), as was China from 1644 to 1912. Despite brief British invasions of Tibet (1903–4), Qing control of Tibet was reasserted. But after the collapse of the Qing Dynasty in 1911 and during the ROC (1912–49), Tibet won *de facto* independence while China did not have a strong central government—amid an era of warlords, civil war and World War II—with which to exercise control not only over Tibet but the whole country (though the Nationalist government under Chiang Kai-shek undoubtedly maintained China's claim over Tibet). In 1951, Tibetan representatives participated in negotiations in Beijing with the then PRC government. This resulted in a Seventeen Point Agreement which enabled the PLA to "liberate" Tibet, and led to the formalizing of China's sovereignty over Tibet, although the agreement was repudiated by the present Tibetan government in exile.

This brief recount of the history of Tibet is an attempt to demonstrate the difficulty of defining what a Chinese nation state is: a difficulty directly related to the struggle to define who the Chinese are. Even if we agree that in terms of ethnicity the Mongolians and Manchus were not "Chinese," politically and geopolitically they were Chinese as they ruled China such that the Manchus eventually identified themselves as Chinese and even lost their own languages (Bell 2013). This is also an attempt to show that whether Tibetans are called Chinese is not just an ethnic issue but a political issue. The Tibetan issue is special not only because Tibetans are not "Chinese" Chinese, but also because it is not a simple instance of ethnic Chinese invading the Tibetans, or one where a Communist China invaded them either.

ETHNICITY, RACE AND NATIONALITY

The majority of the population currently in the PRC, and indeed in Hong Kong and Taiwan, are called *han ren* (Han person). There are some commonly held assumptions about the Han Chinese. For instance, they are supposed to belong to one race, or one ethnicity, though the Chinese official terminology is nationality. They are supposed to be the real Chinese, the "Chinese" Chinese. The main reason for labeling these people together as Chinese is that they speak the so-called Chinese language. The second reason is that they are the people who are supposed to be the inheritors of the Chinese tradition, such as the Confucian doctrine of family and state, Chinese rituals and a belief system that combines three traditions: Confucianism, Daoism (Taoism) and Buddhism (Ge Zhaoguang 1998, 2006).

However, to start with, even the linguistic criterion is very tenuous. In fact many of the so-called Hui persons who are categorized as Muslims do not speak their own language but a version of the so-called Chinese language, as do many Manchus and other nationalities. Second, the Chinese language has been officially identified as having eight to ten major dialects (Gao 2000), and the one that is used as lingua franca, more so now because of market economic penetration, is the Mandarin dialect. But the differences between, say, Mandarin and Cantonese are no less than the differences between, say, Italian and Spanish. In terms of speaking and listening, Cantonese and Mandarin, the so-called two dialects of Chinese, can easily be classified as two languages. My native language in Gao Village is different in accents from what is spoken in the country town Poyang about a hundred kilometers away, which is different from the dialect in a city called Jiujiang, which is in turn different from a dialect in the city of Jingdezhen (once the porcelain capital), which in turn is different from the dialect spoken in the capital city in Nanchang. This linguistic diversity is only within one province of Jiangxi.

The one thing that holds the eight or so major dialects (and so many regional dialects) together is the written script (the han zi). Because the pictograms and ideograms, or the combination of them, instead of phonetic letters, have been kept to represent sounds and meanings, all dialects of the Chinese written language are non-alphabetic and therefore speakers of all dialects can share the same script. For this reason those who invented hanzi—the Han script—read and write them are considered hanren, Han person. But how do we know what nation-alities those who invented the Han script belong to? How do we know those people belong to the same ethnicity, let alone race? Indeed, how do we know who actually invented the characters?

The very term "han" is not a term of race, ethnicity or nationality, but a political-cultural construct. The Chinese were referred to as the Han people by the people outside China during the Han Dynasty when the Silk Road connected China with the other parts of the world (von Richthofen 1877–1912). The fact that the Han Dynasty was called "Han Dynasty" was a historical accident. Toward the end of the first Chinese empire, the Qin Dynasty, there were rebellions rising against the imperial court. Liu Bang was one of the rebel leaders, a warlord who pushed for the final collapse of the Qin Dynasty. He was claimed to be the King of Han zhong during the rebellion, a region around Han shui, the Han River, which is one of the largest branches of the Yangtze River. When Liu Bang finally defeated his strongest rival, the King of Chu, Xiang Yu (*Farewell My Concubine* directed by Chen Kaige is a title that alludes the character of Xiang Yu), he established what was to become one of the most powerful dynasties in Chinese history. He named it the Han Dynasty because before his final victory his military basis was built along the Han River. Hence the people within that dynasty were referred to as the Han people internationally. Obviously the term had nothing to do with ethnicity. As Gladney (1994) argues, the Han nationality is a modern invention, as a political project for the struggle of a Chinese nation state.

The term *zhongguo* (literally "central country") is always translated as "the Middle Kingdom," very often used to infer that the Chinese are Sino-centric. However, another term of translation is not only possible but also presents historical evidence that demonstrates the absence of conceptualization of race and ethnicity in traditional China. In one of the classics, Lie Zi (450–375 BC) describes people of different locations and ways of life as follows:

Persons of southern countries cut their hair and are naked, persons of north countries wrap up their hair and wear leather coats; the central countries persons wear hats and clothes. Because of different conditions persons of nine countries live different livelihoods: some plant, some fish, and some hunt. Just like wearing leather in winter and silk in summer, taking a boat on water and a cart on land, ways of life are not learned but formed according to natural conditions.

There are two important points to be noted here: (1) the differences between people in the north country, south country and central country just amount to clothing and how one gains a livelihood in accordance with the environmental conditions; and (2) *zhongguo* is only a term of location—the speaker talking about surrounding countries is always located in the center in terms of space, just like modern maps in that the country that is the topic is at the center.

The elite Chinese usually claim that they are the direct descendants of Xia, Shang, Zhou people. But during the early stage of an evolving China there were tribes fighting against and interacting with each other. The formation of the Chinese writing system and cultural practice, and whatever came out of the long years of Xia, Shang and Zhou, were the products of these dynamic interactions involving all kinds of tribes and ethnic groups. The Xia period (*c.*2100–1600 BC) is supposedly to be where the earliest ancestors of the Chinese came from. But there is a no good record about Xia and there is hardly any direct evidence of its existence. Therefore it is not clear at all that the Xia people are the ancestors of what are later called the Han people. Though what is usually referred to as the Shang Dynasty (1600–1046 BC) and Zhou Dynasty (1046–356) was recorded extensively in writing, the issue of ethnicity has not been a prominent reference point. According to Xu Zhuoyun (1984 and 2009), the huaxia tribes interacted with tribes who were on the border of what was then central China throughout the Shang and Zhou periods. The tribal people from the east were called *dong yi*, from the west *xi rong*, south *nan man*, and north *bei di*. During the Chunqiu Zhanguo periods, (770–221 BC), the Qi, Chu, Yan, Han, Zhao, Wei and Qin kingdoms were fighting to rule the whole area of China and there is no way to distinguish ethnicity and race. China, in a word, has evolved and developed out of the mixing up of different ethnicities or tribal backgrounds (Zhao Tingyang 2016).

In the Chinese record of history there is a period recorded as wuhu-luanhua (316–439): the rebellions of the five barbarian tribes xiongnu, xianbei, jie, qiang and di that disordered China. The disorder led to huge waves of migration from the north to the south as well as a huge reduction of population. The people who established the Liao Dynasty (937–1125) in the north were not supposed to be Chinese, but they established their capital in what is now called Kaifeng, absorbed Confucianism, built up Confucius temples, adopted Chinese administrative technology and even took up the Mandate of Heaven to justify their rule (Wang Ke 2012).

What this means is that the chaos created a melting pot in which tribal people mixed with each other. As Huang (Huang Guangxue 1987) states correctly, the reason why there are so many Han Chinese is because they absorbed other ethnic groups. One emperor of the Tang Dynasty, for instance, in order to pacify one tribe graced his own family name Li to all the people in that tribe. And that is perhaps why there are so many Lis in China today. The Chinese are a fusion of different peoples. One good example of this fluidity and fusion is what happened to the qiang persons who lived in northern Sichuan. There had been contests between central China and Tibet over centuries, and qiang persons from this area have been stuck in-between and therefore changed their self-identity according to the geographical circumstances: they identified themselves as Chinese when the Chinese were stronger in the area and Tibetans when Tibet was stronger.

As for the inventors or inheritors of the Chinese tradition and culture, again it is not just about the Han ethnic people. For example, the Sui Dynasty (581–618), during when the spectacular Grand Canal and the magnificent stone arch Zhaozhou Bridge were built, was argued by some to be ruled by people other than the Han Chinese. The first and the most successful emperor of Sui, Yang Jian, was most likely of a mixed ethnic background. The first emperor of the celebrated Tang Dynasty, Li Shimin, may have xianbei ancestry and the province of Shanxi where Li was born had already allocated to the xiongnu, the Chinese term for a nomad tribe that is sometimes referred to as the Huns, who had surrendered to the central government. According to Chen Yinque (1997, 2004), the founders of the most glorious dynasty in Chinese history, the Tang Dynasty, Li Yuan and Li Shimin, were not of the Han ethnicity. There is also evidence that Zhu Yuanzhang, the founder of the Ming Dynasty, was of the so-called Hui ethnicity. Even Qin Shihuang, the emperor who unified China the first time, was not of ethnic huaxia, the so-called first Han Chinese. The most well-known Chinese admiral, Zheng, was not a Han Chinese.

The splendid Chinese traditional literature, again, is not simply the result of the so-called Han Chinese writers alone. For instance, the celebrated Tang poet Li Bai was most likely not a Han person (Xinhua

Wang 2017). What was almost certain is that he was born in what was then called the Suiye Cheng, the town of Suyab in the present Kyrghyzstan (Fan 2002). Other well-known poets who contributed to the so-called cannons of Chinese literature such as Liu Yuxi and Bai Juyi were most likely descendants of tribe groups outside China proper (Hechune 2015).

Some of the Qing Dynasty emperors for instance, whose ethnic backgrounds were supposedly Manchurian, were very traditionally cultured in Chinese and their calligraphies and poems are considered among the best examples of Chinese cultural heritage. It was not that the Manchus did not want to protect their national distinctiveness. As Rigger (1996) argues, the Manchus struggled for the legitimacy of their rule over the whole of China by adopting the central Chinese government's institutional practices, while at the same time trying to maintain their cultural distinctiveness through freezing the Manchu frontier, banning inland Chinese migration even at the risk of economic stagnation. Rawski (1998) argues that the Qing fused the Chinese heartland and the Inner Asian borderlands into one empire of greater China.

But the proposition that the Chinese are a fusion of different tribes and ethnicities (Gu Jiegang 1988), and that people other than the so-called Han contributed to the cultural tradition in Chinese history (as stated by Mao) is considered to be Sino-centralism. In her critique of what she considers Sino-centralism—an analysis that has gained momentum in recent years (Elliott 2001, Rhoads 2000, Hermann 2007, Crossley 1999, Hostetler 2001 and Perdu 2005)—and following her Asian Studies Association of America Presidential speech "Re-envisioning the Qing: The Significance of the Qing Period in Chinese history" in 1996, Rawski rejects the "Sinicization" of the Qing Dynasty thesis advocated by Ping-ti Ho (1998) and argues that the Manchus became very good at Chinese tradition and culture not because they were Sinicized, but because they were pragmatic in using elements of Chinese cultural and traditional values to rule the Chinese more effectively. To shift the focus away from the so-called Sino-centered approach to a Manchu-centered approach is refreshing, and to argue that the Manchus wanted to preserve their own identity is probably valid. But this politically correct historical narrative needs to address the question of whether the Manchus, in trying to preserve their own identity while using elements of Chinese tradition and culture, were actually participating in the process of Sinicization: the creation of China. The Manchu-led Sinicization was so penetrating that the Manchus more or less lost their own language by the time the Qing Dynasty collapsed in 1911, even though they were the "colonizers." What is interesting is that when the Manchus were trying, with some success, to "civilize" the "peripheral" ethnic and tribal people in Sichuan and Yunnan, they did not use Manchurian, but the Chinese language and Chinese cultural and traditional values in their civilizing projects (Ge Zhaoguang 2006). This is in contrast to Western and especially anglophone colonizers, who came to dominate the world with their language, their culture and their values.

Before the Manchus conquered China they referred to China as *nikan gurun* (the state of the Han people). But after their defeat of the Ming court, when they became the rulers of the country, they referred to China as *dulimbai gurun* (the central country). Zhao Gang is right when he says "the Qing legacy to modern China included not only just the country's vast territory but also a new concept of China that laid the solid foundation for the rise of its national identity" (Zhao Gang 2006: 4). The Peking Opera (Mackerras 1997) is now considered a quintessential part of traditional Chinese culture, but it was initiated and sponsored by the Manchu Dynasty court and developed by extracting different local opera traditions (Guo Jingrui 2002). Even the lingua franca of Mandarin is a name for how Chinese was spoken at court during the Qing Dynasty by the Manchurian Mandarin officials.

Music, song and dance from other ethnic groups greatly influenced Chinese music in terms of instruments, like the *pipa* and *huqin*, and also in terms of form, like some *cipaiming*, the names of the tunes to which a *ci* poem is composed. Chinese *ci* poetry was mostly formed during the Sui-Tang period when different ethnic people were greatly mixed. Animals such as mules, clothes and footwear such as boots, woolen sweaters and *qipao*, and food such as that made of flour, watermelon, carrots, pomegranate and grapes were present and yet not of Chinese origin.

In the Chinese historical record the "Chinese" Chinese are supposed to be the Hua Xia people, people of *hua* (elegant and pretty cloths) and *xia* (ritual and politeness), and they were supposed to be different from the Yi, Rong and Di who don't have pretty clothing and had no behavioral rituals and therefore were "barbarians." This kind of categorization of the civilized as opposed to the barbarian does have derogative connotations, as is shown by the fact that some characters that have the animal radical as a component refer to "barbarian" people. However, this categorization has nothing to do with skin color or intelligence or even blood. Instead, it is about customs and behavior. In other words, the racial or ethnic categorization as understood in the West is not a traditional discursive Chinese category. With the long history of interaction, persons of north, south, east, west and central countries became one and the same. Finally, even the pre-colonial categorization of tribal Chinese in the Chinese history record is a knowledge constructed by the elite. It is a constructed history with constructed categories.

THE PRC NATIONALITY IDENTIFICATION PROJECT

The preceding discussion of historical evidence shows that the very definitions of ethnicity, race and nationality have to be questioned. In Chinese recorded history there is no such term as *minzu*, meaning "nationality" or ethnicity. The term was first used by Liang Qichao in 1899 (Huang and Shi 2005), who was trying to make use of Western concepts to help the formation of a nation state in China.

This effort of nation building had been continued not only by the Nationalists like Sun Yat-sen and Chiang Kai-shek—which was why they were called the Nationalists—but also the so-called Communists. Upon the establishment of the PRC, the Chinese political and intellectual elite had started what was called a nationality identification or designation (*minzu shibie*) project. The nationality identification project was a huge scholarly as well as political program, the consequences and validity (or even usefulness) of which is hotly debated today. Ma Rong (2012), who is a national minority, argues that China's official designation and recognition of national minorities' status is not good for China's national unity, that nationality issues should be depoliticized and that China's national minority policies are either wrong or outdated because they encourage and highlight ethnic diversities and differences.

Why would a supposedly totalitarian, Communist government of the PRC launch a project that actually invented or reinvented ethnic differences? As already mentioned, the Nationalist leader Chiang Kai-shek only wanted to recognize five branches of "Chinese" of the same lineage.

First let us briefly examine how the project was carried out. In 1953, when the first population census was carried out, respondents were asked to fill in their nationality status, not just to select one of a list of the designated categories but to choose a nationality—the so-called *ming cong zhuren*. The report in 1954 shows that more than 400 different nationalities were named and self-identified, more than 260 in Yunnan alone. It was to deal with this issue that a large number of work teams consisting of linguists and anthropologists, such as the well-known Fei Xiaotong (Fei 1980), and government officials were sent all over the country to find out what the real ethnic situation was. This was the beginning of the hugely consequential *minzu shibie* project, a project of identifying, classifying and finally designating nationality titles.

The criteria for nationality classification was supposedly guided by the Morganian/Stalinist definition: "a stable community with a common language, living in the same area, share the same style of economic life and have the same psychological composition" (Stalin 1934: 68). However, the Chinese reality made the identity process different. For instance, the Hui people are spread all over China and don't have a common language. On the other hand, the tiny Jingpo of about 12,000 residents speak two different languages. Furthermore, Stalin (Suny and Martin 2001), like Lenin (1913), thought nationalities became identifiable through the process of capitalism, before the rise of which there were only tribes and clans. Mao, however, intervened by brushing aside this kind of "scientific" theory, and decided to label all the different identifiable groups as nationalities (Huang and Shi 2005).

As of today the PRC has officially designated 56 nationalities in China. As the Han nationality is by far the largest in population, the remaining 55 groups are labeled national minorities, with the Jinuo nationality designated only in 1979. The PRC government has stopped considering further recognitions of new nationalities, though there are still around 20 identification applications pending.

What was the political motivation behind this huge project? Intuitively, one would think that a non-democratic Communist country would suppress diversity and difference. Instead, the PRC government created and reinvented difference and diversity. Government-assigned scholars even invented written scripts for some of the designated nationalities for them to record their history and literature that had been passed on orally. But why? Thomas Mullaney (2011) thinks that the project was a Communist-era project to determine the precise ethno-national composition of China. This is an accurate but incomplete explanation, which I will explore further in what follows.

A more fashionable and conceptually appealing postcolonialist explanation is that the Chinese nationality designation project was a "civilizing project" by the superior center to develop peripheral people.

The invention of ethnic identities therefore involves the distortion of the past, while the Han Chinese attempted to impose their values (Harrell 1996). Harrell further argues that the Han Chinese "feminized" (the sexual metaphor), infantilized (the education metaphor) and primitivized (the historical metaphor) national minorities. Along similar lines, Gladney (2004) argues, just as the West has defined itself against ethnic Others, so too have the Chinese defined themselves against marginalized groups in their own society. Taking on Said's postcolonial critique of Eurocentrism in its construction of the Asian Other, Gladney employs Michael Hechter's (1975) notion of "internal colonialism" to refer to national minorities as voiceless subaltern groups who have been subjected to various forms of Chinese domination. And the objectified portrayal of minority groups as exotic and erotic is for the construction of the "unmarked," modern, civilized Han majority.

In her review of Harrell, Schein astutely points out that in taking this approach of framing the Chinese as colonialists and imperialists in a civilizing discourse, many authors have relied on reasserting the superior authority of Western anthropological methods. Schein thinks that this method rests on the dubious premise that there is a space for science outside Orientalist discourse (Schein 1996). Gladney, however, does not frame the Chinese outside Orientalist discourse, but rather he stands Orientalist discourse on its head by asserting that in China "Minority is to the majority as female to male, as 'Third World' to 'First' and as the subjectivised is to the objectivised identity." In other words, the Chinese are "oriental Orientalists" (Gladney 1994: 93).

Whether the Han Chinese exercise internal colonialism and imperialism, and whether the national minorities identification project feminized and infantilized the Other, are certainly debated issues. Sautman (2001, 2006 and 2012) points out that Western colonialism almost wiped out the indigenous population in what is now the US and Australia, while indigenous populations like the Tibetans more than doubled in China. The Chinese nationality designation not only preserved the customs and ways of life for national minorities (though they are now under threat because of market capitalism), but also developed their language and even history and literature in written script. Affirmative policies have been designed for them: measures including lower entrance marks to enter higher education, permission to have more than one child per family whereas the Han could only have one, and a financial allowance for Muslims who only eat beef—beef is more expensive than pork in China.

For many non-Han nationality people, the nationality designation project has been a source of good. In cities like Beijing and Shanghai, national minority persons such as Tibetans or Uyghurs may experience discrimination, just as a migrant worker from any part of rural China of another nationality would, but in their own hometowns, research shows that a national minority person is more likely to have a public sector job than a Han Chinese, average years of education are also higher than among Han workers in the region, and minorities do not suffer serious wage differences (Wu and Song 2014).

Scholars like Gladney do admit that there are affirmative policies toward national minorities, and that China does portray itself as a multi-national democratic state and claims that minorities have autonomy. However, Gladney asserts that this is "in name only, since the Chinese Constitution does not allow true geopolitical secession" (Gladney 1994: 104). But multinationalism in China is not in name only: China not only recognizes but has also invented some nationalities. The fact that China does not allow true secession does not mean that there is no multinationalism and multiculturalism in China. These are really two different issues.

Gladney appears to indentify a political motivation behind the Chinese nationality designation project, stating that "The myth of democratic representation is critical to China's construction of itself as a modern multinational state, distinguishing and distancing itself from the ancient feudal Chinese empires that did not allow for representation" (Gladney 1994: 96). This is close to Chinese scholar Shi Lianzhu's evaluation of the project. According to Shi (Shi Lianzhu 1989), there are two reasons behind the rationale for the project. The first was to politically unite all peoples, and to downgrade Han chauvinism demonstrated by the likes of Chiang Kai-shek, who in his book *China's Destiny* declares that all the people are just lineages of the same blood heritage. For the PRC to recognize other nationalities is a step toward national equality. The second reason was to recognize the fact that people of all nationalities contributed to what is called China. However, there is a third reason that Shi does not explore, in the context of post-Mao China: the theory of class and class exploitation. When the national minority classification was designed, one of the guiding ideas was that people of all nationalities have no unresolvable conflicts because they are all oppressed.

The trouble is that some will never take what the Communist government says seriously and will always want to find the sinister elements behind their words. If we review the process we can see that there was nothing sinister behind the national minority designation project. There are three clear motivations behind it: (1) to find out the precise ethno-national composition of China (Mullaney 2011), (2) to promote national equality and economic development (Fei 1980) and (3) to establish national unity by proportional representation in the People's Congress (Cang 2017).

AN ATTEMPT TO BUILD A MODERN
AND PROGRESSIVE STATE

Guided by the Marxist idea of class and class struggle, the CCP under Mao believed that the main contradiction in any society is between the ruling and ruled classes, and therefore the contradictions between nationalities, though they exist, are secondary in nature. Furthermore, the theory of class led the CCP to believe that the ruling class would employ the contradictions among nationalities to divide and rule. Chiang Kai-shek's attempt to define China's national unity in his claim of China consisting of one Chinese lineage of five different branches was seen as typical Han chauvinism that suppresses national diversity and differences. In 1943, the already prominent CCP theoretician Chen Boda penned an op-ed to criticize Chiang's *China's Destiny* along similar lines (Chen 1943). By the same token, Mao, in his political report to the Seventh CCP National Congress in 1945 titled "On Coalition Government," criticizes Chiang as a Han chauvinist. In his speech "On Ten Major Relationships" delivered in 1956 that was not published until 1976, Mao (1976) lists the relationship between the Han Chinese and other national minorities as the sixth most important. Mao is against local nationalism (*difang minzu zhuyi*), but points out that China's policy emphasis should be in opposition to Han chauvinism. Mao states that all the nationalities have made a contribution to the history of China and that the majority Han is in fact the result of a mixture of different nationalities. Mao admits that there have been conflicts between the Han and other minority nationalities who have been bullied by the Han, but for Mao the blame should be placed on the ruling class. Mao thinks that the relationships between the Russians and other nationalities in the Soviet Union are not as good as they should be and that the Chinese government should, instead, sincerely assist minority nationalities with their economic and cultural development. In fact, as early as 1953, Mao (1977: 75–6) issued a severe criticism of Han chauvinism among the CCP party members, and instructed that all who are sent to work in minority nationality areas must not only understand the people in the region but also be sympathetic to them.

THE COMMON PROGRAM

When Mao proclaimed his program of coalition government he was unsure that the CCP could win such an overwhelming victory as they did around four years later in 1949. By using the strategy of United Front, Mao and the CCP were still trying to win over small political parties and society organizations to fight the Nationalists. The narrative at that time was that the CCP would lead a coalition government with other parties, and the social program was what was called New Democratic Revolution. For this purpose a Common Program was drawn up in September 1949 by the Chinese People's Political Consultative Committee, of which Article 50 of the Common Program declared that all nationalities are equal, and that neither national chauvinism nor national discriminations was allowed in the new China. Article 51 declares that "Regional autonomy shall be exercised in areas where national minorities are concentrated and various kinds of autonomy organizations of the different nationalities shall be set up according to the size of the respective populations and regions. In places where different nationalities live together and in the autonomous areas of the national minorities, the different nationalities shall each have an appropriate number of representatives in the local organs of political power" (Li Xuan 2016). Beijing announced that the first People's Congress would hold its first meeting in 1954, and that the Congress would give legitimacy to the state run by the CCP by approving the first constitution; it was required that all nationalities be proportionally represented at the Congress. It was this political rationale that led to the 1952 census, which further led to the rationale of nationality classification and the designation project.

OVERSEAS CHINESE

I have discussed how historical circumstances have made the term "Chinese" complex and undefinable, and how who the Chinese are is constructed knowledge.* I have also discussed the contemporary state of affairs of China's constructed multiculturalism and multinationalism. In this section I will discuss the constructed phenomenon of overseas Chinese. Hoffman and See (2017) claim that more than ten million Chinese nationals currently live outside China. If the descendants of China's historical emigration waves are included, an estimated 40 million Chinese people currently live in 130 countries. In their view, Chinese immigrants tend to maintain their cultural identity and traditions more than other migrants.

But who are they referring to when asserting that there are 40 million Chinese outside China? To conclude this chapter on deconstructing the term Chinese, I will demonstrate that the term "overseas Chinese" has two related referents—"sojourners" and "*hauqiao*"—how the term "overseas Chinese" was produced politically both inside and outside China, and how the term is used politically contemporarily.

The Colonial Manufacture of the Sojourner Discourse

Chinese migrants, especially Chinese from the south, be they Chinese who spoke Cantonese, or Hokkien, or Hakka, had been migrating to South East Asia for centuries (Skinner 1959, Chen 1923, Coppel 1982, Kuhn 2008, Wang Gungwu 1991). The Chinese not only played "a role in bringing Islam to Indonesia" but also "developed ports and city life and supply networks that attracted Muslim traders" (Taylor 2005: 160). But was very little written about them. Only when the Europeans began to colonize did history "begin," and that history included the discourse of the so-called sojourning overseas Chinese (Reid 1996).

One of the consequences of Western colonialism is that it led not only to more Chinese migrants in the form of merchants to South East Asia as "coadjutors" (Kuhn 2008), who played a crucial role in facilitating European colonial governments, but also "coolie" Chinese migrants to the New World that was being colonized. In the process the discourse of sojourners has been constructed. The basic idea of the sojourner discourse is that the Chinese would not and should not be settlers in the New World. The Chinese did not want to take their families when they migrated; they sent money back to China; they did not want to contribute to the building of the new colonies; they were gamblers;

---

* Some of the information and discussion in this section is published in Gao (2017).

they wore strange clothes. The Chinese were always Chinese and they had to go back to where they came from. They were, in the words of the celebrated Australian historian Geoffrey Blainey (1963), "birds of passage."

The categorization of four patterns of Chinese migrants—*huashang* (merchants), *huagong* (coolies), *huaqiao* (sojourner Chinese) and *huayi* (descendants of ethnic Chinese growing up and living outside China) by Wang Gungwu, is actually rather confusing. The coolie pattern fails to make a difference between indentured laborers and gold diggers. In fact all the migrants referred to by the other three patterns can and very often are referred to as *huaqiao* (Chinese residing overseas), even though it has to be pointed out that Wang means this pattern to refer to the nineteenth-century peasantry migration. Sojourner cannot be a pattern by itself because both coolies and merchants may sojourn or settle depending on personal and socio-economic circumstances. The term huaqiao is ideologically controversial (Wang 1991: 8–9) precisely because sojourning characteristics are attributed to it. Wang not only agrees with this kind of characterization but also has a cultural perspective on the sojourning behavior as a product of "Confucian rhetoric" (Wang 2003: 8).

Wang and Ang—a prominent cultural studies scholar—both have the so-called Chinese ethnic background, and have played into racial politics without perhaps realizing it. Wang argues that the term had become a major source of suspicion that the Chinese minorities could never feel loyalty toward their host nations (Wang 1999). Ang deals with the same issue by suggesting that "This ideological China-centeredness and obsession with Chineseness helped fuel anti-Chinese suspicion and discrimination in foreign lands, whether in South-East Asia or in European immigrant societies such as Australia and the United States" (Ang 2001: 82).

The Chineseness and China-centeredness argument is based on evidence that the Chinese tended to stick together and wanted to maintain the Chinese way of life. But there is nothing Chinese about it: the first generation of migrants of any group of the same background tend to stick together. What made the Chinese inclined to stick together particularly was that, as the case of a Chung family in Tasmania (Wu and Gao 2005) shows, economic circumstances (family and lineage sponsorship) were such that a group of Chinese in one particular location tended to be of the same extended family or lineage.

As migrants from China they certainly wished that China was strong and respected: "A stronger China was expected to enhance the status of ethnic Chinese communities abroad, and could be expected to support their interests in confrontations with the colonial states" (Douw 1999: 29). Not surprisingly most migrants of Chinese background would have pro-China sentiments. This was nothing culturally or racially Chinese. The fact that the European migrants did not appear to be defensive of their countries of origins had nothing to do with their racial characters but more to do with the fact as colonialists they were the masters of the New "discovered" World.

Williams (1999) is right in arguing that Chinese traditional ideas and practice of family, extended families and clans are important factors in making the Chinese a well-organized and close community of hard-working men. But these were only enabling factors that had more to do with their sense of self-protection rather than Chineseness or China-centeredness. The knowledge that Chinese migrants were sojourners was produced to serve the political purposes of Western colonialism, to exploit coolie labor when slavery was to be abolished and to justify white colonialist discrimination and their exclusion of the Chinese as settlers.

The Chinese Manufacture of the Nationalist Discourse

The Chinese term *huaqiao* (overseas Chinese) is puzzling in that even second, third or later generations of Chinese emigrants who might have nothing to do with China except their ancestry are called *huaqiao*. It is particularly puzzling if we consider that fact that emigrants of European countries are not called *ouqiao* (overseas Europeans), or *yingqinao* and *deqiao* (overseas English, overseas German). The reason behind this puzzle has to be found in European and especially British imperialism and colonialism. The British and the Europeans would march into a territorial space to claim ownership, to settle it as home. They did not consider themselves to be overseas.

But why do the Chinese also want to call themselves *huaqiao* (overseas Chinese)? In fact, the Chinese state of imperial China forbade Chinese migration overseas and did not stop condemning emigrants as "traitors" until the 1870s (Hoexter 1976). The Qing government (the rulers of which were not supposed to be Chinese "Chinese") at one point went as far as issuing an edict stating that to leave China was an offense punishable by death. But toward the end of the nineteenth century the Chinese state started to tap overseas Chinese as a fruitful source of loyalty (McKewon 1999). In 1909 the Chinese state of the rapidly dying Qing Empire even claimed *ius sanguinis* for all migrants from China and their descendants in its Nationality Law (Douw 1999).

The irony is that while the dying Qing government was trying to tap into overseas Chinese loyalty, the republican activist Sun Yat-sen, a *huaqiao* himself, played the ethnic Han Chinese card to arouse nationalism against the supposedly ethnic Manchu Qing government. Sun therefore played a very important role in constructing the *huaqiao* discourse when traveling to collect donations from overseas Chinese communities for a republican revolution that aimed to overthrow the Manchu rulers whom he did not consider Chinese.

The *huaqiao* narrative was not an ideology of Chinese-centeredness but an elite call for nationalism in response to Western/Japanese colonialism. The authoritative dictionary *ci yuan* (*Origin of Words*) published in 1908 did not even include *huaqiao* as a word (Hsu 2000: 314). It was only when the Western powers started to carve up China and when the Chinese Nationalists started China's nation building that the term *huaqiao* began to be widely used.

The construction of the term took another twist after the CCP defeated the Nationalist government that fled to Taiwan in 1949. This twist is expressed by how the term *huaqiao* is defined in *ci hai* (*Sea of Words*), another authoritative dictionary that was published in 1979: Chinese citizens residing overseas. The referent does not include citizens of other countries who are of Chinese ethnic origin. This reflects the fact that the PRC decided on a policy of encouraging overseas Chinese to adopt local citizenship, as explicitly expressed by China at the 1955 Bandung Conference. This is consistent with the PRC policy of not accepting dual citizenship, a policy designed to alleviate the anti-Communist fear that flared up due to Cold War propaganda outside China. The "reds under the bed" campaign underlined by the sojourner discourse was used to justify, for example, the killing of many Indonesians of supposedly Chinese ethnic background following the 1965 coup.

THE USE OF OVERSEAS CHINESE
FOR CONTEMPORARY POLITICS

Using the term "overseas Chinese" for political purposes has been a continuous practice by Chinese and Western governments, media and scholarship. The utility of the Chinese exploitation of the term is almost self-evident: not only is it politically expedient, as a way of enhancing governing legitimacy (Sow 2013 and Ong 2004), but it is also economically rational. To tap into the capital, and the professional and managerial expertise from overseas Chinese communities is both efficient and effective because of the commonality of cultural understanding and the ease of communication. Again this is not uniquely Chinese. Nobody is surprised, for instance, that the UK and USA have what is called a "special relationship." Nor is it a coincidence that both Australia and the UK were close allies of the US in the latter's aggression in Iraq. The spy network, the so-called "Five Eyes Alliances," is in many ways a rational product of the common British cultural and linguistic heritage (Friedersdorf 2013). Therefore it is not surprising that the current Chinese government also wants to exploit the resources of the overseas Chinese, as demonstrated by Xi Jinping who states that "In the best of Chinese traditions, generations of overseas Chinese never forget their home country, their origins, or the blood of the Chinese nation flowing in their veins" (Xi 2014: 69).

Not without reason, the term "greater China" has come to gain currency (Harding 1993, Callahan 2004), as a result of the fact that the nation state of China is still not a finite entity and that the PRC has successfully made use of resources from people of Chinese ethnic origin from other countries and regions. The Chinese nation state is still not a finite entity because, though the two former colonies Hong Kong and Macau have been handed over to the PRC, they remain autonomous from the PRC. There are still two governments between the Taiwan Straits, the PRC's and the ROC. The economic rise of the PRC, with significant contributions from the Chinese people in Hong Kong and Taiwan, among others, has given rise to anxiety all over the world, but it is especially felt by the West, as its global dominance may be threatened. Under these circumstances the term "overseas Chinese" is often used for political purposes.

Gonzalez-Vicente (2016), for example, accuses the Chinese government of exercising "racial sovereignty" in espousing notions such as that of a "Greater China," and ideas of a cultural and diasporic identity that ostensibly dissociate the nation from territory. Gonzalez-Vicente uses three examples to illustrate his accusation: the abduction in Hong Kong of book publishers critical of the Chinese government; the extradition of Taiwanese citizens from Kenya to China; and the Chinese

CHINESE? WHO ARE THE CHINESE? · 71

government's claim to protect Malaysian citizens of Chinese descent. According to Gonzalez-Vicente, the book publishers—Gui Minhai (a Swedish citizen) and Lee Bo (a British citizen)—were kidnapped by the Chinese government. Because of the lack of transparency and suppression of press freedom in the PRC it is not clear what the real circumstances were. Whether these were acts of thuggery by local security officers we don't know. But it is far-fetched to use this as an example of racial sovereignty, since the Chinese authorities had problems with these two operating in Hong Kong, which is part of China. The situation was complicated by three facts: (1) residents in Hong Kong don't actually have a PRC passport, (2) they have Hong Kong resident status and (3) the PRC does not accept dual citizenship. From the perspective of the PRC authorities, once you have Hong Kong resident status you are a Chinese citizen.

The PRC government also accepted the deportation of eight Taiwanese citizens from Kenya following a case of phone fraud in early 2016. Again this issue is not as simple as the PRC exercising its power extra-territorially. The Kenyan government only recognizes the PRC as a sovereign China and therefore it was diplomatically appropriate to hand over the Taiwanese to its diplomatic counterpart the PRC, since Taiwan is officially part of China for diplomatic purposes. If the Kenyan government decided to hand the detainees to Taiwan there would be nothing that the PRC could do. When the Kenyan government handed over a "gift" the PRC was ready to make use of this opportunity to enhance its claim over Taiwan. It had nothing to do with race, nor was it extra-territorial.

According to Gonzalez-Vicente, the declarations of China's ambassador in Malaysia, Huang Huikang, responding to anti-Chinese protests in Kuala Lumpur's Chinatown that China would not "sit by idly" if the rights of ethnic Chinese were to be violated is a more explicit discourse of extra-territorial sovereignty. It is true that most inhabitants of Chinatown are today Malaysian citizens. Given the history and evidence of how the so-called overseas Chinese were, have been and still are discriminated in some South East Asian countries, this warning might be useful for keeping peace and justice. It is hypocritical for Gonzalez-Vicente to claim that the ethnic Chinese in South East Asia are imagined as *huaqiao*, as part of China's diasporic nation and as "bridges" (this use of *qiao* confuses two different words: one *qiao* for residing and one *qiao* for bridge) to assist with the country's economic and civilizational ambitions while failing to condemn or even mention the history of brutality toward these people.

This is a standard political construction and use of the term "overseas Chinese" by Western governments, media and scholars. When there is a need for discrimination they single out these people as overseas Chinese. These so-called overseas Chinese are Malaysians and Indonesians, and many of them are locals of many generations, some of whom have even abandoned their Chinese names. But they are still being discriminated against as "Chinese," following the "yellow peril" attitude in white colonies or the "reds under the bed" outlook in the non-Communist camp during the Cold War. However, when it is politically expedient they are not considered to be overseas Chinese or even Chinese: the Hong Kongers and Taiwanese are not Chinese in these circumstances: rather they are people of an independent country.

4
Intellectual Poverty of the Chinese Neo-Enlightenment

INTRODUCTION

Since the May Fourth Movement in 1919, the condemnation of Chinese traditions or values has been a dominating trend in China. The construction of China as backward and uncivilized underlines what Chow calls the King Kong syndrome: China as a spectacular primitive monster whose despotism necessitates the salvation of its people by outsiders (Chow 1998). China needs cultural and value enlightenment (*qimeng*) from the more advanced and civilized West. The battle cry of this *qimeng* was that Western civilization of democracy and science was urgently required to enlighten the backward and uncivilized Chinese. For a brief period, roughly during the first 30 years of the PRC, the socialism-to-communism narrative looked like an answer to the question of *qimeng*. Although dangerously challenged during a few months in 1957, the 1949 Revolution narrative remained dominant in the Mao era until the end of the CR.

The increasing critique and condemnation of the Mao era in the 1980s was underpinned by the reignition of *qimeng*, and this was called *xin qimeng* (neo-enlightenment). *Xin qimeng* argues that the 1949 Revolution kidnapped the called-for enlightenment and therefore it has to be picked up again. The conceptualization of *xin qimeng* was crudely but brilliantly narrated by the phenomenal documentary *He Shang* (*The River Elegy*). Although *xin qimeng* suffered some setbacks as a result of the 1989 Tiananmen crackdown it remains a significant conceptualization that not only justifies but also conceptualizes China's rapid development into market capitalism.

DENUNCIATION OF MAO AND FAREWELL TO REVOLUTION

Although publicly and officially Mao is not totally denounced, and although Mao's portrait still hangs on the gate of Tiananmen and his body still lies in state at the memorial hall in the middle of Tiananmen Square, a systematic dismantling of the ideas of Mao and Mao era policies has been taking place for decades. The unofficial verdict has been that Mao achieved nothing positive since 1957 when the Anti-Rightist Movement started. This is the well-known late Mao thesis propagated for instance by people like Li Rui (1999). In the West the onslaught against Mao has gone even further. Through publications such as memoirs, biographies and popular media, Mao is portrayed as "a murderer, a torturer, an untalented orator, a lecher, a destroyer of culture, an opium profiteer, and a liar" in the words of Chang and Halliday (2005: 121). The Mao era was a period of political repression and economic disaster. The CR was a holocaust, the darkest age in Chinese history, producing ten years of calamities.

The Chinese neo-enlightenment intelligentsia have caricatured Mao as one of the emperors in the long stagnant history of China, as if the 1949 Revolution did not take place, as if the idea of the French Revolution, the ideas of Marx and socialism and mass struggle against injustice and oppression all over the world, had never been around and were unrelated to China. Gao Hua, a prominent Mao historian, for instance, asserts that there is a "Mao way of thinking" that can be summarized as: (1) others cannot be trusted; (2) any means to fight your enemy is justifiable; (3) struggle is absolute, everything consists of the two opposites and everything is either black or white; and (4) violent action is the preferable option. For Mao, according to Gao Hua, one is judged by whether one wins, and the winner possesses morality. Gao Hua further asserts that the "Mao way of thinking" is essentially a local Chinese product, grown out of China's vast fertile soil. The Mao way of thinking originated from ancient ruling techniques based on empiricism but is expressed in folk language and is the accumulated residue of grass-root rebellion culture and rogue elements in society (Gao Hua 2008).

Gao Hua's pronouncements of the Mao way of thinking are based on the Chinese neo-enlightenment narrative in a number of important ways. First, they blame Chinese tradition for what is supposedly wrong with Mao, just like the May Fourth Movement blames tradition for what is wrong with China. Second, they are elitist in their contempt toward the lower-class Chinese by treating them as rogue elements. Third, they deny the socio-economic class nature of the Chinese society. Fourth, it avoids any mention of Marxist-Leninist influence on the Chinese Revolution.

Jin Guantao, a very articulate member of the neo-enlightenment intelligentsia, claims that in China the 1980s was the second age of enlightenment, which picked up the ideas of the May Fourth New Culture Movement (Du Guang 2007). Du Guang states that during the time, democracy and despotism fought bare-handed: light and darkness clashed violently. To some Chinese *xin qimeng* intelligentsia, the fundamental way of enlightening the Chinese, i.e. to change their mentality, is to convert them to Christianity. For them it is Christianity that made Westerners individualistic, and taught them to care about human rights. Liu Xiaofeng laments that the greatest mistake of the May Fourth Movement was its failure to make China adopt Christianity. Liu thinks Christianity can save China (Du Guang 2007, Lü Xinyu 2009). Liu Xiaofeng himself would consider his position on Christianity with regard to China as consistent with the enlightenment tradition. But as Lü Xinyu points out, Liu is in fact anti-enlightenment (Lü Xinyu 2009), because to revert to religion is anything but the spirit of the European Enlightenment.

The essential argument of the Chinse neo-enlightenment in the 1980s is more sophisticatedly expressed by Li Zehou, who uses the term "the duet of enlightenment and salvation," to argue that national salvation hijacked enlightenment. Li thinks that the enlightenment thinking of the Chinese May Fourth Movement was passionate but not rational enough. Rationality is what China needs, and that is why the neo-enlightenment should not accept postmodernist Foucault, as Foucault is against rationalism (Du Guang 2007). Li and his neo-enlightenment colleagues fail to realize that Western Enlightenment's stress on rationalism was based on its criticism of what was considered irrational religion. When rationalism translates as *lixing* in Chinese it does not imply any background of secularism against religion. But from the point of view of some European Enlightenment thinkers at that time, Confucianism and the Chinese tradition looked very rational as Confucianism is rooted in non-religious pragmatism.

The Chinese condemnation of Mao has been warmly received outside China and is interpreted as "the Chinese are now telling the truth." In the global intellectual climate of the late 1980s it was easy to ignore the accomplishments of the Chinese during Mao era, such as land reform, the dramatic rise of life expectancy of a vast number of ordinary people, the impressive rise in the literacy rate, the celebrated liberation of women and a sound foundation for modern industry and agriculture.

Instead, one is constantly urged to think about the debris, the ruins, and the cruelty and violence that the Revolution caused on the way. Therefore, ever since the fall of the Berlin Wall it has been fashionable to produce, and easy to sell, anti-Maoism in the "Western" market. The China-made onslaught of Mao the person, Mao's ideas, and indeed the Mao era from 1949 to 1978 has its exported version in the West. Two primary examples of these products are Doctor Li Zhisuis' *Private Life of Chairman Mao* (1994) and Chang and Halliday's *Mao the Unknown Story* (2005).

Publications that included condemnations of Mao from "insiders" such as Li Rui (1994, 1999) and Li Shenzhi (2000) were very popular. Li Shenzhi, who served as vice president of the Chinese Academy of Social Sciences and the first president of the Chinese Association of American Studies, and who is considered the godfather of Chinese "liberalism" by many Chinese neo-enlightenment intelligentsia, asserted that Mao was a bandit, warlord and tyrant and that China had to change, either through peaceful evolution or violent revolution. Li also declared that if China wanted to modernize it had to follow the US and be prepared to be "the grandson" (Zhang Deqin 2006).

The political agenda of the Chinese neo-enlightenment was to bid farewell to revolution: not only the 1949 Chinese Revolution but all revolutions including the French Revolution, while ignoring the fact that the French Revolution was one brainchild of the European Enlightenment. One of the neo-enlightenment heavyweights, Liu Zaifu, argues that the May Fourth Movement was a cultural movement to develop individualism. To him, the 1949 Revolution liquidated individual personality and only in the 1980s did individual personality start to wake up again (Liu Zaifu 1985–6). Liu argues that the May Fourth Movement drove away Mr. Kong (Confucius) but had not really invited in Mr. De (democracy) and Mr. Sai (science) (Liu Zaifu and Li Zehou, 1997).

THE IDEOLOGY OF *QIMENG* AND THE WEST

According to the Chinese neo-enlightenment, China's real progress in humanity, ignited at the beginning of the twentieth century, was interrupted by the Japanese invasion and then hijacked by the 1949 Revolution. Only following the late 1980s did China get back on the right track. China has come full circle: the 1949 Revolution hijacked *qimeng*, and a post-revolutionary *xin qimeng* is required to continue to change the Chinese mentality so as to catch up with the West and capitalism. The editor and managing director of the influential journal *yanhuang chunqiu*, which regularly publishes material framed in the *qimeng* intellectual narrative, has published a widely read book that condemns Chinese culture. The book (Wu Si 2009) is supposed to have discovered the underlying Chinese cultural patterns of behavior that can explain the current bureaucracy, corruption and irrationality. Wu's anti-Chinese political culture narrative is so successful that a word coined by him—*qian guize* (hidden rules)—has become an everyday catchphrase in China today.

The assumption that the Chinese society—the Other—is uncivilized and unhuman, and even man eating (a metaphor used by Lu Xun), is based on the premise that the West—Us—is humane and civilized. They (Us) have democracy to deal with problems in human society and science to tackle nature for the benefit of human beings. We, the Chinese Other, have a "feudalist," "despotic," "dictatorial" or "authoritarian" political system that is oppressive and corrupt. In other words, to the *xin qimeng* conceptualization everything "Western" looks better, sounds better and tastes better. The controversial but hugely successful documentary *He Shang (The River Elegy)* reflects the intellectual mood in 1980s China. China has to bid farewell to the Other—the poor and cruel Yellow River cultural Other and the closed mindedness of the Great Wall Other—so as to embrace Us: the blue ocean culture of the open West.

It is astonishing that in a country that has one of the world's longest continuous civilizations, the people of which have contributed so much material civilization to humanity (Needham 1954–), there exists an idea that almost every educated Chinese is familiar with: worship and have blind faith in things foreign. The social research center of the *Chinese Youth Newspaper*, together with Sina, carried out a web survey of 2,563 young Chinese at the start of the twenty-first century. The results are startling but hardly surprising: 59.2 percent of those surveyed thought that the majority of the people they know of have the mentality of worshiping Western things and 48.7 percent of them do not feel confident being a Chinese (Hu Luobo 2009).

While it can be generally accepted that industrialization and technological innovations have improved material conditions for human life in general, and that human rights struggles such as the Black movement, feminism, the trade union movement, socialism and even the Communist movement have promoted political, social and economic rights for the poor and marginalized, it is also true that science has created new problems in the "progress" of solving old ones. Witness how weapons of mass destruction proved to be more efficient in killing human beings, but have failed to solve the issue of war and peace, and how our environment has been degraded to the extent that it threatens the very existence of humanity.

Nor is it the case that there is no corruption in what are considered to be superior Western societies. Witness the fraud in financial and banking sectors exposed by the recent financial crisis. Are politicians less corrupt in Western societies because there is democracy? In fact, one of the least corrupt societies is Singapore, where there is no democracy and where most of the residents are not from "civilized" Europe but from Asia, the majority of whom are of ethnic Chinese origin.

At the same time, in tune with the international intellectual and political climate, the ideology of *xin qimeng* has taken a new turn, which is that individual human rights take priority over national sovereign rights. The argument, which appears convincing in abstract terms, is that all human beings have basic rights in common, which should be protected by all governments. If and when governments abuse any of those basic rights the international community, meaning those countries that hold the moral high ground of human rights, have the right to intervene, including military attack and occupation of one country by another.

The country that is considered to be the supreme example of human rights protection, to the Chinese neo-enlightenment, is the US, which also has the military, technological and economic power to intervene anywhere in the world. To the *xin qimeng* intelligentsia, it is not a coincidence or accident that the US possesses both qualities: the quality of the most democratic country that protects human rights, and that of the most powerful one on earth. For them it is the former quality that has enabled the US to achieve the latter.

Some of the elite Chinese intelligentsia are so convinced by this argument regarding the American political agenda that in China they are often referred to as whateverists. This crude adversarialism is nicknamed in Chinese online media as two whatevers: whatever it is that China does is wrong and whatever it is that the US does is right. The logic is simple: since the US is the number one liberal and democratic country it cannot do anything wrong, and anything the US government does is legitimate because it is elected by the people, it consists of the people and it works for the people. In contrast, because the PRC is ruled by Communists that are not elected by the people, it does not work for the people, it doesn't consist of the Chinese people and it cannot do anything right or legitimate.

THE POLITICS OF THE CHINESE NEO-ENLIGHTENMENT

The Chinese neo-enlightenment was not just an intellectual trend setter, but was politically backed by people at the top of the CCP. The CCP General Secretary Zhao Ziyang was a major backer until he was toppled following the 1989 Beijing events. Zhao Ziyang (2007) claims that he was responsible for the conceptualization of the prime stage of socialism. When this concept was first officially launched it was not clear what the general party secretary of the CCP meant by it. With hindsight it is clear: China should copy the West. "What is called modernization is just Westernization. What we should do is to do the West way" (2007: 71). "What the West does is the mainstream of the world and China needs to be linked to that track" (2007: 286). Zhao was fully aware that in the process of globalization there is a disparity between rich and poor countries. The gap between the North and South is increasing; the disparity between the poor and rich is increasing. National industries in poor countries are being invaded. All of this will lead to New Left ideas, which will, in the name of national welfare, resist globalization and therefore resist China from marching into modern civilization. These narrow-minded national ideas arouse hatred against the West and it is a great threat to another of China's efforts to enter modern civilization and could lead to another failure (2007: 322).

By using the word "another," Zhao has in mind the effort previously made by China that ended up in failure, i.e. the 1949 Revolution that he himself had participated in. There is no clearer neo-enlightenment message than this. Zhao further illustrates: "Eastern culture is backward; it cannot produce the flower of freedom, democracy and human rights" (2007: 322). In contrast to China, the US is a wonderland; I again quote at length:

> This country's economy has been growing continuously. It is prosperous, developed, and always in a leading position in hi-tech. Its society is stable, and its leadership passes power peacefully and stably. It does not expand its territory; it does not engage in colonialism; all it does is to carry out free trade. Of course the U.S.A. also seeks its

national interest in international relations; but its national interest is the same as the interest of human kind. It develops trade with foreign countries but its foreign policies are governed by domestic values, which aim to promote freedom, democracy, and human rights; these are values of modern civilization for all human society. If we need a leader in human development, that leader is better to be the U.S.A., much better than the Soviet Union, let alone Germany and Japan, because [the] U.S.A. does not have territorial ambition and is not colonialist. (2007: 334–5)

Admittedly Zhao would not have made these remarks when he was still in power, and he might not have been able to articulate them in these terms at that time, even though he was guided by the conceptualization of neo-enlightenment. Zhao made these remarks when he was under house arrest, and must have thought about the matter many times when he reflected on his life and on the cause he had served and on the China that he had led. By any measure these remarks from the former head of the CCP are extraordinary: all the work and struggle carried out by the huge mass of people under the leadership of the CCP for over half a century since 1921 when the CCP was established, the very revolution to which Zhao himself had apparently devoted his life, was misguided and in vain. China had to start again. And the shame of such a failure was supposed to be covered by the fig leaf he claims to have coined: "the primary stage of socialism."

The policy consequences guided by neo-enlightenment are illustrated by the case of Tibet. Thanks to another former head of the CCP, Hu Yaobang, who was held in high esteem by the Chinese neo-enlightenment intelligentsia because he was considered to be liberal and democratic, Chinese government's policies in Tibet were reversed dramatically. By rejecting the theory of class struggle, the idea of socio-economic conflict within Tibetan society was abandoned; temples were repaired and renovated; and for many Tibetans to become a monk was a prestigious life path for males. The former class of the oppressed were urged to think that Mao was a terrible mistake and that the Dalai Lama should be worshiped instead (Wang Lixiong 2002, Wei Se 2006). Hundreds and thousands of those who were labeled as old aristocrats, slave owners and rebellion leaders were rehabilitated and invited to enter the leadership ranks of governments such as the People's Congress, and Political Consultative bodies. The reform in Tibet since Hu Yaobang's intervention meant that the former lower class of people were stripped of any social status and economic protection (Yuan 2009). The class struggle in Tibet was turned on its head by the reform policy, and thus practically handed out a verdict (1) that the pre-1959 system (pre-land reform) was the right one after all; (2) that the Dalai Lama, not Mao Zedong, should be respected; and (3) that the Revolution was a terrible mistake. For many inside and outside China the reverse was a turn for the better for the Tibetans. But the irony that is hardly noticed by the Chinese neo-enlightenment is this: if enlightenment is to make sure that human beings are free of traditional values, especially the benighted religious tradition, is the return of life dominated by religion in Tibet not the opposite of enlightenment?

Is Tibet so special that everything in its society is religious to the extent that it does not experience socio-economic problems? A recent Beijing report (Wong 2009) shows that the March 2008 riots were not just religious, or incited by misguided outside forces, or simply an ethnic drive for independence. The report shows that the riots were caused at least partially by socio-economic complaints. Interestingly, the report points out that the ruling elite in Tibet tries to hide the socio-economic nature of the discontent in Tibetan society and tries to convince Beijing that every time there is a riot it is about independence and incited by outside forces. In this way, the ruling elite is able to extract more resources from Beijing for their own benefit and able to consolidate their own power.

Since the neoliberal guru Milton Friedman's first visit to China in 1980, a neoliberal dynasty has developed (Kwong 2006) that has exercised what Wang Hui (2006: 9) calls the "discursive hegemony" for over a quarter of a century. According to this conceptualization of development, a generation of Chinese has to be sacrificed, and those who are to be sacrificed are the tens of millions of workers who lose their jobs, plus hundreds of millions of rural migrant workers. This is explicitly articulated by celebrity economist, former dean of the prestigious Guanghua Management Institute at Beijing University, Li Yining, who argues that all welfare measures should be abolished so as to maintain work enthusiasm. Chinese society can progress only if the gap between the rich and poor is increased (Li Yining 2009). This is called the primitive accumulation that is required for the development of capitalism, as happened in Britain with developments such as the "enclosure movement." It is ironic that in the name of humanity and civilization, the *Neo-enlightenment* Chinese intelligentsia either publicly or tacitly supports such an inhuman development strategy.

One of the leading and most respected members of the Chinese liberal intelligentsia, Qin Hui, thinks that China's main issue is to promote modernization, not to reflect on modernization. In order to modernize China, rural Chinese have to be turned urban. More importantly, peasant culture, peasant mentality and peasant personality have to be remolded. It is this neo-enlightenment ideology that directs Qin's interpretation of a historical phenomenon in the central Shaanxi Plain: there were actually not many big landlords, nor were there many land tenants, but there were many small and medium-sized landowners who worked on their own lands. The interpretation of this historical fact from one of China's top rural studies experts, Wen Tiejun (2005), is that due to the tension between a highly dense population and little land resources, land in China could not have been concentrated into the hands of very few landlords. Instead, land ownership in China tended to decentralize, and through this process land resources were optimally used and its benefits were maximally utilized. Clearly, under the ecological pressure of a low land to population ratio the most efficient development is more decentralized or more equal land ownership. In other words, this suggests that traditional rural Chinese society was far more civilized than it was given credit for, and in fact far more civilized than the land ownership system in the feudal West. Qin Hui and Su Wen (1996), however, interpret this historical fact very differently. They take the more equal distribution of land as evidence of China being more "feudalistic," and argue that this kind of egalitarianism is the reason for China's lack of development.

Most of the Chinese neo-enlightenment intelligentsia elite hold views of the "West" as idealistic. It is not that they are totally ignorant of the West: they read books about Western philosophy, literature and art and they watch Western television programs and movies, mostly in translated Chinese. They, unlike many American politicians, actually have a passport and travel to, or even stay in, Western countries for a length of time. But they don't actually live like an American or French person and therefore can hardly claim to know anything realistic about the West. They of course would not be interested in reading anything about trade unions, or Communist-inspired protests in Western societies. Therefore, they may not know that a lot of freedoms and democratic rights were not given, as lofty as Lincoln's speech or the American Constitution are, but developed gradually as a result of sustained social tensions during various periods of history, and much of that was won through grassroots struggles. Even today, class interests are entrenched in many Western societies; there is a lot of corruption both in politics and in business; and there are many instances of abuses of human rights. Moreover, democracy and individual rights are ideals that need to be continually guarded and won over. The Chinese have to fight for human rights and democracy, and to do that the Chinese intellectual elite should engage with the working class to improve their working conditions, instead of looking to the West.

CONCLUSION: THE POVERTY OF
THE CHINESE NEO-ENLIGHTENMENT

In this chapter I have outlined the development and main ideas of the Chinese neo-enlightenment. I have argued that the *xin qimeng* narrative has exhausted its intellectual capacity and usefulness. In this brief concluding section I will summarize some features of the poverty of the Chinese enlightenment, old and new.

One feature of the intellectual poverty of the Chinese enlightenment is its inherent social Darwinism, i.e. its admiration for and identity with the strong and powerful on the one hand and its contempt for the week and the poor on the other. This worship of the strong is evident in two major ways. One is its admiration of and identification with the powerful and most affluent nations in Europe and especially the US. It has contempt not only for China but also for other non-Western countries (except Japan, and to some extent successful small coutnries like Hong Kong and Taiwan that are supposed to have "made it") and African countries. In the mind of these enlightenment elite, African and Asian countries, and indeed the rest of the world, have no history, and no civilization to talk about. If China or other nations have suffered from colonial plunder and imperialist invasion they deserved it because it was their fault they failed to catch up with the civilized world.

This survival of the fittest social Darwinism rationale is one of the cornerstones of the Chinese enlightenment intellectual narrative. This is expressed by its intense contempt for poor and disadvantaged social groups in China. It is justifiable and fair for these lower-class people to work like slaves because they are of lower quality (*suzhi di*). Elite Chinese dissidents are seen as heroes symbolizing the national conscience, whereas popular protests or popular opinion (such as the evidential massive support of Mao and his policies) were considered populism that is benighted (*yumei*), and the product of brainwashing and rogue elements (*chunmang*). This blatant worship of the powerful and strong on the one hand, and shameless contempt for the poor and weak on the other, is a sign of the moral decay and intellectual bankruptcy of the *qimeng* narrative.

The second feature of the intellectual poverty of the Chinese enlightenment is its inherent anti-democratic elitism. How can anyone who is not intellectually bankrupt defend the existing system in which "one single country, possessing only about 5 percent of the earth's population, has roughly 20 percent of its G.D.P., spends almost 50 percent of its total defense expenditures, and freely prints bills that account for 65–70 percent of global foreign-currency reserves" (Kennedy 2009). How can anyone defend a development strategy that sacrifices the majority for the benefit of a minority? If the welfare and opinion of the majority can be ignored what is left regarding democratic value and human rights?

The third feature of the intellectual poverty of the Chinese enlightenment is its repetition of May Fourth Movement clichés and its inability to differentiate between liberty and formal institutional democracy. It is true that in traditional Anglo-Saxon societies there was a political culture of individual liberty and personal freedom. The legacy of this tradition is still seen in the UK, USA, Canada, New Zealand and Australia. Much of this tradition has also been spread to other countries, Europe and Asia, including Hong Kong and now China. But although this is related, it is not the same as an institutional democracy of elected representatives through party politics. China needs liberty and individual rights protected by law, but the way to achieve that is not through enlightenment clichés.

The fourth feature of intellectual poverty of the Chinese neo-enlightenment is its failure to conduct empirical research in the social sciences. This may either have something to do with its contempt for doing the hard work of empirical research, or to do with the issue of limited resources.

The fifth feature of the intellectual poverty of the Chinese neo-enlightenment is their refusal to be critical of modernity. As discussed above in the case of Li Zehou, China is considered to be at a lower stage of human development that needs Westernization, but it cannot talk about postmodernism. They refuse to see that all the postmodern or modern problems are with us in China today, including alienation, environmental disasters and a reduced quality of life. They do not realize that the Mao era was modern, and in many aspects the ideas and practices in the Mao era were actually postmodern, postcolonial and deconstructionist, as I will argue in Chapters 6 and 7 on the CR.

The Chinese intellectual idea of modernity is sometimes expressed through crude materialism. Professor Xiao Zhuoji of the School of Economics at Beijing University, for instance, is reported to have said that one indication of China's modernization is that professors at Beijing University all have cars and holiday villas (Mei Hua 2009). Surely it is a sign of intellectual poverty if you cannot think of an alternative to a development model that has resulted in so many problems. Unlike the Chinese enlightenment narrative, intellectual discussion originating from other non-Western countries is at least forward looking and critical. For instance, way back in the late 1940s, the Singer–Prebisch thesis was put forward by non-Western economists, and was later developed into the theory of dependence as an alternative narrative to explain the Latin American situation, in reaction to some theories of development and as a criticism of modernization theory (Amin 1994). By the 1970s, South Asian scholars also developed subaltern studies, challenging the hegemonic intellectual narrative of the Western academic world (Spivak 1999). What have mainstream Chinese scholars done in their intellectual discourse, apart from repeating clichés?

5

The Coordinated Efforts
in Constructing China

INTRODUCTION

The biotechnology scientist Li Jiayang is an important techno-bureaucrat in China, as he is the vice president of the Chinese Academy of Sciences, dean of the School of Agricultural Sciences and the deputy minister of the Chinese Ministry of Agriculture. Professor Li was a member of the external biotechnology advisory panel of DuPont from 2007 until 2012, when he was exposed for serving as an advisor to a transnational company. DuPont quickly had his name removed and announced that Li had stopped being a member in 2011 when he was appointed vice minister of agriculture (*Beijing Youth*, 2013). But according to the New York Stock Exchange report on October 14, 2013, Li was still a member of the company's advisory panel (Lv Yongyan 2016). Li, a distinguished scientist, became a controversial figure because of the debate on the issue of DNA-engineered crops, and because there was a call for food sovereignty among some Chinese academics (Yan Hairong 2015).

Is the importing of engineered seeds from transnational companies like DuPont good for China's national interest? Is there a conflict of interest for Li, who is in a position to make policies on such issues in China while at the same sitting on an advisory panel of a company whose aim is to penetrate the Chinese market? For scientists in developed Western countries there might be no dilemma of this kind, since to serve their national interest is often very good for transnational interests, as these countries dominate in the fields of science and technology.

This chapter attempts to get into the complex issues involving the Chinese political and intellectual elite, not only regarding the issue of nationalism versus transnationalism, but also regarding constructing the PRC. The Chinese political and intellectual elite are of course not one and the same entity. But apart from the fact that many of the intellectual elite, like Li Jiayang, are also the political elite, and the fact that

one of the criteria for selecting the Chinese political elite is credentials in academic and intellectual studies—a kind of meritocracy legacy
from traditional China—the Chinese political and intellectual elite in
post-Mao China have two things in common: (1) class interests and (2)
intellectual conceptualization as the foundation of their knowledge of
China and the world.

This chapter argues that the common class interest of the Chinese
political and intellectual elite means that they are not only more likely
to degrade the Mao era, but are also inclined to surrender themselves
to transnational interests. As an analytical category, "comprador" may
be an appropriate term to use for this class of people, as they tie their
socio-economic interest to transnational capital. A particular member
of a class may or may not be conscious of his or her class interest, but
the class as a collective is aware of its class interest in its conceptualization of China and the world. The chapter also argues that the Chinese
comprador conceptualization of China and the world was triggered
by the post-Mao backlash against the CR, from the Literature of the
Wounded, developed from the *suku* (telling bitterness of the past)
literature, to bidding farewell to the Revolution by picking up the
enlightenment theme, and finally to embracing neoliberalism.

NEO-ENLIGHTENMENT THAT HAS INSPIRED THE
CHINESE POLITICAL AND INTELLECTUAL ELITE

As discussed in Chapter 4, since the late 1970s—with the appearance of the Literature of the Wounded and the promotion of horror
stories such as that of Zhang Zhixin (a story that I deal with at length
shortly), coupled with exposure to the material affluence not only of
developed Western societies but also the "tiger" economies in East
Asia—the Chinese political and intellectual elite in post-Mao China
suddenly came to the understanding that China was even more uncivilized and backward than it was before 1949. To their understanding,
the Chinese May Fourth Movement that was meant to enlighten the
Chinese was hijacked by nationalism/communism that was perceived
as necessary to save China from oblivion. To their shock they "discovered" that there was nothing revolutionary about the 1949 Revolution,
that there was nothing modern about the CCP and that the system
dictated by Mao was feudal. An ideological and political denigration of

China's past, including the 1949 Revolution, was called for. Hence the neo-enlightenment (*xin qimeng*).

How do we understand the self-hatred displayed by this group of Chinese who were participants in, and in many ways definers of, a revolution that irreversibly changed nearly a quarter of the human race, but who now say it was all wrong? The explanation lies in unpacking the Chinese as a general category. As I argued in Chapter 3, there is no such thing as "the Chinese" ethnically. As I will argue in this chapter, there is no such a thing as "the Chinese" politically. There are Chinese of not only different political positions and of different economic interests, but also of different conceptualizations of China and the world. The fact that "political opposition" is not allowed openly in China does not mean that there are no political differences. The fact that they are "Chinese" does not mean they don't identify with interest as well as intellectual conceptualization that is non-Chinese. In fact the Orients can be Orientalists.

THE CHINESE INTELLECTUAL ELITE AND THE WEST: THE CASE OF LIU XIAOBO

Liu Xiaobo is one of those 1980s Chinese enlightenment intelligentsia figures who took cultural essentialism seriously—unlike Wei Jingsheng, an electrician, who put up a wall poster that advocated the controversial notion that what China needed was the "fifth modernization," i.e. democracy, with a reference to the Chinese government's declared program of Four Modernizations first raised by Zhou Enlai in 1973 (four modernizations of industrial, agricultural, national defense and science and technology); or Li Zehou, who developed the idea that there was tension between the narratives of Chinese nationalism and the Enlightenment and that the tragedy for China was that the Enlightenment had to give way to nationalism amid foreign invasions. What made Liu Xiaobo stand out was not original ideas but his sharp way of articulating something that he knew would shock his audience. For instance, he declared that the reason why Hong Kong was so civilized and modern was that it had been a British colony for 200 years. Therefore for China, a country so big and backward, to reach the status of Hong Kong, 300 years of Western colonization would not be enough (Sautman and Yan 2010, Chen Weisong 2017).

Parallel to Liu Xiaobo's self-hatred of China and the Chinese (Li Channa 2010), he sang the praises of the West, especially the US. For instance, Liu Xiaobo supported the US invasion of Iraq in 2001 (Liu Xiaobo 2002, Sautman and Yan 2010). When the 1989 Tiananmen events were taking place, Liu Xiaobo was actually in the US as a visiting scholar. Liu immediately flew back to Beijing to take part in the events: he was among those who staged a hunger strike to support the student protests. One has to admire his courage and conviction. Liu in this instance overcame the weakness of the Chinese intellectual elite's lack of engagement with grassroots struggles advocating for rights. To his credit, Liu was also one of the few people who helped to get the students out of Tiananmen Square in time to avoid further casualties, during the last phase of the Beijing events. What finally got Liu into more trouble with the Chinese authorities was his work of getting people to sign and publicize what was called the 2008 Charter. Shockingly, the Chinese regime arrested Liu Xiaobo and put him in jail. This act of cowardliness on the part of the Chinese authorities demonstrated its insecurity and lack of intellectual conviction.

Most likely it was this cowardly act that prompted the decision to give Liu Xiaobo the 2010 Nobel Peace Prize. The award generated fierce debate (Fallows 2011), to the extent that the Nobel Peace Prize committee felt pressured to respond. One committee member, Geir Lundestad, claimed that Beijing's decision to jail Liu "solved the problem" of how to recognize Chinese activists. He said the judges gradually came to believe that they had to "address the China question." In his talk at Oxford University, Lundestad said "If we had given a prize to a dissident from Cuba or Vietnam, fine, there are difficult situations in those countries, but the question would then be: why don't you address China?" (Lundestad 2010).

These remarks reveal that to committee members the prize not only had to be awarded to a dissident, but also a dissident in a Communist country. They would not consider awarding the prize to dissidents in countries such as the US, like Noam Chomsky, or a dissident in Saudi Arabia or Israel (Ali 2011). One can easily name tens of countries where human rights abuses are worse than those in China. The award has to be granted in accordance with the geopolitical interests of Western powers, whatever that interest is perceived to be in any particular year. That is of course why the American National Endowment for Democracy paid Liu Xiaobo for his dissident activities.

RE-ORIENTALISM AND THE WESTERN
TRANSNATIONAL INTEREST

As Lisa Lau (2009) argues, the "Orientals" can, and some Chinese Orientals do, perpetrate Orientalism no less than "non-Orientals." These Orientals can "self-Other" by having an intimate relationship with transnational capital, a relationship that is closer and of more immediate significance than their relationship with their compatriots. Guo Songmin (2016) calls these Orientals engaged in intellectual discourse the "comprador intelligentsia." Guo argues that the main feature of the comprador intelligentsia is that their politic-economic and social status interests are closely related to Western transnational capital. The more Western transnational capital penetrates China the more they benefit. Furthermore, Oriental Orientalists work together with their mentors to develop an Orientalist narrative of their own country. For example, the post-CR term for the Chinese Literature of the Wounded was co-constructed by the intellectual elite in the West. Bian Qin (2016) points out that in his interview with the Phoenix media outlet the then young author Lu Xinhua (it is his work *The Wounded* that prompted the name of this genre) admitted that the Chinese did not have the conceptualization to name the immediate post-Mao literature as the Literature of the Wounded. It was the Associated Press that coined the name, which was then reported by Chinese Reference News. It was the Literature of the Wounded that announced the arrival of the anti-CR, anti-Revolution and anti-Mao discourse which further led to Orientalist Orientalism and that conceptualizes the first 30 years of the PRC's history from 1949 to 1978 as a total failure.

As Lau (2009: 40) argues, the Oriental Orientalists had to "utilize positionality to prove eligibility as representative and validity of testimony to join their Western colleagues. The oriental Chinese Orientalists' claimed status is almost that of 'witness', which is a far less empowered position than that of Orientalists, who saw no reason to justify themselves." The Chinese witness is nonetheless powerful because it rings true of "the Chinese themselves say so." In what she calls Occidentalism, Chen Xiaomei argues that it is impossible to divorce Western influence from what is "authentically Chinese" because the latter concept "has already been 'contaminated'" and even constructed by cultural and intercultural appropriations that belong to the whole of Chinese Western relationships (Chen 1995: 4).

The post-Mao neo-enlightenment could not bring itself to admit that, despite the ups and downs, including turmoil, the 1949 Revolution did change China, mostly for the better. Logically, therefore, they would deny the fact that like any other country, China's economic development was path-dependent and that the Mao era laid the foundation for not only the runway but also the engine for the post-Mao economic take-off. This denial is best illustrated by the 2008 Beijing Olympics Opening Ceremony directed by Zhang Yimou: the grand narrative of China's history leaves the 30 years of the Mao era blank. How do you explain the sudden jump from a poor and economically collapsed country to the world's second largest economic power in 30 years, according to this construction of contemporary China? "Miracle!" everyone shouts.

THE CHINESE ELITE AND GLOBAL CAPITALISM

China's economic power on the international stage has brought enormous prestige and wealth to the Chinese intellectual and political elite. Nowadays it is hard to invite a prominent Chinese scholar to a speaking engagement without paying for a business class ticket. The amount of wealth plundered by the *guan er dai* (princelings of the veteran revolutionaries) from the Chinese state assets that had been accumulated during the Mao era is nothing short of being spectacular. According to AFP (2016), the Panamanian law firm Mossack Fonseca, which was at the heart of a massive leak of offshore banking records, has more offices in China than any other country. At least eight current or former members of China's Politburo Standing Committee, the ruling party's most powerful body, have been implicated, according to the reports. The British-based *Guardian* newspaper said an internal Mossack Fonseca survey found the biggest proportion of its offshore company owners came from mainland China, followed by Hong Kong.

The Chinese media has largely avoided reporting on the leaks, and social media has eliminated all references to them, with reportage by foreign news broadcasters such as the BBC blacked out. Corrupt Chinese officials have moved more than US$120 billion overseas, according to a 2011 report by the central People's Bank of China. Mossack Fonseca's offices in China include the major financial centers of Shanghai and Shenzhen, as well as the port cities of Qingdao and Dalian, but also lesser-known provincial capitals such as Shandong's Jinan, known for its links to China's coal industry, and Hangzhou in Zhejiang, along with Ningbo, also in the eastern province.

Another example is Li Xiaolin—daughter of Li Peng, a former premier—whose fortune is estimated at US$550 million, and who has made a name as China's "power queen" after a career spent running electricity-generating businesses. Li was (until Xi Jinping's anti-corruption campaign) noted in China for conspicuous consumption—her appearance in a pink Pucci trouser suit at the annual meeting of a top government advisory body prompted a widely shared social media post that suggested the 12,000 yuan (US$1,500) price tag was equivalent to warm clothes for 200 poor children. Previous International Consortium of Investigative Journalists investigations have linked her to two other British Virgin Islands companies, and to Swiss bank accounts. Li and her husband, Liu Zhiyuan, were revealed as the beneficiaries of five bank accounts that together held as much as US$2.48 million in 2006–7. Li's identity became known to Mossack Fonseca when BVI regulators asked for information about COFIC Investment Ltd. in 2015, and inquiries were made with the Geneva law firm that represented it. Cofic's directors at this time were two partners in the firm, Charles-André Junod and Alain Bruno Lévy. Its shareholder, however, was a secretive Liechtenstein entity called Foundation Silo, whose beneficial owners were named by Junod as Li and her husband.

Zeng Qinghong was China's vice president until 2008. His younger brother, Zeng Qinghuai, is well known in Hong Kong, having worked there as an envoy for the Ministry of Culture. He was a consultant to *Beginning of the Great Revival*, a state-produced propaganda movie which, according to the *New York Times*, "exemplified the hand-in-glove relationship between business and politics." The Panama Papers revealed that Zeng Qinghuai is a director of a company called Chinese Cultural Exchange Association Ltd, registered first in the tiny South Pacific island of Niue, then in Samoa. He sits on the board alongside another princeling, Tian Chenggang, son of former vice premier and Politburo member Tian Jiyun.

A 2012 court case, in which Tian Chenggang unsuccessfully sued a developer called Beijing Henderson Properties, shed new light on the business dealings of the red nobility. The court in Hong Kong heard that Tian and a company linked to Zeng had been separately engaged to lobby regulators on behalf of Henderson when it was under investigation for breaching foreign exchange regulations in 2006. An exchange of letters disclosed in court suggested that Tian's father had written to the regulators to plead leniency. In the event, the fine imposed was smaller than expected. Companies linked to Zeng received fees of US$2.1 million. Henderson rejected Tian's demand for US$5.5 million, so Tian sued for the money but lost. The judge's summing up said of him: "He tried to project an air of superiority … His attitude was contemptuous and disrespectful" (Garside and Pegg 2016).

CHINA TURNED NEOLIBERAL

China has gone a long way toward becoming a market society. Observers of China are intrigued by the assemblage of labels to describe China as an example of existing capitalism, with market-friendly policies and Leninist institutions of the post-Mao Chinese political economy. China has been alternatively labeled as "nomenclature capitalism," "bureaucratic capitalism," "capitalism with Chinese characteristics," "com-capitalism," "market Leninism," "state capitalism" and "mercantilist capitalism" to name just a few (Baum and Shevchenko 1999: 333). Whatever one calls the post-1989 China, one point is clear: from farewell to Revolution to the neo-enlightenment, and from the dismantling of collective farming to "development at all costs," China has unceremoniously embraced neo-liberalism. As insightfully pointed out by Wang Hui (2006), the tragic events of 1989 were crucially important to enforcing a neoliberal logic in China. That year was not just one of suppressed of liberty: it led to the order of neoliberalism and a kind of market economy that is a suppression of democracy and freedom. In doing so, China actually saved capitalism.

Drezner, in response to the thorny question of why the system of global economic governance fared better than expected after the 2008 recession, claims: "We can tentatively conclude that both the power of the United States and the resilience of neoliberal economic ideas were underestimated during the depths of the Great Recession" (Drezner 2013: 124). Drezner has missed the point entirely. As Johan Lagerkvist argues, it was China that kept the system going. "Thus it is crucial to conceptualize China's political economy as neoliberalizing, albeit in a state-capitalist form, otherwise the surprising robustness of the global neoliberal project is exaggeratedly credited to the United States" (Lagerkvist 2015: 7), and "that the Chinese government was able to stabilize its own economy was centrally important in preventing an even deeper collapse in the global economy after 2008" (Nolan 2014: 2).

How did a country that was supposedly run by the world's largest and most powerful communist party turn into a neoliberal market economy that saved global capitalism? First of all, it started from the very top, as I discussed in Chapter 4. The once top boss of the CCP, Zhao Ziyang, a man fond of playing golf, wanted China to catch up with capitalism in the name of the "primary stage of socialism." Zhao was of course supported by Deng Xiaoping, the power behind the curtain, who did a favor to US capitalism early on by invading Vietnam in 1979 in the name of "teaching them a lesson." Since the 1990s, the revolutionary conceptualization of the CCP "to serve the people," the very rationale for its existence, was systematically hollowed out. More and more Chinese have been invited to join the CCP, but those who do are most likely to join for the purpose of career progression and power.

The current CCP leader Xi Jinping was sharp enough to realize this and wanted to reverse the tide not only by launching an anti-corruption campaign, unprecedented in Chinese history, but also by reminding the CCP not to forget the original intention (Xi Jinping 2016). However, it is unclear how Xi is going to accomplish the original aims of the Revolution in the context of current China.

China is such a big country, as discussed in Chapter 3, and the Chinese are so diverse a people that to hold the country together the most difficult task for Xi, or anyone, is to get the people organized. The CCP under the leadership of Mao managed to get the Chinese organized because they managed to work out organizing principles within what I term a Maoist discourse (Gao 1994). One of these organizing principles was the structure and activities of grassroots organizations of the CCP. In every work unit, be it a department of human resources or a factory floor, there was a CCP party branch, and in every branch there was a leading group composed of the core members of the CCP in the work unit. Every member had to pay membership fees and regular meetings were held once a month. This was called "organization life." In those meetings, the CCP party policies and politics were studied and the political situation and daily problems of the work unit were reviewed.

That organizational principle now seems to have collapsed. Professor Kong Qingdong of Peking University, a self-claimed Maoist, complained that there was no CCP party organization anymore, and that the members of the CCP did not even pay membership fees. Kong said that in order to maintain the appearance of the party unit he, as the branch secretary, had to pay the membership fees for his colleagues from his own pocket (Kong Qingdong 2016). Kong complained that the CCP now looked like an underground organization because it was afraid of being seen for what it truly was. Moreover, as a teacher, one was afraid to even talk about Marxism or Chairman Mao in the classroom. From Deng Xiaoping to Hu Yaobang, from Zhao Ziyang to Jiang Zemin and Hu Jintao, the CCP ideology and organizational principles all but collapsed. It is under these circumstances that current leader Xi Jinping wants to tighten ideological control. My friends and colleagues in China informed me, for instance, that in 2016 members of the CCP all over China were mobilized to pay their overdue membership fees. But it may be too little, too late for him.

HOW DO THE NEOLIBERAL ECONOMISTS CONSTRUCT CHINA?

As the director of the CCP Party Construction Department at the Central Party School in Beijing, where senior CCP officials are trained for promotion, one would expect Professor Wang Changjiang to talk about the organizational principles of the CCP and its ideology. Instead, Wang is reported to have argued that the CCP as a revolutionary party is not legitimate in current China, that the idea of revolution should be abandoned and that a party in power should not follow the idea of Marxism but that of market capitalism, because only the market economy fits the natural order of individual pursuit of self-interest (Chou Niu 2016). Nothing short of dismantling the CCP would be Wang's ideal scenario.

Here is another example of how the Chinese neoliberal literati constructs contemporary China, as detailed by Lao Ji (2017). The role played by what is called the Chinese Archive Institute is to compile, write and publish historical information about the leading figures of the CCP. Long Pingping, the director of the Third Department of the Chinese Archive Institute, specializing in the field of Deng Xiaoping, played a major role in the publication of *Selected Works of Deng Xiaoping, A Chronicle of Deng Xiaoping, Selected Important Documents of the CCP Since its Fourteenth Congress* and *The Development and Formation of the Important Policies Since the Third Plenary Session of the 11th CCP party Congress.* These are important publications that construct China's contemporary history. Long was also the director general of the television series *Deng Xiaoping in Historical Transition*.

In order to construct a politically correct Deng Xiaoping, the series not only selects data but also fabricates information. For example, Deng is presented as a principled fighter who was firmly and clearly against the CR. But Deng never aired his opposition against the CR when Mao was alive, and even on July 20, 1977 when Deng was participating in a meeting chaired by the then CCP Chairman Hua Guofeng after the death of Mao, Deng was perpetuating the CR discourse of condemning Liu Shaoqi, and celebrating the removal of Liu as a victory.

In the series Deng is credited with the restoration of China's tertiary entrance examination system (*gaokao*), whereas in fact as late as July 30, 1977 Deng was still on record speaking affirmatively about the CR education practice, and the *gaokao* was approved by Hua Guofeng on July 5, 1977. In the series Deng is credited with the development of the Shenzhen Special Economic Zone, whereas in fact it was Hua Guofeng who argued that the approach to its development should be bolder, faster, more experimental and more liberal. Another truth manufactured by the series is that Deng took the lead in the abolition of the lifetime position in the system. But it was Ye Jinaying, Li Xiannian and Chen Yun who retired, whereas Deng was chairman of the CCP central military commission until 1989 when he was 85, and chairman of the PRC military commission until 1993, retiring at the age of 89.

The Chinese neoliberals have been working hard to construct a contemporary Chinese history in which Deng is promoted as the transformer of Chinese society, while Mao is being consigned to the dustbin of history. They achieve this task by selectively excluding negative information about Deng during the Mao era, while crediting Deng with positive policies which he was in fact not responsible for.

Along the same lines of constructing a neoliberal China, the Chinese intellectual elite firmly place the blame for the phenomenon of corruption on the public ownership of means of production (Zhang Weiying 1997, Fan Gang 2005). For this proposition to be logical (Zhang Weiying 1997) one has to argue that corruption existed even in the Mao era when there was full-scale public ownership of means of production, in spite of the contrary evidence that there was hardly any corruption at that time. Contrary evidence also includes the fact that in 1999 the ten most corrupt societies in the world were all market economies, according to the Transparency International. To the Chinese neoliberals, the way forward in countering corruption is full-scale privatization that allows the market economy to play its role (Zhang Shuguang 1994, Zhang Wuchang 1997). Zhang Weiying even goes as far as to argue that without privatization, managerial corruption is a Pareto improvement—a suboptimum solution, the best possible one given the circumstances (Zhang Weiying 1997). One of course cannot blame the neoliberal economists personally for China's rampant official corruption in post-Mao China, but the emergence of the saying that "corruption is the lubricant for reform" is an indication of how corruption is justified through the ideology of neoliberalism.

CONSTRUCTING MAO

Gao Hua's construction of Mao is another example of how the Chinese literati systematically construct contemporary China. The post-Mao Chinese intellectual elite, supported either directly or indirectly by the Chinese political elite, has systematically hollowed out the intellectual idea of Mao, and constructed a Mao who was a ruthless maniac whose sole purpose in life was to gain personal power. The two accounts along these lines best known in the West are Jung Chang and Halliday (2005) and Gao Hua (2000, 2011).

As detailed by Li Xiaopeng (2016), Gao Hua is right in claiming that the Yan'an Rectification Movement was Mao's attempt to get rid of the influence of Soviet-trained theoretical authoritative CCP leaders such as Wang Ming, Bo Gu and Zhang Wentian. But is it right therefore to declare that Mao wanted to attack those so-called Internationalists so as to establish his absolute ruling position in the CCP? The *prima facie* evidence seems to be supportive of the Gao Hua narrative: when the CCP Seventh Party Congress was held after the Yan'an Rectification, Mao's opponents were demoted while those who followed Mao like Liu Shaoqi were promoted. This looks like proof that Mao used the Rectification Movement to consolidate his position and gain absolute power. But when we carefully examine this, the claim of a ruthless personal power struggle seems problematic: those who were demoted also included Kang Sheng, who was one of the most active people in the Yan'an Rectification. On the other hand, Zhou Enlai, the very person who—together with Wang Ming, Bo Gu and Zhang Wentian—was largely responsible for giving Mao a hard time immediately before the Long March, was also drawn into the inner circle of decision making.

As Li Xiaopeng (2016) argues, an entirely different construction can be made regarding the final distribution of power within the CCP after the Seventh Congress in Yan'an: the fact that Wang Ming and others of the Internationalist group still kept their positions as members of the CCP Central Committee, that Kang Sheng was demoted due to the personal injustice he did to many in the party and that Zhou Enlai kept his important position because he understood the political narrative of the Yan'an Rectification, demonstrates that the Yan'an Rectification was not about Mao's personal power struggle but about the very direction of the CCP and the Chinese Revolution.

Gao Hua wants to present Mao as a sinister person and a double dealer. This is again supported by *prima facie* evidence that is well known: there were two organizational principles developed by Mao in order to win power in China. One is reflected in the well-known saying "political power comes out of the barrel of the gun" and the other in "the army has to be commanded by the Party." Gao Hua constructs the two principles as Mao's double dealing for personal success: Mao used the first principle to gain power and the second principle to control the army. This construction disregards the bigger picture of how to make a successful revolution, by hollowing out the political contents of the two principles. The political content of the first principle is that, since in the context of a weak working class in China the organization of workers' movements in urban centers would not lead to a successful revolutionary cause, the CCP had to organize armed struggle. In other words, the CCP had to have its own army to gain power so as to create a successful revolution. The political content of the second principle is that the army had to be guided by political programs of socialism so as to be different from the armies of the warlords and the army of the KMT. The army was not just a military force but also a political organization for the purpose of changing Chinese society. The CCP continued the organizational principle that the military must be placed strictly under the command of the CCP, until 1989 when Deng Xiaoping ordered the army to roll tanks onto the streets of Beijing to suppress the student protest, while at the same time forcing Zhao Ziyang, the supposed top boss of the CCP, to resign.

THE CASE OF ZHANG ZHIXIN

In "A report written in blood" published on June 5, 1997 in the *Guangming Daily* Chen Yushan portrays Zhang Zhixin as a heroine against Jiang

Qing and Lin Biao and as a communist revolutionary saint—beautiful, kind, brave and talented. Chen further claims that Zhang was executed by the Gang of Four and their follower in Liaoning, Mao Yuanxin. But in 1975, the same year Zhang was executed, Su Tieshan (2015), who was also accused of the crime of being against the Gang of Four, and Lin Biao were released. Su Tieshan wanted to find out why the two came to such different ends, despite being accused of the same crime.

One explanation is that Chen's report is very selective in presenting information and leaves out some vital facts of the Zhang case. Su found out a major difference between his case and that of Zhang Zhixin: Zhang wrote anti-Mao slogans repeatedly, such as "Down with Mao Zedong," "Oil boil Mao Zedong," "Hang Mao Zedong" and "cut Mao into pieces," while Su did not. The media event that propagated the Zhang Zhixin case did not point out this fact. Another fact not revealed by Chen was that Zhang also attacked Zhou Enlai. In 1973, during a mass meeting which involved criticizing Lin Biao and Confucius, Zhang shouted that "the ultimate root of CCP right wing politics is Mao Zedong." In other words, Zhang was executed not because she was anti-Jiang Qing or Lin Biao, as documented in the Chen report, but because she was seen to be attacking Mao—not Mao's ideas, but Mao personally.

The Chen report also fails to place the case of Zhang in its historical context: according to the Six Articles on Public Security published in 1967, anti-Mao slogans were a reactionary crime to be punished. In other words, no matter how absurd or unreasonable the rules were judging by post-revolutionary values, rule procedure was observed in the Zhang Zhixin case. The Chen report also fails to mention that the death sentence decided by the local court had to be approved by the provincial court and the provincial court decision in turn had to be approved by the Supreme Court in Beijing. The execution of Zhang followed this procedure. On April 3, 1975 the Supreme Court in Beijing approved the execution of Zhang in the name of the Lord President of the Chinese Supreme Court Jiang Hua, who also chaired the later trial of the Gang of Four.

What was also important for Chen in constructing the case of Zhang Zhixin is to point the finger at Mao Yuanxin, because the case occurred in Liaoning where Mao Yuanxin was a leading member of the Liaoning Provincial Revolutionary Committee. In his "why cannot the law of the people protect Zhang Zhixin," published by the *Guangming Daily* on July 17, 1997, Ma Rongjie asserts that the sworn follower of the Gang of Four in Liaoning ordered the immediate execution of Zhang Zhixin without any appeal. On August 7, 1998 the *Southern Weekend* claimed that "there are more secrets in the case of Zhang Zhixin"—Zhu Jianguo (1998) asserted that in an interview with him, Chen Yushan (1979) declared that Mao Yuanxin insisted that a life sentence was not enough for Zhang. "Kill her" was what he said. In his interview, Zhang Yueqi, the secretary of Ren Zhongyi (who chaired the rehabilitated Zhang Zhixin), is reported to have said that it was Mao Yuanxin who killed Zhang Zhixin.

All the fingers were pointed at Mao Yuanxin, who happened to be the nephew of Mao Zedong, the real target of the Zhang Zhixin story, who could not be named. In spite of all these accounts, Su Tieshan does not think there is enough evidence to claim that Mao Yuanxin was the person who decided to kill Zhang. Mao Yuanxin's defense lawyer Zhang Haini also argued against such an accusation when Mao Yuanxin was tried in the 1980s. Mao Yuanxin was responsible but so were the others because it was a collective decision. Pointing a figure at Mao the nephew was politically convenient for the condemnation of Mao the uncle.

What made the production and consumption of the Zhang Zhixin story so sensational at that time when the backlash against the CR was at its height was not just that a pretty young woman was killed for saying something in words, but the accusation that her throat was cut before her execution to prevent her from shouting reactionary words on the execution ground was also shocking. In a stereotypical Peking Opera production, Chen Yushan describes the scene: several guards pull Zhang down to the ground and cut her throat to take away her right to express the truth. However, the good daughter of the Party does not show any change of the color on her face, but straightens her chest and stares in a dignified manner at her executioners.

In fact Zhang's throat was not cut. A brutal measure was indeed taken that was approved by the justice of the Shenyang Court for the medical clinic of the Shenyang Public Security to cut off Zhang's vocal cord before her execution. The detailed description of witness accounts by both Chen and Ma show that Zhang's throat could not have been cut because if that were the case Zhang would have died straight away and would not have been able to walk toward the execution ground heroically.

Su Tieshan also points out a significant development: for three months from June to September 1979, the media was full of journalist reportage of Zhang Zhixin, but then suddenly the reportage stopped and the case was off the agenda. As more and more readers of this media sensation demanded justice and wanted to punish those who were behind this horrendous crime, the official media declared in a September 12, 1997 editorial by the *Guangming Daily* that the murderers of Zhang Zhixin were of course the Gang of Four and its sworn followers. Finding out who was individually responsible for Zhang's murder is not undertaken because, like so many other cases, the responsibility lies collectively with the Gang of Four. The official truth of the Zhang Zhixin case brainwashed a whole generation of Chinese youth at that time.

THE CASE OF LI RUI

In the Chinese elite construction of contemporary China, Li Rui, born in 1917, is something of a legend. Intelligent, articulate and spirited, Li Rui is an ideal prototype Chinese literati. Having studied mechanics in Wuhan University, Li was one of the highly educated young Chinese who went to Yan'an to join the Communist Revolution. In 1952, just three years after the establishment of the PRC, Li was appointed the head of China's water and electricity department. 1958 was the cusp of Li's career when, impressed by his argument against the idea of building a dam at the Three Gorges to generate electricity, Mao asked Li to be his "part time correspondent secretary" (*jianzhi tongxun mishu*). Mao gave several people this title so as to get more diverse information. Nobody except Li Rui claims to have been Mao's secretary. Within a year after this appointment Li only wrote three letters to Mao (Yu Jiaxue 2017). Though Li's 1958 appointment of a correspondent secretary lasted about a year until 1959 when Li got into trouble at the Lushan Conference, Li often uses the title of Mao's secretary to boost his credibility for his criticism of Mao.

In 1958, Li became the rising young star in the CCP hierarchy, which he embraced. Li's ambition was not groundless. Li was more than a bureaucrat: he was a prolific author and writer, publishing frequently in official media outlets even in the early years of the PRC, again something that made Li stand out since most of the top CCP officials had no formal education. In the eyes of the Chinese elite, Li fits the image of a gentleman scholar in traditional China, who not only had the ability but also the duty to maintain order under heaven. Li's most influential publications are *Revolutionary Activities of the Early Comrade Mao Zedong*, a collection of his writings on Mao (1957), *An Actual Record of*

the Lushan Conference: on the Spot Notes from Mao's Secretary (1994) and
Mao Zedong's Tragic Late Years (1999).

Apparently, one cannot find a more authoritative and more authentic
account of the construction of contemporary China than that offered
by Li Rui. Li appears to be authoritative because he is a participant at
the very top of the CCP hierarchy, as shown in his Lushan book. The
authority appears even weightier since Li, as the cleverly marketed title
of the book shows, was Mao's secretary. Li appears authentic when he
critiques Mao as his writings on the young Mao initially inspired Mao's
personality cult.

One of the major propositions of the post-Mao construction of contemporary China is the late Mao thesis (Li Rui 1999), which holds
that Mao would have been a great Chinese leader had he died in 1956,
the year before the Anti-Rightist Movement. From 1957, to the GLF
started in 1958, finally to the CR from 1966 to 1976 when Mao died,
China was a total disaster and it was all Mao's fault. At least some of
the Chinese political elite may have some reservations regarding this
late Mao thesis, but the Chinese literati elite love it. For them this is the
correct history. For them this is not a construction but a factual record.

However, a crackdown on Li's credibility began in 2009 when a
document posted on social media by a person named Zhang Jie spread
like wildfire (Zhang Jie 2009). The Zhang Jie document is in the form
of an interview with Zhou Hui, who was born in 1918, and, like Li Rui,
went to Yan'an to participate in the Revolution as a young enthusiast,
appointed to be a party secretary of Mao's home town in Hunan
Province after the success of the 1949 Revolution, a position higher
than that of Li Rui. Like Li Rui, Zhou Hui got into trouble during the
1959 Lushan Conference. Like Li, Zhou was rehabilitated during the
late 1970s and appointed to important positions in the CCP hierarchy.
What is explosive in this interview is that Zhou places the blame of
the disastrous outcome of the Lushan Conference, including his own
victimization, on Li Rui, who himself was also the victim. Zhou claims
that Li Rui was largely responsible for the outcome at Lushan because
not only did he make blunders, but he was also treacherous.

During the fatal 1959 Lushan Conference, which aimed to correct
the too-radical GLF and to make adjustment in policies, General Peng
Dehuai wrote Mao a letter criticizing the GLF, and Mao in turn made
copies of the letter for every conference participant to read and comment
on. On July 23, Mao made a speech in which he criticized both the

"radical" Left and the "conservative" Right regarding the GLF, but Mao's tendency seemed to favor the Left. In the evening, Zhou Hui, Li Rui and Zhou Xiaozhou—the first party secretary of Hunan Province—went to see Huang Kecheng, the PLA's chief of staff at that time. Then Peng Dehuai came to join them. Together they complained that Mao was behaving like the late Stalin, tricky and inconsistent, and covering up the truth of the GLF. When they came out of Huang's residence they happened to bump into Luo Ruiqing, the minister of public security and Mao's top personal guard.

Naturally they were worried that they would be asked what their meeting was about. Li Rui thought that the best way to anticipate the likely inquiry was to write a letter to Mao to explain what had happened, since he believed that he had Mao's trust. However, in the letter Li Rui not only left out much of the contents of the meeting but he also swore what he had stated in the letter was the truth, the whole truth and nothing but the truth. He further stated that he would accept punishment if he had lied. Mao immediately copied Li's letter and distributed it to the conference. However, when questioned, Huang Kecheng admitted something that Li was trying to hide, that they had talked about Mao behaving like the late Stalin. As a result, trust was broken for everyone, not only among the conversation group but between the conversation group and other conference participants, and of course between them and Mao. The five of them were seen as untrustworthy, and accused of forming an anti-Mao and anti-Party clique.

It can be argued that Li had acted with good intentions as he was writing the letter to protect everyone involved. But the next blunder made by Li is harder to explain. On August 11, Li changed his position 180 degrees: he pleaded guilty to anti-party and anti-Mao activities, a cowardly act that Li admitted to years later in his own account (Li Rui 1994). In his interview with Zhang Jie, Zhou claimed that Li went to Mao personally not only to confess his mistakes so as to win back Mao's trust but also claiming that there were clique activities within the CCP, and that Zhang Wentian (a former top CCP boss, demoted during the Yan'an Rectification Movement, and deputy foreign minister during the GLF) read Peng Dehuai's letter before Peng sent it to Mao. Li Rui also told Mao that Zhang Wentian even added the words describing the GLF as "petty bourgeoisie fanaticism" in Peng's letter. Li further revealed to Mao that Zhang Wentian's three-hour speech criticizing the GLF was also read by Peng prior to its delivery on July 21. So Li seems to have presented evidence that an anti-party clique was forming and that the criticism of the GLF was not an individual act of conviction but a premeditated group activity. Li got everyone into trouble.

In the practice of Western democracy, interest group activities are the norm and different interests are supposedly represented by different group activities. However, in the CCP politics of consensus, which is a legacy of the Chinese tradition, group activities are seen as divisive and conspiratorial. The irony is that although Li made such a huge effort to redeem himself in his confession, Mao did not lift a finger to save him. Li had believed that Mao would favor him, but instead Li was dismissed from all his official posts. Li was, therefore, understandably a very bitter man after the Lushan Conference.

As Zhou Hui passed away years ago, the authenticity of the Zhang Jie document is yet to be confirmed, although doubts were raised, especially by the anti-Mao journal *yanhuang chunqiu* (Han Gang 2013). A statement signed under the name of Hui Haiming (2017) was posted on social media to declare that Zhou Hui's family denied the authenticity of such an interview. But again that is not confirmed, as it is posted under a pseudonym. Zhang Jie (2017) even published an open letter calling Li Rui to challenge the interview account. After considering skeptics such as the veteran and dissident writer Dai Qing, self-proclaimed historian Chun Ming (2016) states that the Zhang Jie document is believable because the sequence of events is confirmed by Li's own account (Li Rui 1994) and confirmed by Quan Yanchi and Huang Lina (1997).

Recently a significant publication by Qi Benyu (2016) seems to confirm the Zhou Hui interview account. According to Qi, the Minister of Public Security Luo Ruiqing did not just bump into the members of the conversation group at Huang's Lushan residence that night. In the system every party official has bodyguards who report directly to the public security headquarters and who are duty-bound to record official activities. Therefore the so-called secret meetings between Peng, Zhang, Huang and the Zhou's were not secret. Qi states that when Li Rui made confessions to Mao that night, Mao's personal secretary, Lin Ke, was present. According to Lin Ke, Li Rui also told Mao that during the meeting at Huang Kecheng's residence, Peng made phone calls to the army. As a minister of defense there was nothing unusual about him making a call to the army. But Li's insinuation was that this was clique activity, which later led to the label of a "military club" because both Peng and Huang were in the military.

SELECTIVE DATA FOR THE LATE MAO THESIS

One major building block for constructing the late Mao thesis is that Mao and Mao alone was responsible for not only the "holocaust" of the CR but also the disaster of the GLF. The usually straight-talking Deng was circumspect when he talked about the responsibilities of the GLF. In his supposed defense of Mao, Deng claimed that Liu Shaoqi, Zhou Enlai and himself were also impetuous during the GLF, and that even Chen Yun, the most cautious of all, did not air his opposition. But as Lei Shen (2009) points out, this is a cunning way of shifting responsibility to Mao. In fact it was not just that Deng was not against it, he actively supported it. Lei Shen details the speeches and activities that Liu and Deng made during the GLF in supporting reckless policies. In his memoirs the then general editor of the *People's Daily*, Wu Lengxi (1995), admits that Mao asked him to resist pressure to publish materials encouraging reckless-ness. Wu confesses that he made mistakes by ignoring Mao's warning and by surrendering to pressure from other leaders.

This is confirmed by careful research by Yang Lianshu (2009). Yang finds that in the second volume of Liu Shaoqi's *Selected Works*, covering the period between 1957 and 1961, for the five years in question seven pieces were chosen, not one of which opposed the radical GLF. More remarkable is the blankness of the three years between May 1958 and May 1961: Liu was not supposed to have said anything or given any instructions. Liu was appointed to replace Mao as the president of the PRC in April 1959, and yet until May 1961 nothing said or instructed by Liu was included in his selected works. Two speeches by Liu made in May 1961 are included, but this was after the CCP's adjustment was more or less complete.

The same selective approach to excluding information that may damage Liu's reputation is also applied to Zhou Enlai in the *Selected Works of Zhou Enlai*. And the same is also applied to Deng Xiaoping: not only there is no evidence of Deng opposing the GLF, but there is a blank space covering more than three years. In other words, for more than three years Deng said nothing and instructed nothing when he was the active and practical manager of the CCP Central Committee as the general secretary of the CCP.

On the other hand, an irony that escapes every commentator and every scholar in the field is that in the *Selected Works of Mao*, more than 20 pieces, speeches and instructions that are included were all aimed at opposing radicalism and at suppressing fanaticism. And yet everyone points a finger at Mao and Mao alone for the disaster of the GLF. The famine that resulted from the GLF is even named Mao's famine. Liu Shaoqi did become very critical and worried about GLF policies in the spring of 1961. But before that Liu was an active advocator and promoter of the public canteen and concept of commune. Liu even thought that China could catch up with the UK in one or two years in iron and steel production and therefore supported the idea and practice of backyard furnaces.

CONCLUSION

Form the Literature of the Wounded to the farewell of revolution, from the neo-enlightenment to the late Mao thesis, from the dismantling of collective farming to the assembly line of the world, and from the denunciation of Mao—especially through the events of the GLF and the CR—to the neoliberal narrative of market economy and privatization, constructing contemporary Chinese history and China's political development have advanced in parallel. To justify China's entry into global capitalism, revolutionary theory and practice—i.e. the basis on which the CCP is built—has to be denounced, and the political content and revolutionary ideas of Mao have to be hollowed out. In this process there have also been two sets of coordination: coordination between the Chinese intellectual elite and the Chinese political elite, and coordination between the Chinese intellectual elite and that of the West. In many cases the Chinese intellectual elite and political elite are one and the same. However, in many cases the Chinese intellectual elite, including Western-trained Chinese economists—trained either through short courses and study tours or degree courses—either propagate neoliberal conceptualizations or construct contemporary history to justify political actions. The set of coordination between the Chinese intellectual elite and that of the West, through foundations, scholarships, prizes and awards, is demonstrated by setting up the media agenda, conceptual paradigms and support for political dissidents.

6

Why is the Cultural Revolution Cultural?

INTRODUCTION

"[L]a Chine n'existe pas" (Natacha 1975: 44–45). China exists only in the mind because there is no history of China unless someone writes about it and there is no knowledge of China unless and until someone produces and consumes it. The history and knowledge of the CR is what is written on paper or now among the cloud of the internet. Memories of the CR don't last unless they are passed on orally or in writing. With modern technologies, producers of knowledge of the CR can be even more powerful with audio and visual images. But as we know, memories can be faulty, and what one remembers and does not remember about the CR is very much directed by conceptual values and beliefs, the empirical facts and theoretical implications of which I have dealt with extensively (Gao 1994, 1998, 1999b, 2002, 2006).

In this chapter, and Chapter 7 on the CR, I will demonstrate how different data and information can be selected to confirm or to argue for different constructions of the CR. As a case study of how China is constructed and for what purpose, this chapter aims to demonstrate not only that data and information can be selected for specific political constructions of the CR, but also (and more importantly) that the CR was indeed cultural.

TWO DIFFERENT CONCERNS FOR
THE PRODUCTION OF KNOWLEDGE

During the years of the CR, there was one set of conceptual values and beliefs that inspired young and radical Chinese to participate in what they believed to be a revolution to change mentality. They were passionate and genuine in wanting to break the old in order to build up the new in thinking, in cultural practice and in ways of life, in the process of which they left a trail of destruction and human suffering. Related conceptual values and beliefs also inspired some young intellectuals and students in Europe (Fields 1984) and in American academia, when a group of young American scholars who, disgusted by what was seen as a bankrupt Western imperialism demonstrated by the unjust, inhuman and cruel Vietnam War, thought that they had found an alternative: a third way that was different from both the Stalinism and Western capitalism—Maoism—most actively on display in the CR. Between 1968 and 1979 a group in the US called the Concerned Asian Scholars mounted a fierce attack on the conceptual values and beliefs held by the older generation of Asian studies in general and China studies scholars in particular. For the young and the radicals in China and the rest of the world, "The Cultural Revolution addressed issues that could not but call into question the daily experiences of students and teachers everywhere: the division of manual and intellectual labor, the role of science and objectivity, the relationship between politics and knowledge and the ideological structure of the transmission of learning" (Lanza 2017: 9).

However, after the death of Mao in 1976, and soon after the arrest of the so-called Gang of Four, one of whom was Mao's wife Jiang Qing, very few radicals left in the West were prepared for the sudden change of political course in China, as Lanza narrates below:

> Between 1976 (the death of Mao) and 1981 only three or four essays on China were published in the *Bulletin* and none of them addressed directly the radical shift in Chinese politics that began in 1976 and its potential consequences. China basically "disappeared" from the journal's pages, it became a conspicuous absence, the veritable elephant in the room. When it reappeared, in a double issue in 1981, the contributors to the *Bulletin* struggled to cope with the new China and the very different image of Maoism it presented. Gone was the optimism towards the Chinese model, gone was the possibility of alternative policies, but also gone was much of the grounding that since 1968 had provided a foundation to the collective subject of the Concerned Asian Scholars. (Lanza 2017: 7–8)

When I was a young academic and naïve about the politics of scholarship and academia, I wrote a couple of pieces on the CR which were published in the *Bulletin of Concerned Asian Scholars*, the journal mentioned above, launched by the Concerned Asian Scholars Committee. The then dean of humanities and social sciences at Tasmania University, the sociologist Professor Malcom Waters, said to me that "bulletin" did not sound scholarly and nor did "concerned" sound academic. As an indication of the change the *Bulletin* changed its name to *Critical Asian Studies* in 2000.

In fact it is not entirely "the end of concern," as termed by Lanza. There is concern from the other side of politics, the concern of human rights victims of the CR in general and about the CR in particular. The Belgian Australian scholar Pierre Ryckmans, who wrote under the pen name Simon Leys, asserts that the CR had nothing revolutionary about it except the name and nothing cultural about it except the pretext (Leys 1977). To him it was a power struggle between a handful of men behind the smokescreen of a fictitious mass movement. Ryckmans was hailed as a prophet by the new generation of scholars, because he has been confirmed by the post-Mao Chinese who "themselves say so."

In post-Mao China, total denunciation of the CR has been the official edict and unannounced denegation of Mao has been the unofficial practice. One can blame anything on the CR. He Weifang (2016), one of the so-called "contacts" of the US embassy in Beijing and a law professor well known in journalist and academic circles in the West because of his dissident views regarding the Chinese regime, claimed to be an "outstanding" member of the CCP (He Weifang 2012). Yet in his interview with Sohu, he argued that the CR had made China cruel and numb to the extent that all current problems are related to the CR (Fuxingwang 2016). One can make any accusation about China under the leadership of Mao, no matter how absurd it is. Former Italian Prime Minister Silvio Berlusconi once declared that the Chinese would boil babies to fertilize land in the Mao era (*Los Angeles Times* 2006). Mao and the CR, like Stalin, are the key words of the black book on communism in today's political discourse.

Chronicles, annals, gazetteers, a collection of speeches, academic and scholarly endeavors and hundreds of concentrated media outlets have all been out to produce one conceptualized knowledge of the CR: "a ten year disaster or holocaust," "unprecedented in Chinese history" and the "darkest period of Chinese history." Had it not been for the invention of the Internet, which provides an alternative venue for dissenting voices and for sharing different datasets and different interpretations of this data, it would have been the end of history for the CR.

CONSTRUCTING OF THE CULTURAL REVOLUTION
REGARDING THE PERSONALITY OF LIU SHAOQI

A discussion of the CR has to deal with the personality of Liu Shaoqi. I will start with Dikötter (2016), who claims that Mao was insensitive to human loss, nonchalantly handing down killing quotas, and that the CR was about an old man settling personal scores at the end of his life. What happened to Liu Shaoqi is typically narrated in the literature as Mao's personal revenge. Not only was Mao said to have used ideological differences as an excuse, but Liu was also said to have died strapped to a prison bed, untreated by doctors.

If the CR was meant to get rid of Mao's opponent Liu Shaoqi, then one has to explain why the CR lasted ten years, since only three months after the official launch of the CR in 1966 Liu was already demoted to number eight in the CCP hierarchy. Furthermore, in October 1968 the CCP Central Committee Congress passed a resolution not only to strip Liu of all his official positions in the CCP and the Chinese state, but also to expel him from the Party, a disciplinary act considered the most serious punishment for anyone in the system. If the CR was just a personal power struggle then there was no rationale for the CR to continue toward the 1970s until Mao died in 1976.

In fact there had been continuous differences between Mao and Liu in terms of the conceptualization of China's development. According to Liu Shaoqi's wife, Wang Guangmei (Wang Guangmei, Liu Yuan, et al. 2000), an intelligent and courageous woman who not only lost her husband but also suffered personal humiliation during the CR, it was based on Mao's own suggestion that a collective decision was made that Liu was assigned to work on the front line of the state while Mao retained power behind the curtain. Therefore it was not the case that Mao lost power to Liu after the failure of the GLF, an assumption that is almost universally held.

Mao's decision to demote Liu was based on profound conceptual differences. From the 1950s, Liu's thinking and working style had already become different to that of Mao's, and when Mao had new ideas, Liu found it difficult to follow. However, as Wang points out there was never a power struggle and the two got on well personally (Sun Xingsheng 2010).

In fact, fundamental differences between Liu and Mao existed before the CCP takeover of power in 1949. Liu was a strict and efficient administrator who advocated Party discipline as a tool to tame its members. In his *On the Cultivation of CCP Members* published in 1939, Liu issued a disciplinary statement to CCP members: to be a docile tool of the Party is a test of the member's character. A real Communist must be the Party's docile tool, and must obey the Party unconditionally and work for the Party tirelessly. Mao (1942), however, in 1942, declared that a CCP member has to think about the issue carefully to find out whether it is realistic and reasonable. One should not follow blindly and should not be a good slave.

Of course, we should consider the different ideas in their historical context. Liu's focus then was on CCP party discipline whereas Mao had in mind the audience who followed the Soviet Russian-trained Internationalists headed by Wang Ming. While the CCP was still struggling to survive, the difference between them not only did not matter but was also useful: Mao targeted those at the center whereas Liu targeted the CCP members as a collective. But after the CCP took over power in China and when Mao had different ideas about the future direction of China, these kind of philosophical differences started to matter, as I will discuss shortly, and mattered fatally. Mao and Liu were two different personalities not only in their working style but also in their conceptualization of China and the world.

This is evident in what happened during the large 1962 conference of 7,000 participants: a conference that reflected the failure of the GLF, which gave the specious perception that Liu wanted to blame Mao for the GLF failures; hence the rationale for the anti-Maoist producer of the truth that the CR was a personal power struggle. Gao Wenqian (2007) thinks that the forever-suspicious Mao launched the CR because he was jealous of Liu, as Liu's reputation rose after the GLF. But the fact that Mao was angry with Liu was nothing personal: they simply had profound conceptual differences on the future direction of China. Again, Wang Guangmei understands this very well in hindsight: Mao thought that the practice of "contracting farming to the households" was a road to capitalism and Mao blamed Liu for not stopping the practice (Sun Xingsheng 2010).

This conceptual difference between Mao and Liu came to the surface again in January 1965 at a Central Committee work conference, when Mao warned that the Socialist Education Movement (SEM) should be aimed at solving the contradictions between socialism and capitalism, whereas Liu thought the SEM should just cleanse the CCP officials who had problems with practical work, organizational matters and financial irregularity or corruption. According to Liu Yuan (Sun Xingsheng 2010), one of the most articulate of Liu's children, when Liu realized that Mao was not happy with the way Liu ran state affairs, Liu went to Mao to apologize for his not "respecting" the chairman, to which Mao replied that this had nothing to do with respect but with Marxist principles, with which he was not going to make concessions. In 1979, when Sun Xingsheng interviewed Wang Guangmei, he asked one direct question: did Mao want to launch the CR to get rid of Liu? Wang replied clearly: no, the CR had a lot to do with the SEM. It was not personal. To Mao the development of the SEM had already shown two issues that were crucial to the development of the CR: (1) the problem with the CCP was not just a matter of discipline, or even corruption, but a matter of principle regarding the direction that China was to take—a contest between socialism and capitalism—boiling down to the issue of whether to maintain collective agriculture; and (2) how to conduct political movements—from top to bottom or from bottom to top—to let the masses master their own affairs with CCP guidance or to impose party control and discipline so as to maintain order.

On both issues, Mao failed. Collective agriculture was dismantled and China became naked capitalism. No mass movement was allowed and top to bottom control was maintained at all costs: an approach symbolized by the crackdown of the Beijing protests in 1989. What Deng Xiaoping, who was named the number two capitalist roader, did after the death of Mao proved exactly what Mao had feared: China's road to capitalism started with the dismantling of collective farming.

THE DIFFERENCES BETWEEN LIU AND DENG

Deng had survived the CR to fulfill his vision of what China should be like, but the top capitalist roader died a miserable death in 1969. When Deng was evacuated to a remote place in Jiangxi as Liu was to Kaifeng, Liu was already on his deathbed without any members of his family around him, whereas Deng lived in a huge house with his wife. Mao protected Deng but not Liu.

However, there was one crucial difference between Liu and Deng in this respect that is often ignored: Liu's wife was under official investigation whereas Deng's was not. Liu's wife, Wang Guangmei, was not only personally humiliated in public but also under a high-level investigation and prosecution at the beginning of the CR because she was involved in two events that were crucial to the development of the CR: the SEM and a work team at Tsinghua University. Wang headed a team and implemented Liu's idea and practice of the SEM and produced a report called the "Taoyuan Jingyan" ("Taoyuan Experience"). At the beginning of the CR, when the "work teams" were sent to various schools and universities, Wang headed a team posted to the most important centers of student rebellion at Tsinghua University. Wang was accused of suppressing the masses on both occasions, the two occasions that reflected profound conceptual and political differences between Mao and Liu Shaoqi. The official post-Mao publications invariably accuse Mao's wife Jiang Qing of doing things that she had no right to do, but never offer an explanation of why Liu arranged for his wife to engage in such important tasks. In other words, when the CR started, Wang Guangmei was not treated as just Liu's wife but as a political figure expected to answer for her own political activities.

There was also a personality difference between Liu and Deng: Deng was flexible and knew how to enjoy life outside work. He liked to play bridge and drink Maotai, he smoked heavily and let things go if required. Liu was everything that Deng was not: stubborn and stern, not only to the people who worked with him and his family but also to himself. So when Liu heard the news that he was expelled from the Party he could not take it and his health went downhill.

The crucial question is: why was Liu expelled from the Party but not Deng? Liu was expelled from the Party not on the basis of any of the conceptual and political differences with Mao mentioned above, but due to the tripartite crime of *pantu*, *neijian* and *gongzei* (turncoat, hidden traitor and scab). All the accusations had something to do with the fact that Liu was doing underground work organizing workers' protests during the early period of his Communist career (MacFarquhar and Schoenhals 2006). Deng, however, seemed to have a "clear" past, though one accusation sticks to him even today: during one fierce battle, Deng, one of the top commanders, disappeared from the fighting front and turned up later in Shanghai. Otherwise Deng had a credible past, proved himself in the "Red Area" (remote rural areas with the Red Army), had gone through the Long March and commanded armies in battles. Liu Shaoqi was different: he used to work in the "White Area," urban areas occupied and administered by the Nationalist government. Liu, like many underground Communists, was arrested and came out of jail, apparently unharmed. As was well known, the Nationalists were brutal to the Communists and many were simply shot if they did not confess or hand over information about their comrades. Suspicion was raised about the circumstances under which Liu was released from jail.

Again, in the production and consumption of knowledge regarding the CR, the difference between Deng and Liu is not discussed and not stressed enough. Among many of the high-ranking army officers and officials with a Red Areas background there was not only a suspicion of those who worked underground in the White Areas, but also a sense of unfairness. This sense was enhanced by the fact that many of the most important state machine positions were occupied by those of the White Areas background, as they had more formal education and seemed more articulate. The sense of deservedness by the Red Areas veterans resulted from the fact that the CCP won power because of their life-and-death fight, not because of a working-class movement. It did not take much for some to be unsympathetic to Liu and his wife Wang, considering also that she was highly educated and from a wealthy capitalist family background and used to have personal contacts with Americans before she joined the Revolution.

There was supposed to be a lot of evidence, after a lengthy investigation, to "prove" the allegations that Liu betrayed the party and the working-class movement. But what actually happened is still one of the darkest secrets of the CCP (MacFarquhar and Schoenhals 2006, Han Suyin 1994). According to Gao Wenqian (2007: 178–82), Zhou Enlai, who was assigned head of the special case of the Liu Shaoqi investigation, knew that the accusations against Liu could not be sustained and therefore slowed the process of the investigation. Frustrated by Zhou's delaying tactic, according to Gao Wenqian, Mao "replaced him as head of the special investigative group with Jiang Qing and appointed Kang Sheng, the security chief, to assist the Madam" (2007: 178). Gao Wenqian asserts that it was Jiang Qing, helped by Kang Sheng, who framed Liu Shaoqi and Zhou Enlai and was forced to cave in by putting his signature on the final verdict that was the basis for expelling Liu from the Party. Though Gao Wenqian is treated in the West as some sort of authority on the life of Zhou Enlai, I am not convinced by his account. There are three problems. First, there is no evidence offered regarding the assertion that Mao urged Jiang Qing to frame Liu. Second, the claim that Zhou was forced to sign off the paper and the assertion that Jiang Qing replaced Zhou as head of the investigation are not coherent.

Zhou's signature was not required as a formality if Jiang Qing was the head of the investigation. Finally, in signing the paper Zhou appeared to have written a long text condemning Liu (Gao Wenqian 2007: 181). But if he was forced to do something against his conscience he did not need to go to such lengths, because a simple yes would be enough to save his own skin. It is most likely that some evidence was manufactured and some data were selected, while other information that proved Liu was innocent were not included so as to prove a predetermined decision. Though Liu was rehabilitated posthumously, the circumstances by which he might have been framed still remain murky.

THE DEATH OF LIU SHAOQI

The post-Mao reconstruction of Liu aims to show that Liu was maltreated, by excluding data and information that he was in fact looked after, at least medically. That Liu Shaoqi was untreated and uncared for is a narrative repeated in Chinese official publications (Li Chao 2010). The motivation, as with Dikötter, for such selective use of information is first to construct the image that the CR was personal, and second that Mao was an evil monster. That there is information that shows otherwise hardly makes a dent in the accepted truth of the CR because of the political conviction that the evil Communist regime led by the monster Mao could not treat its opponents in a humane way.

According to Gu Yingqi (2016), there were not only regular nurses but also a chef to look after Liu when he was ill. Gu, like Li Zhisui who participated in the manufacturing of *A Private Life of Chairman Mao* under the guidance of his American mentors (Gao 2008), was a health care physician at the central office of the CCP, looking after leaders like Liu Shaoqi. Gu was also an attending doctor at the Beijing Hospital, the deputy director of the Zhongnanhai compound (where the top Chinese leaders were residing at that time), a principal military medical officer and later deputy minister of health. Gu was assigned to look after Liu. In June 1968, when doctors advised that Liu's daily consumption of six eggs should be reduced to two and the Liu should eat less pork but more beef, soya products and vegetables, the staff acted accordingly. Gu insists that there was no negligence.

Through Wang Dongxing, the director of the CCP Central Office, Mao and Zhou had instructed the medical personnel to do everything possible to treat Liu. When Liu was seriously sick in July 1968,

Professors Tao Leheng, Huang Wan and Dr. Dong Changcheng of the CCP central leadership at the Zhongnanhai compound actually worked and lived in Liu's house. There were also four nurses, some of whom had to sleep on the floor. In doing so they rescued Liu seven times from serious pneumonia. When Liu could not get off the bed there were nurses to wash him. The forever cautious Zhou Enlai instructed the medial staff to take photos of the bedroom where Liu was treated to make sure that there was enough light, that the room was clean and that the bedding was washed clean white. From July 1968 to August 1969 a total of 40 consultation treatments took place at Liu's home when his life was in danger, involving a group of the best doctors in China. The best medicine available was used, some of which was imported.

Like other top leaders of the CCP such as Deng Xiaoping, Chen Yun, Chen Yi and Ye Jianying, in an apparent effort to anticipate a possible Soviet Russian military invasion, Liu was evacuated and flown to Kaifeng on the 17th October 1969. Dr. Dong Changcheng and nurses Cao Bing and Ji Xiuyun accompanied Liu with emergency medical equipment to Kaifeng, but the duty of care was handed over to local medical staff on November 6, 1969. On November 10, 1969 Liu passed away. Liu was certainly in poor health since 1968 and would most likely have lived longer had he not been politically victimized. The evacuation probably accelerated the bad health situation, but to say that Liu was not treated humanely is not true, according to Gu, as someone responsible for looking after Liu.

THE CULTURAL IS THE POLITICAL AND
THE POLITICAL IS THE CULTURAL

Mao liked operas, especially Chinese traditional ones, but, as his disappointment with his colleagues on the issue of collective agriculture grew he was increasingly unhappy with the content in the field of Chinese art, especially the performing arts, as he thought they were all about emperors, ministers, scholars and pretty women. They did not reflect contemporary society and did not have working and laboring people playing any roles. To sooth Mao's anger at the Ministry of Culture for what Mao termed a "dangerous revisionist" phenomenon, the mayor of Beijing, one of the most powerful figures at the time, Peng Zhen, headed what was called the Cultural Revolution Group of five people in 1964 to carry out the task of reforming literature and the arts, especially the performing arts. So the supposed CR had already started in 1964, two years ahead of the official CR in 1966.

As Clark (2008) convincingly documents, the CR was not only intended to be cultural, with its origin years before, but also achieved innovation and vitality which impacted years later. However, by 1965 Mao was increasingly frustrated by Peng Zhen's Cultural Revolution Groups for not making any substantial progress—not because Peng did not intend to do something, but because he understood the task of cultural reform as purely involving the cultural aspect.

While Mao gave up hope in the Beijing Cultural Revolution Group, some radicals in Shanghai, organized by Mao's wife, Jiang Qing, and clearly encouraged by Mao himself, published a critique of a play titled *The Dismissal of Hai Rui* in the Shanghai-based newspaper the *Wenhui Daily*. Hai Rui was a Qing Dynasty official (1514–87), one of whose most controversial acts was to expropriate the land that had been annexed by the rich and powerful and redistribute it to the original owners. The author of the critique of the play, which was written by the accomplished writer Wu Han who was then deputy mayor of Beijing, was the then unknown personality Yao Wenyuan. Understandably, Peng Zhen was not happy with the direct attack from Shanghai on one of his colleagues, especially when he did not know that Mao was behind the attack. Peng demolished the publication and would not allow it to appear in media outlets in Beijing: an act that led to his own downfall.

What Peng Zhen and his colleagues did not, or pretended not to, understand was that for Mao the cultural was clearly the political. At the Lushan Conference in 1959 the then minister of defense, Marshal Peng Dehuai, was dismissed in the aftermath of the GLF, a fatal event after which Wu Han wrote *The Dismissal of Hai Rui*. Mao related the dismissal of the historical figure Hai Rui to the dismissal of his Defense Minister Peng Dehuai politically because of the crucial issue of land ownership. As discussed in the last section, and according to Liu's wife, Wang Guangmei, Mao was unhappy with Liu in 1962 for failing to stop the practice of household farming contracts. For Mao that risked dismantling the system of collective agriculture. Mao wanted to apply the critique of *The Dismissal of Hai Rui* to counter-attack the critique of the dismissal of Peng Dehuai in relation to the issue of redistribution of land as a measure to destroy the collective system.

Again as confirmed by Wang Guangmei, in 1964 Mao was not happy with Liu because of the latter's working style with respect to the SEM.

For Mao, the SEM should not have been directed at a vast number of ordinary CCP party members, but at those CCP cadres in leading positions at various levels of government. At the same time, Mao made a range of critical remarks regarding the Chinese state machine, labeling the Ministry of Health as the Ministry of the Urban Lord because most of the meager resources were allocated to the urban sector whereas the majority of Chinese lived and worked in the rural sector, and he criticized China's education system for not only damaging the health of students but for being out of touch with reality.

For Mao the cultural and the political could not be separated. But for Peng Zhen and his colleagues the cultural was just a scholarly debate that should be politically neutral. Therefore, in a document called "Outlines of the Report on the Current Academic Debates" drafted in February 1966 under the supervision of Peng Zhen as a Cultural Revolution Group document, one of the most controversial statements was that "everyone should be equal in matters of truth" in scholarly debates. For Mao there was no politically neutral scholarly debate. Mao decided to take action and called an enlarged Politburo meeting during which a document titled "Notification by the CCP Central Committee" was issued on May 16, 1966, hence the official starting date of the CR. The notification declared that there were figures such as Khrushchev who were asleep in the Party. It was also at this meeting that the Cultural Revolution Group headed by Peng Zhen was dismissed. Instead the new Cultural Revolution Small Group was set up and headed by Chen Boda, Kang Sheng and Zhang Chunqiao from Shanghai, with Jiang Qing as the deputy. In this notification some main ideas of the CR are laid out: "one has to break the old before one can establish the new," "the cow ghost and snake spirit"—an earthy Chinese way of referring to demons and monster of bad characters—have to be criticized. Then in August 1966 the Eleventh Plenary Session of the Eighth CCP National Congress of the CCP was held in Beijing, during which Mao wrote a few lines on a piece of used newspaper attacking Liu, resulting in Liu's demotion to number eight in the CCP hierarchy.

The main CR document, the "Sixteen Articles", was issued by the conference, in which some of the major CR ideas and practices were promoted, including the idea of mobilizing and relying on the masses, the idea of bombarding the capitalist headquarters, of breaking away with the "four olds" (old ideas, old culture, old habits and old customs) and the "four big freedoms" (freedom of putting up posters, freedom of debates, freedom of protest and freedom of criticism), which were to be written into the Chinese Constitution in 1969 but abolished after the death of Mao. The "Sixteen Articles" document also stresses that the struggle should be carried out in words, not in physical fighting, and that the majority of the party officials are good and that even the bad ones should be allowed to change and should be welcomed back if reformed. As the CR was meant to be cultural, the document specifically points out the necessity of an educational reform, the contents of which included the shortening of the length of schooling, simpler courses and students' engagement in other forms of learning such as farming, working in a factory and in military affairs. It also points out that measures should be taken to protect scientists, and that the aim of revolution was not to disrupt economic activities but to promote production.

VIOLENCE, AND CHINA AS A METHOD

The Red Guards, the Gang of Four, and most of all Mao himself, have been condemned for the violence and cruelty that occurred during the CR. This officially sanctioned and widely accepted historical knowledge has been supported by the production of the "literature of the wounded," of memoirs and autobiographies by well-known writers such as Ba Jin and Ji Xianlin, by Nien Cheng and the even more popular Jung Chang, and by the production of media sensations like the execution of Zhang Zhixin. As someone who was a teenage Red Guard during the CR, I witnessed violence and cruelty, though on a very small scale and to a lesser degree in the area of a rural village. The empirical evidence and human suffering cannot be denied.

I was spoon-fed quotations from Mao's *Little Red Book*, quotations taken out of context; those most frequently recited include "revolution is not a dinner party, nor embroidery or writing an essay" and "the crux of Marxism is that rebellion is justified." The theoretical origin of violence and cruelty blamed on Mao is identifiable. Based on this kind of evidence the historical knowledge of the good against evil and of humanity triumphing over the inhumane monster Mao is simple and easily explained. From this perspective it is totally incomprehensible and utterly perplexing, as Jung Chang reminds us, that the Chinese have not removed the portrait of Mao from the Tiananmen Rostrum and removed his body from Tiananmen Square. China has not changed and will not change so long as the CCP is in power. Thus China is a method, and the CR is a particularly convincing element to be used to demonstrate not only the evil of communism but also the necessity of getting rid of it.

Simplicity is beautiful, as Einstein famously said. But historical reality is never simple. Human beings want comfort but historical reality is never comfortable. Regarding the CR, if we probe the question of the origin of the Red Guard, the question of who carried out the violence and the question of how a cultural revolution turned into a violent physical one, then nothing is simple and comfortable for either the victims or the producers of knowledge about the CR.

THE ORIGIN OF THE RED GUARDS AND DIFFERENT CONCEPTUALIZATIONS OF THE CULTURAL REVOLUTION

The person who coined the term Red Guard is Zhang Chengzhi, then a teenage student who is a well-known contemporary writer. The term was first used in public in a poster on May 29, 1966. To be a Red Guard became fashionable largely because Mao, on August 18, was wearing a Red Guard band on his arm on the Tiananmen Rostrum during one of the eight inspections of millions of students in the square. The first groups of the Red Guards were from the elite schools in Beijing and most of them were sons and daughters of high-ranking CCP party officials and army officers. It was these people who first put up posters criticizing their teachers and school administrators for imposing overly strict academic standards that had allowed the enrolment of students who had non-revolutionary family backgrounds. However, when students of non-revolutionary backgrounds rose up to rebel in the name of Red Guards, their attempted targets were not teachers, but the power holders at their schools. Violence and fractions arose between May and August 1966, referred to as the 50 days.

Fractions arose because there were mainly two groups of students, both claiming to be Red Guards defending Maoism. There was the fraction of the establishment consisting of students whose parents were power holders. It was the princelings who initiated the Red Guards organization and took the CR as a movement to attack the taken-for-granted class enemies like the Rightists, former landlords and capitalists, and those of so-called counter-revolutionary backgrounds. There was also a group of students whose parents were professionals from non-revolutionary backgrounds who would be happy to attack the power holders so as to claim a space in the ruling hierarchy and the state machine. Both groups could claim Maoist legitimacy depending on how the CR was interpreted. Take the CR idea of tackling the four olds—old ideas, old culture, old habits and old customs—as an example. If one interpreted the four olds idea as the four olds belonging to Chinese society in the past, then the former landlords and capitalists would be the CR targets, as understood by the princeling Red Guards. If one interpreted the four olds as the cultural, the mentality that the CCP, the government and army power holders could and had taken on themselves, then the contemporary power holders would be the targets, as understood by the Rebel Red Guards. Clearly there were two kinds of conceptualizations of CR targets. Both groups of students understood their own conceptualization instinctively but neither was theoretically articulated at the beginning of the CR. If anything, the princeling Red Guards' conceptualization was more readily acceptable and understood. Hence the difficulty for Mao and his radical colleagues.

Violence arose precisely because of the contest between these two understandings of the conceptual framework of class enemies. This is also closely related to another issue, that of working style, which Mao took to be crucial because he saw it as a political issue: whether the masses were allowed to mobilize and take matters into their own hands. The power holders headed by Liu and Deng would certainly not allow that. Take the example of Beijing Normal University, where one of Deng Xiaoping's daughters, Deng Rong, was a student. Through his daughter Deng was informed of the development and therefore directed the CR at Beijing Normal. Hu Qili, then a rising young cadet at the Youth League, a cradle for Communist officials and bureaucrats, was received by Deng at his home on May 7, 1966, together with two student representatives, Liu Jin and Song Bingbing, both children of high-ranking CCP officials. In early 1967, Hu Qili (1967) wrote a poster, "Deng Xiaoping is the Black Commander of Suppressing Students at the Middle School for Girls at Beijing Normal University," a poster that revealed the content of Deng's reception. Deng instructed that no organization should be allowed to appear without permission or they would be categorized as illegal, and that the CR had to be managed by the Party organs at all levels. In fact later in April 1967, when the situation changed dramatically, Deng Rong (1967) wrote a poster criticizing her father along the same lines as Hu Qili, which was published by the *Liberation Daily* and *Guangming Daily*.

VIOLENCE

Liu himself admitted that he could not follow the CR because he was just an old revolutionary who came across new problems. It is quite likely that Liu did not really understand what Mao wanted the CR to do. In running the day-to-day work, Liu as the first deputy of Mao and Deng as the general secretary of the CCP Central Committee would not allow the bottom-up approach and wanted to maintain tight party control over the students. So they decided to send "work teams" to the schools and universities to manage the increasingly agitated students. However, the work teams sent by them were not "moderate," as suggested by Johnson (2016). They wanted to suppress the student movement as they did during the 1957 Anti-Rightist Movement. During the 50 days from May to August 1966, from a total of around 300,000 tertiary students and teaching staff in 53 institutions in Beijing, 12,802 of them (10,211 students and 2,591 teachers, about one in every 23 people) were victimized as Rightists or counter-revolutionaries by the work teams. That is the reason behind Mao's assertion in his poster attacking Liu in August 1966 for suppressing different opinions by "white terror" and practicing dictatorship against the masses, a suppression that was "left in form but right in essence." Mao further points out that Liu did the same thing during the SEM, implicating the "Taoyuan Experience" report, which largely led to the misfortune of Wang Guangmei.

The work teams' approach to the CR during the 50 days was later summarized by the Rebel radicals as "attack the broad masses of people so as to protect the small number of power holders." The princeling Red Guards not only reported to their parents what happened at their schools but also supported the work teams. The way the CR was conducted at the beginning in Beijing also spread to other parts of the country. In Wuhan University, for instance, 1,242 students and staff were victimized by the work team. While the work teams and princeling Red Guards were conducting the CR according to their conceptual understanding and based on their political interest, the Rebel Red Guards were increasingly encouraged by the CR radicals represented by the new Cultural Revolution Small Group dominated by Jiang Qing. On July 1, 1966 for instance, the main "theoretical" CCP journal the *Red Flag* published an editorial stating "have faith in the masses and rely on the masses," the spirit of which was clearly contrary to what the work teams were doing. Resistance against the work teams was gaining momentum, especially after the two CR radicals Wang Li and Guan Feng paid a visit to the Tsing Hua University Rebel "hero" Kuai Dafu, who was detained by the work team headed by Liu's wife Wang Guangmei.

Clearly violence during the first 50 days period of the CR was carried out by the work teams, organized by the central government led by Liu and Deng. The victims of violence were students, teachers, professionals of non-revolutionary backgrounds, noted scholars and writers, and some party officials. The fraction that actually understood the real intention of Mao and the CR was suppressed. It was the August 1966 decisions which issued the "Sixteen Articles" and demoted Liu Shaoqi that "liberated" the Rebel Red Guards. However, this political reversal invoked a violent backlash from the princeling Red Guards, who finally realized that the CR did not match their understanding of it.

XIJIU (WEST DISTRICT POLICING) AND *LIANDONG* (UNITED ACTION)

One leading figure of the princeling Red Guards was Kong Dan, whose father was the minister of investigation, and whose mother was the deputy director of Zhou Enlai's office. According to Kong Dan (2015a), what was called *xijiu*, whose members were teenagers who issued general orders concerning the running of the CR and China, was headed by Kong himself as the general commander, with Chen Xiaolu (son of Minister of Foreign Affairs Chen Yi) and Dong Lianghe (son of Dong Biwu, vice president of the PRC) as deputies. Kong reveals that most of the 13 General Orders issued by Xijiu were drafted by Li Sanyou, whose father was deputy minister of public security. In fact Zhou Enlai's office provided logistics support for *xijiu* and Zhou Enlai even asked *xijiu* to keep order at Beijing Railway Station (Kong 2015). Kong admits that *xijiu* was an instinctive reaction among the princelings to the development of the CR when it was clear that it was directed toward old revolutionary officials. Kong admits that *xijiu* was a reaction to the CR: we have to protect our parents and keep the order of the state (Kong Dan 2015a). Kong not only thought that what he and his princeling Red Guards comrades did was natural but also legitimate. However, what Kong Dan does not state is what they actually did, especially in terms of the violence committed (Wen Bei 2015).

By the standard CCP knowledge framework of class struggle, *xijiu* members, including Xu Wenlian (son of General Xu Haidong) and

Deng Xiaoping's daughter Deng Rong, wanted to direct the Red Guard movements toward the old six black categories of class enemies—the landlords, rich peasants, counter-revolutionaries, bad elements, Rightists and capitalists—so as to defend their powerful parents. They even set up torture rooms, jails and labor reform detention centers. In these detention centers in No 1 and No 6 Middle Schools where princelings were heavily concentrated, 200 were tortured, some to death. Those who died during this period include playwright Bai Xin, archaeologist Chen Mengjia, editor of the *People's Daily* Chen Xiaoyu, historian He Ji, pathologist Hu Zhengxiang, educationalist Huang Guozhang, General Huang Shaoxian, writer Kong Jue, early communist revolutionary Li Da, journalist Liu Keling, entomologist Lu Jinlun, classical literature expert Xi Luxi, geologist Xie Jiarong, Kunqu opera actor Yan Huizhu, conductor Yang Jialun, educationalist Yu Dayin, journalist Chen Zhengqing, secretary of the Youth League as the school attached to Qinghua University Liu Shuhua and the well-known author Lao She (Wen Bei 2015).

Qi Benyu points out that well-known figures such as Shangguan Yunzhu and Ma Sicong also died during the period. Jiang Qing even wanted to find out who was responsible for the death of these artists (Qi Benyu 2016). In their fourth General Order the *xijiu* teenagers ordered the targets of class dictatorship to move out of Beijing, and 85,198 Beijing residents were repatriated to their original hometowns. The practice of *chaojia* (search one's house and confiscate personal properties) was also widely carried out by *xijiu* (Qi Benyu 2016). They would wear army uniforms and ride brand new bikes, and some of them even had jeeps and used the slogans like "long live red terror" to justify their detention and torturing. The Beijing Daxing Massacre was one of the most horrendous crimes at that time. If one searches the key words "Beijing Daxing Massacre" on the internet there are many entries describing the brutality, and some explicitly blame Mao and the CR radicals for what happened. However, according to Qi Benyu (2016) it was the princeling Red Guards who were responsible and it was the CR radicals who stopped them.

Were their parents behind this kind of organized and planned violence? Kong Dan admits that they thought they had the backing of Zhou Enlai (Kong Dan 2015a). Kong says that all the general orders to these teenagers, issued as documents from the Central Committee of the CCP, were read by his mother who affirmed her support, though Kong

Dan also states that his mother read them only after they were issued and he and his comrades did not get direct guidance from either his mother or Zhou. On August 31, 1966 General Ye Jianying was reported to have said, when receiving Kong Dan on the Tiananmen Rostrum, that general orders by *xijiu* were good (Wen Bei 2015). Veteran Communist leaders Tan Zhenlin and Li Xiannian also praised the actions by *xijiu* and Zhou Ronxin, director of Zhou Enlai Office, allocated office space for the *xijiu* headquarters (Wen Bei 2015).

It is possible that neither Zhou Enlai nor the teenagers' high-ranking party officials and army officer parents were behind the princeling actions. However, what is clear is that those teenagers talked and acted with confidence as they were the masters of the country and of the state.

In December, two of the *liandong* members were caught stealing by the Rebel Red Guards of the Beijing University of Aeronautics and Astronautics and were handed over to the Ministry of Public Security. *Liandong* immediately organized a rescue of the two by attacking the Ministry of Public Security. They were violent to the members of the ministry and succeeded in rescuing captives during their second attack. *Liandong* organized six such attacks on the Ministry of Public Security and brought their hatred of the CR Small Group to the surface by shouting "boil Jiang Qing and down with Chen Boda." It was only then that the Minister of Public Security Xie Fuzhi ordered a crackdown of *liandong*, and with the help of Rebel Red Guards the leaders of *liandong* of various schools were arrested. The Rebels listed the crimes committed by *liandong* and connected what they did with what the work teams sent by Liu and Deng did, to formulate a narrative that a reactionary capitalist headquarters headed by Liu Shaoqi and Deng Xiaoping wanted to stop the CR. But the arrested leaders of *liandong* were soon released because Mao could not afford to offend so many veteran leaders personally by detaining their teenage children. *Liandong* died down, but some of them would not lie down. After their release some of them were reported to ride bikes in gangs, shouting "long live Liu Shaoqi" and "we will see in ten years whether Chairman Mao is correct." How confident and prophetic they were (Lao You 2011).

EDUCATION, CULTURE AND THE CULTURAL REVOLUTION

One of the most prominent features of the mainstream construction of the CR is that it destroyed Chinese culture and education. There are at least two sets of *prima facie* evidence frequently presented for this construction of the CR, one set of evidence being the humiliation and torture of producers of culture which led to the death of some, such as the much-admired writer Lao She, and another being the destruction of traditional cultural objects and relics, vividly demonstrated by photos of books being burned by teenage Red Guards. Regarding education, the evidence appears even more apparent, as education institutions stopped running for some time all over the country.

EDUCATION

Let me deal with the issue of education first by looking at the current situation of education in China. In the year 2017, on WeChat and social media there is a post that has been widely shared: "two German teachers left China in anger and thus boxed loudly the ear of China's education" (Shijie Huaren Zhoukan 2017). One German who taught in Suzhou for eight years decided to leave China because he complained that he could not see any real education developing in China in his lifetime. For him China's education is all geared toward gaining high marks. Another German teacher had lived and worked in a remote village for more than ten years at his own cost. The idealist young German first taught at a country school but was sacked because the parents had complained that his teaching did not help students in getting good marks. While in the village the young German lived, worked and played with students in the field, in painting, with music and so on. He was accused of not doing proper work.

What is interesting is that the Chinese themselves are not happy with the current education system that puts undue stress on marks and examinations. In all these years, during my conversations with people in the education system, from students to parents and from teachers to bureaucrats, there is not a single person that is happy and not a single person who does not complain. I ask every time: but why don't you change? Their answer is always more or less the same: there is nothing they can do about it. They find it so hard because change requires a revolution, a revolution in thinking, a cultural revolution.

One overriding argument for the examination system is equality: everyone is supposed to be judged equally by marks, irrespective of family background, social standing and wealth. In other words, impartial, closed and strict academic examination would reduce the influence of Bourdieu's tripartite of the economic, cultural and social capitals (Bourdieu 1986) to a minimum.

In fact the thorny issues surrounding China's education are not new. In 1964, two years before the start of the CR, there was already student unrest in the elite schools in Beijing. In the aftermath of the GLF failure, China implemented a more stringent examination system in the schools that stressed academic achievement. The princelings, with social capital, or rather political capital, at these elite schools were not happy because children from families that had cultural (artists and high-skilled professionals) and even economic capital (remember that until the CR, as Nien Cheng confirms, the former capitalists were still paid dividends and interest on their wealth before the Communist takeover in 1949) were apparently doing better in the system. The unrest in 1964 was in many ways a preview of what happened at the beginning of the CR (Gao 2015). The two fractions—the old elite from the pre-1949 Revolution years and new elite, the princelings—were competing for the ruling positions.

As Andreas (2009) demonstrates convincingly, with the failure of the CR, the two fractions, in their common fight against the ideas and practices of the CR, accommodated each other and joined together as the ruling class, the "Red Engineer class" in current China.

In fact judgment by examination is never equal because there is no equality at the start and therefore none at the end. This should be obvious for at least two reasons. One is that a child from a rural village can never compete with an urbanite equally in China; hard work and talent play only a part, perhaps a small part, in whether one succeeds in examinations. To be equal requires affirmative action that favors the disadvantaged. The other reason is that different people with different talents and academic aptitudes are inherently unable to accommodate those differences.

Here came the CR experiment: abolition of academic examinations and tertiary enrolments were to be recommended from grassroots organizations with paper examinations only as a reference. Years of education in school were shortened so as to make more time for practical work such as engaging in agricultural and industrial production. Textbooks, if used at all, were more relevant to contemporary society instead of the history of the rich and famous of the past and should be more Chinese instead of foreign. Students were educated to be both Red and Expert, not just the latter. Finally, the teachers had to be re-educated so as to be equipped for this approach. What was also required was a whole package because one area of this experiment could not succeed without the implementation of all the others. Hence the CR, at least theoretically speaking.

This was indeed revolutionary: a *cultural* revolution. But to start this revolution, the old practices would need to stop first, hence the shutdown of schools. The conceptualization was that one could not establish the new without making a break with the old. In this process there would be interruptions, disruptions and even destruction in the normal sense of the word. It is understandable therefore that there was resistance, because the revolution placed high demands on those who had to give up their privileges or at least get out of their comfort zone. It was such a massive undertaking that Mao and his radicals called for the masses to "educate themselves" and to "liberate themselves." When the masses were involved there might be misunderstanding and even deliberate "mob" behaviors, and therefore there would be violence and unnecessary destruction.

However, the post-Mao political and intellectual elite construction of the CR doesn't see the attempted change in this conceptual framework; whether they believed it then is a different matter. They go as far as to say, as the example of Ji Xianlin shows, that the CR was a crime that involved sabotaging Chinese education and culture. They do not even mention the word "experiment" let alone "revolution." In all the condemnation of the CR, one question is never asked: why would the Gang of Four, or Mao, want to destroy China's education and culture? Without a rational inquiry, they do not want to mention the fact that primary schools were stopped for only a short period of time (for one or two years varying from place to place), or the fact that primary and secondary education expanded greatly in the early 1970s (Gao 1999a, Pepper 1996).

The post-Mao political and intellectual elite argue that the number of graduates was hardly enough for China and that the kind of education they had was not of a high standard: if anything, it was Maoist propaganda. Again, *prima facie* evidence of this proposition is plentiful: like the Mao quotations in textbooks, like the personality cult of Mao in the form of Mao badges and Mao busts. Again, a rational inquiry would show that the issue of personality cult was not as straightforward as it seemed. It is true that there was a need to boost Mao's prestige and emotional power to the populace so as to lead a revolution of this nature, this scale and this magnitude. And Mao knew it and therefore allowed a degree of personality cult. Apart from the well-known letter that Mao wrote to Jiang Qing as early as July 8, 1966 expressing his skepticism about Lin Biao's promotion of the Mao personality (Qi Benyu 2017: 460), Mao was trying to cool down personality cult practices that he considered not only unhelpful but also absurd. On December 6, 1969, a document titled "On Several Issues Concerning the Propaganda of Mao Image" was issued in the name of the CCP Central Committee which instructs that just as it was instructed in a decree issued on July 13, 1967 no statue of Mao should be erected without approval, that no Mao badges should be made without approval from the center, that newspapers should no longer use Mao's portrait as the head picture, that no product packages including porcelain vases should have pictures of Mao and that "loyalty" activities such as "morning instruction from Mao and evening report to Mao," Mao quotations before a meal should be all stopped.

CULTURE: KANG SHENG AND JI XIANLIN

Kang Sheng was first portrayed as an evil genius in Byron and Pack (1992), not only as head of the secret police that arrested and victimized his opponents or people he did not like without any scruples, but also as a hypocrite who advocates the destruction of traditional Chinese culture on the one hand but plundered objects and treasures of traditional Chinese culture for himself. The post titled "Kang Sheng Plundered More Than 10,000 Precious Cultural Objects During the CR" is pasted on Wangyi, which attributes the original post in 2007 to Heilongjiang xinwen wang. Wang Li, who was one of the victims of Kang Sheng and who did not have any motivation to say good things about the latter in a publication after Kang's death, states that Kang Sheng was not only a very cultured man, whose calligraphy was probably one of the best among high-ranking CCP leaders, but also one of those who tried very hard to protect traditional Chinese cultural objects. Kang collected a lot of cultural objects from possible destruction and donated all of them to the state without any compensation before his death (Wang Li 2008). In fact the CR was not the most destructive period even in terms of traditional Chinese cultural relics and objects; it was during the 1990s when the real estate boom started in China, as an expert Xie Chensheng (2017) points out.

Kang Sheng is also constructed as currying favor with Jiang Qing so as to be in Mao's good books, and is seen as collaborating with Jiang Qing in persecuting good people (Byron and Pack 1992: 148–9). However, according to at least one insider, Kang Sheng's personal secretary (Yan Changgui 2015), Kang was against promoting Jiang Qing to be a member of the Politburo Standing Committee during the CR. On the other hand, the post-Mao construction of the Deng does not want to reveal the fact that Deng Xiaoping actually respected Kang and had a very good relationship with him (Yan Changgui 2015).

While Kang Sheng has been constructed as a saboteur of culture, the Chinese literati like to present themselves as victims. Professor Ji Xianlin is a well-known example of this largely because of his "cowshed" memoirs (Ji 1998). But a court case in 2013 has caused many to question the authenticity of Ji's memoirs. Ji's family brought Peking University to court because of a dispute over whether 577 valuable cultural antiques and objects, of which 207 were priceless old paintings, should be the property of the university or his family. Social media posts demand to know whether Ji was really the victim of the CR, whose home was supposed to be searched and properties confiscated. Questions were also raised regarding how Ji had come to possess so many valuable objects when he was just a professor without a huge family inheritance (Wang Yi 2013). It emerged that Ji was far from a passive victim, but a political activist. In 1957, Ji chaired the anti-rights movement in the Department of East Languages at Peking University and had several colleagues and students labeled as Rightists (Xin Hutochong 2014). It was also revealed that during the CR, according to Nie Yuanzi for instance, Ji was one of the Rebel leaders of the Jingganshan Rebel group (Nie 2005).

CONCLUSION

There are many conclusions that can be drawn from the above discussion of the CR in terms of it being a *cultural* revolution. The first obvious conclusion is that the post-Mao construction of the CR, instead of blaming Mao for it directly, denounces Lin Biao, the Gang of Four, and especially Jiang Qing and characters like Kang Sheng and Nie Yuanzi for the violence and disorder. Relevant to this is the conclusion that the Party officials and army officers who were victimized during the CR are being constructed as the "good guys," and for whom any evidence that might show otherwise has to be excluded from contemporary Chinese history. Another major conclusion is that this construction of the CR cannot but frame its origin as a personal power struggle. The profound conceptual and ideological differences between Mao on the one hand, and Liu, Deng and the whole CCP hierarchy on the other, are excluded from the discussion. The ideas of Mao and the contents of the CR that are profoundly culturally revolutionary, in areas such as education, healthcare and the arts, are hollowed out.

7
Why is the Cultural Revolution Revolutionary? The Legacies

INTRODUCTION

In Chapter 6, I argued how the post-Mao construction of the CR hollows out the ideas of Mao and the contents of the CR that are *cultural*. From seemingly irrefutable facts—such as the unfair dismissal of Peng Dehuai in 1959, the death of Liu Shaoqi, the work teams, the CR violence and factions, the horrible death of Zhang Zhixin or the ambiguous career of Ji Xianlin—very different understandings can be produced and consumed. Data and information are selected and processed either deliberately or even unconsciously to include some elements while excluding others for a specific type of knowledge consumption. In this chapter, the concept of selection is used to demonstrate some of the positive legacies of the CR.

The start of the CR took place 50 years ago—a long time in contemporary politics, but a short time in the scale of human history. Whether the highly respected Zhou Enlai really said that it is still too early to comment on the French Revolution is questionable, but what is beyond doubt is that whether the CR is relevant to China will be made clear in years to come. Precisely because of its relevance, the post-Mao Chinese authorities forbade any discussion and debate about the CR, even after 50 years. However, for many years the intellectual and political elite were not only allowed but encouraged to write memoirs and autobiographies condemning the CR as *shi nian haojie* (ten years of calamities) for the Chinese people, and as the darkest time in Chinese history. The post-Mao Chinese political and intellectual elite are afraid of free discussion of the CR not only because they know that their version of the CR is one-sided but also because they know their anti-Maoist development policies are not welcomed and not accepted by some sectors, especially lower classes in Chinese society. That is the fundamental legacy of the CR.

MAO, THE EVIL MONSTER OR THE LEADER OF THE CCP? WHO DEFINED THE DISCOURSE?

In a sense, every Chinese political actor at that time contributed to the development of the CR. Peng Zhen contributed by suppressing the publication of Yao Wenyuan's commentary on the play *The Dismissal of Hai Rui* in early 1966. Liu Shaoqi and Deng Xiaoping contributed by instructing the work teams to use the anti-Rightist method of putting down criticism of authorities in May 1966, especially university students and staff who were involved in what was called the June 18 Incident who were labeled as "organized counter-revolutionaries" (Gu Zhang 2016). In fact that was one of the main reasons why Mao wanted to take down Liu Shaoqi, as he expressed in his own "big poster" in August 1966. Zhang Chunqiao contributed by encouraging the workers in Shanghai to take over power from the CCP party authorities. Jiang Qing contributed by representing the CR radicals and by reforming the Chinese performing arts. Wang Li, Guan Feng and Qi Benyu contributed by expanding, explaining and elaborating Mao's ideas, often expressed by Mao in random talks. Chen Boda contributed by writing the editorial that launched the anti-four olds movement, which led to the destruction of various traditional cultural relics. Zhou Enlai contributed by apparently supporting the notorious *xijiu*, which was responsible for a lot of early CR violence, by making concrete measures to protect some power holders while victimizing others, and above all by managing to get the two fractions, the CR radicals fraction and the conservative power holders fraction, together to run the day-to-day work of the nation. Last but not least, to use a cliché, the Red Guards and Rebels contributed by participating in the CR according to their understanding and their socio-economic interests. Surprisingly, new evidence seems to suggest that the widely portrayed "evil" Kang Sheng actually contributed very little to the CR, for better or worse (Qi Benyu 2016, Nie Yuanzi 2005).

Nonetheless, any evaluation of the CR cannot be separated from an evaluation of Mao because Mao was not only the initiator, the ultimate arbitrator and policy decision maker, but also the main source of ideas of the CR. From evidence that has emerged in Chinese sources on Mao and on the development of the beginning of the CR, such as the ruthless crackdown on students by the work team sent by Liu and Deng (Wang Li 2008, Qi Benyu 2016), and from what Deng had done since the death of Mao, especially in his treatment of Mao's wife Jiang

Qing, in his decision to invade Vietnam in 1979 and his ordering the armies and tanks to undertake a bloody put-down of protesting students and citizens in 1989, one could argue that Deng Xiaoping was a more ruthless political leader than Mao.

Mao was powerful before and during the CR not because he was ruthless. Mao had the ultimate say in CCP politics not only because he was the "Chairman" of the CCP but also, and more so, because he was a towering figure intellectually. In a word, Mao was the embodiment of what the Chinese officially term as Mao Zedong Xixiang (Mao Zedong thought) and what I term Maoist discourse (Gao 1994). Unless and until the Maoist discourse (or paradigm, or narrative) is replaced, those Chinese leaders, though giants in their own right, are defenseless in dealing with Mao. That is precisely why the post-Mao regime finds it hard to settle a narrative for the future of China: to discredit Maoist discourse is to discredit the whole CCP enterprise, on which their very existence depends, and at the same time a new narrative is needed to justify what has actually happened that has been anti-Maoist.

Some might argue that Mao was anything but intellectual. Chang and Halliday (2005), for instance, portray Mao as nothing but a power-hungry monster. Even though Chang has been thoroughly repudiated, for instance by Benton and Lin Chun (2009), the knowledge of Mao produced by Chang and her co-author husband was consumed with relish, largely because of her successful book *Wild Swans* (Chang 1991).

Chinese leaders such as Zhou Enlai, Deng Xiaoping, Peng Dehuai, Lin Biao, Chen Boda, Wang Ming, Zhang Guotao and Zhang Wentian had enormous political, military and intellectual abilities in their own right. These prominent figures in the CCP suffered political defeat at one time or another at the hands of Mao. They either had to follow Mao or had to be demoted because of the tide of revolutionary discourse led by Mao. That the highly committed, highly educated and extremely intelligent CCP leaders were totally convinced of Mao's leadership role can be confirmed by the diaries of Yang Shangkun: for example, in one of the 1949 entries Yang commented how Wang Ming was a low-quality leader compared with Mao (Yang Shangkun 2001).

When Deng Xiaoping (Deng 1980) said, in his interview with the Italian Journalist Oriana Fallaci, that without Mao "the Chinese people would, at the very least, have spent much more time groping in the dark" he was referring to this discourse. By saying this Deng, always the straight talker, was not being modest or politically expedient because he made the utterance at the height of his political career when he would not have to answer to anybody: Mao was dead and the so-called Gang of Four were in jail. Deng had, for the first half of his life, followed Maoist discourse under the leadership of Mao, but wanted to change course during the second half of his life. For the pragmatic Deng who genuinely wanted to see a strong China, there was no intellectual dilemma in this change of direction precisely because he was not intellectual enough. It was Mao who dictated the intellectual design for the CCP and China until the 1970s. Therefore a discussion of the legacy of the CR is also a discussion of the legacy of Mao in many, though not all, ways.

With the above as context in mind, I will now outline the CR legacies in seven areas that are revolutionary: intellectual ideas, economic development, improvement in health and education in rural China, technological development, guiding principles in China's ethnic and foreign policies, gender equality and Xi Jinping's leadership.

INTELLECTUAL IDEAS

We have to remember that the CR is not called the *cultural* revolution for nothing. It was aimed at cultural change, as argued in Chapter 6. It is easier to change a regime than a culture and mentality. The CR failed and was in many ways bound to fail as a political movement at that time, but this is not necessarily so in the scale of history. One of the most repeated and prevalent slogans at that time was "fight with ideas not arms." From the very beginning the CR was about intellectual ideas. The fact that the CR had roller-skated into the chaos of fighting with arms and even military weapons was not what was designed, nor was what was expected. It was meant to be about ideas, about mentality and about subjectivity. Therefore when we talk about the legacy of the CR we need to start from the very concept of intellectual ideas.

China in both traditional and modern times has imported paradigm-changing intellectual ideas and grand narratives. Two notable examples are Buddhism from India and a Marxist-Leninist version of communism from Europe. But what intellectual ideas or grand narratives has China exported? Arguably the one and only intellectual idea of any discursive significance that is exportable and visibly exported from China in modern times is what is called Maoism. Cook (2014) noted how the French postcolonialist and post-structuralist intellectuals, the Black movement in the US and the struggle for land reform and for self-liberation through guerrilla warfare today is inspired by Maoism (Roy 2011, Wang Hui 2015a). In this respect Julia Lovell's (2016) recent contribution is worth exploration: she cites the Maoist Naxalite movement as being inspired by the CR, a movement that is considered the single biggest security challenge to the Indian state (Chakrabarty 2014, Roy 2011). Sanjay Seth links Indian Maoism with the emergence of postcolonial and subaltern studies: Naxalite Maoism, he writes, made Indian intellectuals "engage with and in peasant struggles in a manner that left them more receptive to peasant consciousness" (Seth 2006: 602). Citing Wang Hui (2009), Wolin (2010), Wang Ning (2015), Wolin (2010) and Niccolai (1998), Lovell points out that a connection can be drawn between CR-inspired rebellion and the epistemological skepticism of post-structuralism—Michel Foucault went through a Maoist phase in the early 1970s. Andreas Kühn (cited by Lovell 2016), in his monograph on the German K-Gruppen, argues that numerous West German ex-Maoists have enjoyed vigorous afterlives in mainstream politics, for the most part in the green movement. As Lovell (2016) argues, Maoism greatly inspired the Black movement in the US. It is worth quoting at length as I could not put in a better form:

> The Cultural Revolution's rhetoric of anti-authoritarian rebellion inspired revolts outside China that took aim at a broad range of political, cultural and social customs: at domestic and foreign policy; colonial rule; electoral representation; relations between the sexes; education, film and literature. The impact of the Cultural Revolution (upper-case) is part of a much more diffuse (and often liberalizing) process of a cultural revolution that has transformed society, culture and politics since the 1960s, especially in the developed West. In countries riven by deep historical, ethnic or socio-economic fault lines (post-fascist Germany and Italy; post-segregation America; post-independence India), the Cultural Revolution's legitimization of political violence served as the spark that lit a prairie fire—a fire that in some instances is still burning today. The United States is regularly jolted by revelations of racist police brutality; for veterans of the 1960s and 1970s African American liberation struggle inspired by Cultural Revolution Maoism, some of the political ideas suggested by their readings of Maoist theory and practice remain relevant. (Lovell 2016: 649–50)

With the gradually developed Confucian values of obedience and hierarchy entrenched in China's long tradition, and with the Leninist tradition of organizational control, the intellectual idea of "to rebel is justified" urged by Mao during the CR was tremendously exhilarating and liberating and therefore inspired many idealistic young Chinese, who ironically—or perhaps Mao would say not ironically—rebelled against the official authorities they knew of and eventually against Mao himself. Examples of these rebels include the Hunan Shengwulian (Wu Yiching 2014) led by the then 17-year-old Yang Xiguang in the later 1960s, the Guangdong Li Yizhe group (Chan et al. 1985) in the early 1970s and the dissident writers, artists and political activists in the post-Mao era. In other words, the CR inspired grassroots participation in management and substantive democracy (Perry 2003). For the purpose of personal power and for the purpose of stable economic development it would be totally irrational for Mao to call the young and the radicals to rebel against his own party. The only rational explanation is that Mao wanted a cultural and intellectual change in Chinese society.

As discussed in Chapter 6, a fashionable and politically correct construction of Mao's launching of the CR is that it is not about ideas but about power struggle. A sophisticated version of this model of a power struggle (MacFarquhar 1974) is that due to the disastrous failure of the GLF during the late 1950s, for which Mao was held responsible, Mao was forced to retreat from the center of power. The CR was Mao's way of gaining his power back by knocking down his opponents. If one wants to select "facts" to support this line of argument they are easy to find: Mao did complain that documents and policies were issued in the name of the state without his approval and Mao did give up the position of chairman of the PRC in 1959 to Liu Shaoqi. This seemingly logical explanation has many flaws when all the evidence is taken into consideration. First, it was as early as 1954, long before the GLF even started, and Mao himself who proposed to give up the position of chairman of the PRC so that he could have time to think about larger matters (Xinhua Wang 2013). Second, the chairman of the PRC was and still is largely a ceremonial position, for duties such as receiving heads of the state of other countries. The first candidate put forward to take over this position was actually not Liu Shaoqi but Zhu De, the highly respected military commander during the long years of the CCP's struggle for victory (Renmin Wang 2016). Third, nobody did or could take over the ultimate power from Mao as he had kept the two most powerful positions in the system, the chairman of the Military Commission, without whose permission no military action of any kind could be mobilized, and the most important of all, the chairman of the CCP. It is the most important position in the hierarchy because it is the number one position *de jure*—according to the PRC Constitution, every institution, be it the State Council or the People's Congress, must be placed under the leadership of the CCP. It was a *de facto* situation that had existed since the 1940s in the Yan'an days: Mao was the ultimate decision maker. Finally, precisely because it was Mao who set the discourse for the CCP and the PRC up to the 1970s, he did not have to do much to take down his opponents. In August 1966, during the Eleventh Plenary Session of the Eighth CCP Congress, Liu was already demoted from the number two position to number eight in the hierarchy, only three months after the CR was supposed to have started. This is why, as pointed out in Chapter 6, Liu's wife, Wang Guangmei, denies that the CR was about a personal power struggle. Fundamentally the CR was about ideas. Of course, in order to implement his ideas Mao had to exclude those who did not like or did not understand them. It is this logical necessity that makes the power struggle construction sound reasonable.

One of the principal ideas developed during the CR, but not sufficiently articulated at the beginning and then hollowed out by the post-Mao construction of the CR, was that the CCP could change into a party for capitalism unless a profound transformation of mentality took place for the members of the CCP, especially those who held main positions of responsibility. To push that transformation forward the CR radicals, guided by Mao, issued instructions, not through the normal bureaucratic procedure of going through every level of the CCP party hierarchy, which was how it was usually done, but through the media (*liang bao yi kan*) (two papers and one journal: the *People's Daily*, the *People's Liberation Daily* and the *Red Flag* journal), like Donald Trump who apparently wants to be connected with the electorate through Twitter to avoid what he calls "fake news" outlets. They called directly for the masses at grassroots level to "bombard the headquarters of the capitalist road," that is, to struggle against the main leaders of the CCP party organs at every level. One can imagine what kind of havoc this loosening of governmentality would bring to a country of such size, of such diversity of ethnic groups and of such diverse class and social interests. Fractions of rebels and class conflicts as analyzed by Chan et al. (1980), Perry (1996), Andreas (2009) and Gao (2015), and ideological differences analyzed by Wu Yiching (2014), are only part of the whole mess. It would have been miraculous if there had been no personal humiliation, individual suffering, violence and death. Indeed, it was a miracle that there were no large-scale civil wars. By 1968, Mao had to get the soldiers from the barracks to restore order all over the country.

The idea of changing the mentality of the party power holders had been trialed when the majority of the CCP party officials went through *pipan hui* (being criticized and humiliated in a mass meeting) by the rebels and "the masses." Almost all of them had to and did make self-criticisms orally at this kind of mass meeting and in writing. Some were forgiven for their "mistakes," a few became rebels themselves, while more of them could not understand what was happening. A large number of them remained apprehensive at best and resentful at worst. One of those who appeared to have understood the idea and came out triumphantly was Ji Dengkui, who was promoted from a middle-ranking CCP party official to that of vice premier, and who had played an important role in the transition from the CR period to the post-Mao period.

Some ideas advocated during the CR, such as the ideas of using the West to serve the Chinese and using the past to serve the present, the idea of breaking the old before building the new, were guiding intellectual ideas that inspired the reform of Chinese literature and arts, most notably in performing arts because Mao's wife, the radical Jiang Qing, happened to be an expert in performing arts. The ballet opera of the Red Regiment of Women is the best example of using the West to serve the Chinese, and the model Peking operas are good examples of using the past to serve the present (Clark 2008): traditional opera in form and revolutionary in content. The artistic attainments achieved by artists like Yu Huiyong, an accomplished artist who was promoted to become minister of culture during the CR, but committed suicide after the post-Mao regime put him in jail (Dai 1994), are unprecedented (Zhang Guangtian 2016), even though some intellectual elites like Ba Jin (1991) would not admit it.

The idea of recruiting students directly from rural villages, factory floors and army units, recommended by grassroots organizations to tertiary institutions, the idea of abolishing the traditional style of examinations, and the idea of open schooling so that students would acquire direct knowledge and experience of production activities, are not only revolutionary, but postmodern ideas in education. The idea of the "barefoot doctor" that stresses prevention, hygiene education, a system that makes the medical doctor not only live but also work as a member of the community, proved to be affordable and effective in rural China and recommended by UNESCO. The idea and practice of such a medical service serves not only as an example for poor developing countries but also provides inspiration for affluent developed societies such as the US, where health care costs are so high that the lives of the poor are threatened. These ideas are about mentality and subjectivity and require profound political and cultural change.

The idea of "white collar" managers participating in practical production by engaging in direct labor activities on the factory floor while "blue collar" workers participate in management by being listened to with formal and informal representations in management, as reflected in the Angang Constitution (Cui Zhiyuan 1996), is revolutionary in forging new citizenship, in substantive democracy and in subjectivity. Equally revolutionary is the idea of institutionalizing leadership positions that consist of personnel of three age groups: the old, the middle aged and the young—the old to pass on experience and maintain stability, and the young to provide vitality and new ideas.

The idea that those who are engaged in mental labor should do some manual labor, and those who are mainly engaged in manual labor such as workers and farmers should also engage in intellectual studies; the idea that even a soldier should also participate not only in production activities such as growing food, but also in intellectual activities like studies and discussions and debates; the idea that rural people should not only farm but also engage in industrial activities such as manufacturing, underpinned the development of township and village enterprises that were advocated during the CR, were all spin offs from what was called Mao's May Seventh Instruction. It was to implement these ideas that a large number of bureaucrats were sent to the countryside and many of the Chinese intelligentsia in the state sector were gathered together in what was called the May Seventh Cadre School, which was later condemned by the post-Mao anti-Communist intellectual and political elite as "cowsheds" (Ji Xianlin 1998) or "labor camps." For many in the political and intellectual elite—as people who used to take comfort and convenience for granted—life was indeed harsh in terms of physical work and living conditions when they were transplanted into a rural area without running water and electricity. But the majority of the Chinese, i.e. the rural Chinese, had been in "labor camps" for generations. If anything those transplanted urbanites lived much better conditioned lives during the hardest of their times (Gao 2003). What is not mentioned is the intellectual discourse that the May Seventh School was designed for: cultural and mental change so as to create new subjectivity.

Some argue that the Chinese "mass line" ought to be acknowledged in the liberal world as "a form of democracy" (Lindblom 1977: 262), and that those non-liberal systems which prioritized public welfare and enjoyed popular support "have a genuine historical claim to the title democracy" (Macpherson 1966: 3). Formal democracy theorists of the Western model might be baffled by this kind of informal but substantive democracy (Sartori 1987: 183–4). As Womack (1991) argues, democracy in China must be understood and judged in terms of the desires, interests and situations of the Chinese people. In hindsight, however, we are now seeing how the electorate in formal Western democracies have become disillusioned with party politics and how they vote just for the sake of destabilizing the establishment. The importance of getting people to connect with democracy can never be overestimated.

ECONOMIC DEVELOPMENT

In order to change the mentality of the people and change the rational discourse of human development, the CR risked the destabilization of the whole bureaucracy and chaos in the whole of society. But Mao and his colleagues, especially those headed by Zhou Enlai, had always in mind the importance of China's economic development. This is not surprising because it concerns the livelihood of so many people. In the intellectual battlefield of assessing economic development in the Mao era, the claim that the CR brought China's economy to the brink of collapse persists in spite of statistics that indicate otherwise, as Kraus (2012) argues by citing respectable political economists like Naughton (1991) and Riskin.

The Clashing Views: A General Picture

The post-Mao regime, in order to justify their development into capitalism, exploited the backlash against the extremity of class struggle and political movements and mobilized every propaganda means possible to demonize the CR, including the declaration that the Chinese economy during the CR was on the brink of collapse. This line of construction regarding the CR has one problem: if the economic situation was so bad how can China's economic take-off in the 1990s be explained? One often-touted conceptual framework is that post-Mao China has adopted the market economy on the one hand and received Western support on the other. The word "miracle" is frequently used by China experts (Webster 2013), a miracle made possible because of Deng Xiaoping who said "to get rich is glorious" (MacFarquhar 2016: 600).

A more reasonable conceptualization is that during the CR, the economy was not as bad as is presented by the post-Mao political and intellectual producers of knowledge, that post-Mao economic development is not as good as is touted in the media and that the Mao era laid a sound foundation for the later economic take-off. However, this sensible conceptualization, which is supported by a massive amount of evidence, is unacceptable to mainstream scholarship both inside and outside China because it is intellectually unexciting and politically incorrect. How, therefore, to make sense of the supposed rupture between the economic wasteland ten years before and a thriving economy a decade later? Has the vulgar Orientalist saying of Deng Xiaoping, "to get rich is glorious" (a saying that has been repeated again and again without any reference), been that miraculous? Do we still need biblical language to produce knowledge?

One way to get around this is to say that there is a connection between the economic wasteland of the CR and the economic take-off soon after: the paradoxical and unintended consequences of the CR. Along these lines, the prominent American sociologist and specialist on Mao and the CR, Andrew Walder (2016), claims that one of the reasons why the economic reforms of the Soviet Union failed whereas China under Deng Xiaoping succeeded is that economic and technological backwardness fostered by the CR left little support for maintaining the status quo. But there is no paradox here because if one removes the colored glass of personal power struggle one can see clearly that the CR intended to break down the status quo. It is not that there was little support for maintaining the status quo, but that there was no entrenched status quo, precisely as intended by the CR.

Along similar lines, and on the conceptual assumption that China under Mao in general and the CR in particular would not and could not have achieved any good, Dikötter argues that what undermined the deadly planned economy was rural residents' "myriad … dispersed acts of resistance during the last years of the Cultural Revolution" (Dikötter 2016: 796). But the decentralization and the mobilization of local initiatives were heavily promoted policies, first during the GLF and then restarted during the CR, the outcomes of which were the emergence of the township and village enterprises (then called *shedui qiye*, the Commune and Brigade Enterprises or CBEs). They were not acts of resistance from the bottom, but acts encouraged from the top.

In order to prove that the CR forced economic backwardness, Walder lists per capita a GDP figure in China in 1976 that it was only US$852, "slightly below India (US$889), and well below Indonesia (US$1,598), Pakistan (US$1,006) and Malaysia (US$2,910). South Korea's per capita GDP was four times higher than China's (US$3,476), and Taiwan's per capita GDP was more than five times higher (US$4,600)" (Walder 2016: 622). But talk about GDP figures and growth rates does not reflect the economic reality of China at that time. First, much of the economic activity could not be included in such calculations, as the case of the Gao Village study shows (Gao 1999). For instance, agricultural produce from private plots (land that was not collectivized, about 5 percent to 10 percent of total land varying from place to place and time to time) has never been included in the measurements. Second, comparing a non-market economy with a market capitalist economy is like comparing oranges and apples. How do we calculate the price or value of virtually free housing, free education and free health care in the urban sector? How do we evaluate the purchasing power at any particular time across economic models internationally? In a non-commercial economy, many of China's economic activities and incomes were not even counted or could not be priced. For instance, the enormous amount of irrigation infrastructure work was accomplished by the rural labor force without a price. Or taking housing as an example, the majority of urban residents suddenly found themselves rich in assets from the late 1990s when apartments that had been allocated to them for free in the Mao era had a value on paper because housing became commercialized.

Moreover, Walder does not take into account the Cold War circumstances under which economies like Japan, South Korea and Taiwan benefited not only from enormous amounts of aid of all kinds from the US but also from the Korean and Vietnam wars. China, on the other hand, was under harsh economic and technological sanctions from the whole of the Western world, on top of the fact that China had to bear the costs of these two wars.

Therefore, a more reasonable comparison of China is not with Japan, South Korea or Taiwan, the focal areas of the Cold War where the

US exercised virtual occupation, but with other developing countries, like India.

One should of course point out that China also obtained support from the Soviet Union. But a comparison of that with US support of Taiwan is instructive. Up to 1958, the total value of Soviet loans and aid projects to China averaged less than 50 US cents per head annually, compared to the US$30 per head that Doak Barnett estimated America invested in non-military aid to Taiwan and its population under Chiang Kai-shek up to 1958. China received no free economic aid from Russia; Soviet loans (as apart from trade agreements) amounted to only US$430 million (1,720 million rubles), and were all repayable. US economic aid to Yugoslavia during the same period amounted to more than that, and American loans to India were more than four times as much. "Soviet loans and/or 'free aid' for military equipment made during and after the Korean War had been variously estimated in the neighbourhood of $2,000,000,000" (Snow 1971: 201–2).

Aside from 1967 and 1968, the two most chaotic years when economic and production activities were interrupted, Chinese economic growth was higher on average than most developing countries at that time (Meisner 1999, Bramall 1993). Just as with indicators of growth, iron and steel production increased 2.6 times, crude oil 9.2 times, coal three times and grain 1.6 times (*China Statistics Year Book* 1994). In 26 years from 1952 to 1978, China's annual GDP growth of an annual average of 6.5 percent, is, compared with the global average of 3 percent, very impressive. This could only be a rough estimate, for the reasons mentioned above, because China was not a commercial economy and much of its economic activity was not counted as such. China's industrial capacity was the equivalent of Belgium when the PRC was established in 1949, and by the time Mao died in 1976 China was already the sixth largest industrial power in the world (Meisner 1999). By then China was already the third largest coal producer, the largest cotton-spinning producer and the second largest producer of grain and cotton.

Because of the Cold War environment, when China felt threatened on all fronts, what were called Third Line industrial strategies started to take place after the US started to bomb North Vietnam in August 1964, with the intention of moving important heavy and defense industries inland and to their third-tier areas in case there was a war. By the end of the 1970s, fixed assets of the Third Line industry increased from 29.2 billion RMB to 154.3 billion. Covering 13 provinces, the Third Line industry lasted for nearly 15 years and China invested 205 million RMB and set up several thousand projects (Qi Benyu 2016), including China's nuclear industry in the Sichuan and Shaanxi areas, aviation industry in the Sichuan, Shaanxi and Guizhou areas, and missile and rocket industry, including the now well-known Xichang satellite launching station. In order to break the transportation blockage and difficulties between and among these areas and other parts of China, large-scale railway and road construction took place in these areas, and ten main railway lines (a total of 8,046 kilometers, or 55 percent of China's newly built railways) were constructed. Roads also increased by 220,780 kilometers during this period: more than half of China became connected to newly built roads. More than anything else, the Third Line industry invested heavily in iron and steel production. Panzhihua, Chongqing, Changcheng and Chengdu iron and steel plants were results of these investments.

In October 1966, far away from the political turmoil in Beijing, China successfully exploded the first ballistic nuclear weapon, and in December that year successfully launched a medium-range land-to-land missile. In 1970, China succeeded in launching its first two-stage rocket and in the same year their first satellite. In 1975, China succeeded in launching three satellites. Late in 1975, China launched its first recoverable satellite (Ma Quanshan 1998: 3).

It is important to point out that I do not praise nuclear proliferation when I state that China "succeeded" in conducting nuclear tests by launching missiles during the CR. Nor do I deny that from the perspective of efficiency, investment return in dollars and productivity in terms of profit, the Third Line industry was not the best economic strategy or plan. By citing the above statistics and facts I aim to reinforce two arguments: (1) the post-Mao construction of the CR and the GLF in particular, and the Mao era in general, is always selective in including and excluding information and data; and (2) the conceptual framework adopted by the producers of knowledge dictates their selection. The anti-Communist conception automatically excludes any information or data that shows the CR in a positive light, and the neoliberal economic rationalist conception excludes the historical context of the Third Line industry. Such a conception will lead one to think that the Third Line industry was a waste of resources which could have been much better used to develop light industries for consumer products that benefited the livelihoods of the Chinese people, or that it would have been more efficient to invest them in the first-tier areas along the south-east coast.

In hindsight, both conceptualizations—anti-Communist and neoliberal economic rationalist—will lead one to conclude that Mao was not only a bad economist but also a paranoid, bellicose and power-hungry mad man who did not care about human life, as indeed Chang and Halliday (2005) and Dikötter (2010) claim.

The historical context is that there was a serious threat of war against China, and the Korean and Vietnam wars show that China was never far away from war threats and even nuclear war threats from the US. It is all very well for Western scholars in their ivory towers, or Western-trained Chinese, to portray Mao as irrational when they live and work for the power that dominates the world, and when they could bomb, invade and humiliate the people of any nation at any time. We cannot understand China if we don't place ourselves in the position of China at that time. We cannot understand China if we only consider thngs from the Western viewpoint, which dominates our conceptual framework, sets research agendas and regulates scholarship standards.

Agricultural Infrastructure

One of the reasons for the good record of grain production in the post-Mao era is that the huge amount of work invested in irrigation projects, especially those carried out during the CR, happened to pay off during the years immediately after the death of Mao. From 1966 to 1977, 56,000 middle- and small-sized electric stations were built that connected 80 percent of communes and 50 percent of production brigades with electricity. Irrigation powered by electric pumps reached a capacity of 65 million horsepower. More than 20,000 electric-powered wells were made that could irrigate more than 700 million *mu* of land (one *mu* is about 0.0667 hectares). Compared with 1965, China's irrigated land increased by 51 percent, electricity consumption in agriculture increased by 470 percent, electric-powered water wells by 935.89 percent, land areas irrigated by electric power by 355.58 percent, available tractors increased 5.7 times, and hand tractors increased 65 times (Zhongguo nongtian shuili 1987: 25–43).

Huge irrigation projects such as the Haihe Project, which was completed in 1973, took ten years to build and involved 4,300 kilometers of dykes, 270 dredged channels, rivers and brooks, and more than 60,000 culverts, bridges and sluice gates. The Liaohe Project, completed in 1972, built 4,500 kilometers of dykes, 220 reservoirs and 920 electric-powered irrigation stations. Up to 1977, China built nearly a hundred rivers and more than 70,000 large or middle-sized reservoirs. The so-called "man-made heavenly river," the Linxian Red Flag Canal completed in 1969, is 52 kilometers long and has expanded the irrigation areas to more than 60,000 *mu*.

Enormous amounts of infrastructure work done during these years involved millions of people and trillions of hours of work that was virtually free, as shown in the case study of Gao Village (Gao 1999a). If these kinds of infrastructure works were attempted today, they would require an astronomical amount of financial investment that can be accounted as GDP. Instead of a positive assessment of such work as a contribution by rural people to their own livelihood and the public good, the post-Mao neoliberal market intellectual elites interpret this as slave labor. It is also worth revisiting Walder's GDP assessment to point out that the economic and financial value of such infrastructure work as done by the Gao villagers has never been included in the numbers added to growth rates for those years.

The relevance of this is demonstrated by the fact that the "Number One Document" issued in 2011 is about irrigation in rural China. According to the Xinhua website, the official interpretation of this document, Beijing plans to spend four trillion RMB on rural irrigation in the next ten years. The reason why this is interesting is that it took 30 years for the Chinese authorities to realize that they could not ignore the investment any longer. The Chinese state could afford to ignore irrigation infrastructure for 30 years because of the fact that the sound irrigation infrastructure that was built in the Mao era worked well for so many years. The dismantling of the collective system meant that even elementary maintenance has been neglected. A lot of the infrastructure fell into disuse, and the drought in north and south-west China have shown the effect of this neglect.

According to one study, the 1988 statistics in Anhui show of the 98 middle-sized reservoirs, 70 were built between 1966 and 1979, and of the 2.79 million *mu* of irrigated land, 1.96 million *mu* were built in this period. There was a severe drought in 1978, but grain production was not affected as a result of the irrigation infrastructure built in the Mao era (Li Changping 2011, Xu Hailiang 2000). Li Changping further argues that although four trillion may sound like a lot of money, compared to what had been invested in the Mao era, it is not very much. According to Li, on average there had been at least 200 to 300 million laborers working on irrigation projects during winter each year. If each laborer worked 30 days each winter at the cost of 100 RMB a day, at today's value the investment on irrigation each year was about 600 to 900 billion RMB a year.

Rural Industry

The second development is the rise and expansion of township and villager enterprises (TVEs). In his critique of Stalin and the Soviet model of economic development, Mao developed the idea of decentralization and of encouraging local initiatives in industrialization. Mao summed up the idea in the earthy saying, "walking on two legs"; the leg of the central planned economy of state-owned enterprise and the leg of locally developed collectively owned enterprises. These ideas were initiated and developed during the GLF, but were shelved after its failure. They emerged again during the CR, which gave rise to TVEs. Many of those TVEs were not only transitional to but also inspired the development of the Chinese private sector that exists in the economy today (Wong 2003). It is worth pointing out that the ideas of decentralization and promoting local initiatives have laid the pathway for the economic take-off in post-Mao China, as local governments were the real actors behind the development. It is worth repeating that the local initiatives which started during the GLF years reignited during the CR and were called CBEs. Take the province of Jiangsu as an example. The total value of TVEs in 1975 reached more than 244 million RMB, an increase of 2.22 times compared with 1970 (this is calculated at the value of purchasing power at that time), a 20 percent annual increase (Mo Yuanren 1987: 140).

IMPROVEMENT IN HEALTH AND EDUCATION IN RURAL CHINA

Another important development is that the CR period had provided a healthy and educated rural workforce in huge numbers who later became migrant workers—the numbers reached 200 million annually in the post-Mao period. This is a matter of huge significance, but it is hardly ever discussed. The practical and affordable medical care of the barefoot doctor system invented during the CR was the direct result of Mao's intervention through his condemnation that the Ministry of

Health served only the urban lords (Cui Weiyuan 2008, Worsley 1982). As I have described in the case study of Gao Village (Gao 1999a), it was during the CR when all school-aged children were able to attend school for the first time in the village's history. This was more or less the same nationwide (Pepper 1996). In a word, it was the great advancement of education and health care during the Mao era in general, and during the CR in particular, that prepared the workforce and was vital for the eventual economic take-off. "Specialists on India's economic development, for example, credit Mao's mass literacy and public health mobilization campaigns with laying the social foundations for a post-Mao economic take-off that has permitted China in recent years to surge ahead of its South Asian neighbour" (Perry 2016: 116).

TECHNOLOGICAL DEVELOPMENT

Another development during the CR that is relevant to the post-Mao economy is the development of technology. It is worth repeating here Walder's (2016) assertion of "forced technological backwardness" by the CR. First it is again necessary to repeat the historical context that the West placed technological, and even traveling sanctions on China. So China had to rely on herself. This is worth pointing out because anti-Communist and neoliberal economic rationalists tend to exclude this aspect, instead of saying how well China has done in spite of this deliberate policy of strangulation. Once the West relaxed its grip, after Henry Kissinger's visit in 1971, China started to seek advanced Western technology. China invested US$5,000 million and imported 26 large projects, including 13 large chemical fertilizer plants, four chemical fiber plants, three petrol chemical engineering plants and ten alkylbenzene plants. It was with these imported technologies that the Beijing, Shanghai, and Shandong Petroleum Chemical Plans were set up, as were the Shandong Shengli, Liaoyang, Beijing and Helongjiang chemical fiber plants. Other fertilizer-producing factories were set up in Daqing, Nanjing, Liaohe, Dongting, Luzhou and Guizhou. This had nothing to do with post-Mao reform.

The self-reliance technologies that developed during the Mao era and the CR that benefited post-Mao economic development are just too numerous to list. The development of hybrid rice seeds is an excellent example because it boosted output by somewhere between 15 and 20 percent. It was during the Mao era and especially the CR that scientists like Yuan Longping started to work on these kinds of projects in coordinated teamwork, the achievement of which not only brought benefits to post-Mao economic development but also helped other countries in the world. In relation to this it is worth pointing out that the one and only Nobel Prize for science won by a Chinese of the PRC origin is Tu Youyou, for discovering the compound Artemether that cures malaria. Tu, again, worked and achieved the results during the CR. It is important to stress that these two scientists worked with their teams and it was their teamwork that achieved the results. For this reason it was difficult for some years for the global scientific community to pick out one individual to nominate as a Nobel candidate for the Artemether discovery. The Nobel Prize assumption of individual discoveries is contrary to the CR idea of teamwork and its contribution to the public good. It is interesting to note that Yuan Longping now takes the credit for himself and runs a company that makes a profit, while parroting the clichés of condemning the Mao era, and not surprisingly has been berated by thousands over social media (Si Min 2017).

By the time Mao died, China had fought two large wars, the Korean War and the Vietnam War, with the US, the technologically, economically and militarily most powerful country in the world, and two small wars—one with India (1962) and one with Russia (1969). China had developed into a formidable industrial country with sufficient national capabilities, including nuclear weapons, to defend itself. It even managed to send a satellite into space. Taking into account the fact that China benefited greatly from Soviet Russia's generous help, these achievements are remarkable as Soviet assistance was cut off toward the end of the 1950s. There would have been no way to achieve this development without the policy of self-reliance and collective efforts, given the circumstances of the Cold War, which led to capital, economic, technological and trade sanctions against China. It was the Maoist discourse that held the collective together during this historical period.

The anti-Communists would of course bring attention to the economic scarcity in the Mao era, to justify their conceptualization framework. In those days even basic daily items such as soap were rationed. This is often cited as evidence for the bankruptcy of a planned economy run by a Communist regime. Only a market economy can achieve miracles, and the post-Mao economic reform proved that, as the Chinese not only no longer had to ration but there was an oversupply of commodities. Apart from the fact that even in developed Western societies affluence is a recent phenomenon, the Chinese state had to ration daily necessities at that time as a strategic choice, a choice made during the height of the Cold War. The PRC faced hostile forces all around, because by the late 1950s China had split from the Soviet Union, and had to extract and save every penny to develop national defense industries rapidly. The Chinese farewell to consumer goods scarcity became possible when the Cold War became warmer in the early 1970s because of decisions the US made, and only then was China able to have a seat at the United Nations. Those international geopolitical changes paved the way for China to shift investment strategy from heavy and national defense industries to light and consumer industries. At the same time China could start to import Western technology and foreign currencies and even investment from the overseas Chinese community. The truth according to anti-Communist Cold War propaganda is that in the Mao era, China isolated itself from the outside world and it was only when Deng Xiaoping came to power that China started to open up.

GUIDING PRINCIPLES IN CHINA'S ETHNIC AND FOREIGN POLICIES

The Marxist philosophy of class struggle laid the foundation of Mao's ethnic and foreign policies which were pushed to the extreme during the CR. The theory of class struggle and its practice in the Mao era, although it should be critiqued in terms of its excess and condemned by its victims, had consequences that still vibrate today. One example is that ethnic tensions in regions such as Tibet have been increasing in the post-Mao era. There are of course many interrelated factors in this development, but one could argue that an important factor is the abandonment of Mao's intellectual discourse of class. While class theory alienated the elite and upper class of Tibetans, it played a role in uniting the lower classes under the official line that people of the exploited and oppressed classes are brothers. Because values and identities were not premised on ethnicity but on class (Wei Se 2006), the logical extension is that the majority of the Tibetans and other ethnic Chinese should not have unresolvable contradictions among themselves. It is based on this guiding principle that the Chinese authorities implemented measures in dealing with political and socio-economic issues. Once the principle was thrown out by the post-Mao regime, ethnicity emerged as the focus of conflict.

It is the same case with foreign policies. Even for Mao, China's national interest should be considered a priority, just like it is for any national leader. But what was different for Mao was that he wanted to differentiate the people from the ruling classes, and therefore for him, to support and defend the interests of the people of other nations is the same as supporting and defending the interests of the Chinese people. Thus in China's relation with Japan, Mao would say that the Japanese imperialist invasion of China was a crime committed by Japan's ruling class at that time, and therefore the people of both countries were victims. It was under this intellectual understanding that Mao even thanked, with his typical humor and irony, Japan for helping the CCP win power (as the Japanese invasion distracted Chiang Kai-shek's anti-Communist efforts), and that China was willing to give up the demand for monetary compensation from Japan when the PRC and Japan finally established diplomatic relationships in 1973. Again, once that principle was gone, the historical damage incurred by Japan's invasion of China has become the nationalist or even racist issue, as it manifests itself today.

As a last example we can observe China's relationship with Vietnam. During the Mao era, especially during the CR, China under Mao supported the Vietnamese fight against US imperialism. Again this was guided not only by national interest but also by the theory of class struggle. For Deng Xiaoping, however, foreign policies guided by the theory of class struggle would damage China's national interest. He would forego class theory so as to embrace capitalism to develop China's economy. It surely was not a coincidence that Deng launched an invasion of Vietnam in 1979 as soon as he had returned from his visit to the US. Other factors, such as the fact that Vietnam joined the Soviet-dominated Council for Mutual Economic Cooperation (Comecon) and signed the Treaty of Friendship and Cooperation with the Soviet Union in 1978, and the fact that in December 1978 Vietnam began a full-scale counter-attack against Kampuchea (today's Cambodia), played their roles in China's decision to "punish" Vietnam. Domestic politics might also have been a factor, as Deng wanted to launch the war to consolidate his grip on the CCP (Thayer 1987). These considerations relating to international geopolitics and domestic politics regarding the Sino-Vietnam War contain elements of truth, but what has often been ignored is the difference between Mao and Deng in how they conceptualized the world. Specifically, unlike Mao, Deng did not conceive the dynamics of class theory, in whereas Mao did. Just as Deng would abandon class theory as a necessary principle guiding China's domestic policies, he would not even contemplate class theory in assessing international geopolitics. Deng clearly got support for his determination to "teach Vietnam a lesson" during his trip to Washington, DC in January 1979 following the formal normalization of ties. Brzezinski's memoirs go into this. During Deng's trip he was given a classified briefing on Vietnam's order of battle. And as the fighting raged, Brzezinski convinced the White House not to cancel Treasury Secretary Michael Blumenthal's trip to discuss trade issues. The declassified record of Deng's conversations with Carter have Carter opposing the attack, but not adamantly (Zhang Xiaoming 2015).

GENDER EQUALITY

According to a recent US Bureau of Labor Statistics report, the Chinese women's labor participation rate of nearly 70 percent is the highest in the world, even higher than the French male labor participation rate of 62 percent (International Labor Comparisons 2011). This may well be a mixed blessing for women, because it mostly means that Chinese women work extremely hard not only earning an income but also doing most of the housework, which includes more responsibilities in looking after children. But there are two compensating points. One is that most Chinese parents help look after their grandchildren. The other is that even a professional woman in China may be able to afford domestic help either part time or full time. In any case, the fact of a woman earning an income is an indication of subjectivity and independence. This has a lot to do with the 1949 Revolution and the Maoist legacy.

Mao's idea of gender equality can be traced back to his famous "A Report on Hunan's Peasantry Movement" in which Mao hailed the rise of women that shook the foundation of Chinese male dominance. Then in 1928 the Three Major Disciplines and Six Points of Attention to discipline Red Army soldiers were released, the instruction of "avoiding women when having a bath" was added in 1929 and later changed to "not to molest women." In December 1955 Mao made a comment on the article "Women March on the Labour Front" that the broad masses of women should be mobilized to participate in labour to build socialism and that women and men should be paid the same for the same labor and that this could be achieved in a socialist society (Peng Shicheng 2017). Mao's famous saying that "women can prop up half the sky" is known all over the world as an inspiration even in protests against Donald Trump.

That the 1949 CR has generated its spin-off—the gender revolution—is beyond dispute in the field, though it is true that the achievements have not been as good as was officially claimed. The CR pushed the Chinese gender revolution further to the positive side. It is true that China today is still a gender discriminatory society in which women do more work but are less recognized. However, China has made great strides in promoting the status of women owing to the efforts of the CCP government of the PRC in general and also to Mao himself. Given how entrenched traditional discrimination against women has been since ancient times, these achievements are even more impressive.

The distinctive gender equality agenda pushed by the CCP demonstrates how the issue was dealt with as a matter of urgency when the PRC was established. In April 1949, six months before the declaration of the People's Republic, the first national women's conference was held and the All-China Federation of Women was established. By 1952, two years before the Chinese Constitution was enacted, the Marriage Law was already in place. All the discriminatory customs imposed on women—most significantly, polygyny, foot binding and female infanticide—were declared illegal by this and other legislation.

Meanwhile, women were encouraged to participate in political life as well as to work outside the home. A recent study by Yao Yang and Wuyue You (2016) of Peking University is an insightful indication of these achievements. Female membership in the CCP increased steadily and peaked in the mid-1970s. In 1949, women accounted for 11.9 percent of the CCP membership. By 1976, this figure had increased to 13.5 percent. The increase in female membership was especially notable in the countryside, rising from 8.5 percent in 1949 to 13.2 percent in 1976. In 1973, the number of female members in the CCP's Central Committee reached a record high of 17 percent. The Yang and You study shows that one of the consequences of women's political participation was a decline in the gender population imbalance due to a drop in infanticides and mistreatment of young girls. Data collected from the county chronicles of approximately 1,200 counties, the CCP's statistical publications and the 1990 census, indicates a causal relationship between a higher female Party membership and the decline of gender population imbalances. Female membership in the Party in 1950 strongly correlates with the change of the population sex ratio between 1950 and 1980. Based on their analysis, increasing female party membership can explain 17 percent of the decline in gender imbalance across the population between 1950 and 1975. More rigorous econo-metric analysis based on an instrumented panel method qualitatively confirms this baseline result.

Since the 1980s onwards, a more stringent one child per family policy was implemented in rural China. The sometimes ruthless policy measure ignored the socio-economic as well as traditional values of rural com-munities by imposing prohibitive financial penalties and forcing brutal abortions. As a form of passive resistance many rural people tended to abort a female in favor of a male. The urban political elite who designed this brutal policy did not pause to reflect on that fact that it is easier to implement a one child per family policy in the urban sector because they had social security and welfare provisions which were absent for rural people. A rural family would prefer to have a male child because the parents would need a son to look after them when they were old, since a daughter would be married into the family of the husband. Therefore, logically and rationally a rural family is in favor of the underground practice of aborting female children.

What is interesting and significant is that even under these circum-stances, the political participation of women has a positive outcome in terms of gender balance. As the intellectual discourse of the CCP is that there should be gender equality, once you are member of the CCP, a woman, either by mentality or by discipline or both combined, is less likely to choose abortion. The Yang and You (2016) study shows that female party membership had a strong impact on family planning. In other words, female representation in the CCP seemed to have a direct positive impact on the number of surviving female newborns, either before or after the stringent family policy measures were taken.

The liberation of women triggered a dramatic change in Chinese society. But this change cannot be taken for granted because change of this nature is political and needs the political will of the state, which in turn is guided by a political agenda. The contrast between what was achieved before and what happened after Mao clearly shows not only that there is a long way to go to achieve gender equality but also that development can be reversed if there is no political will to make progress. As the Yang and You (2016) study shows, women's political participation has been slowing since China entered the reform age. Nationwide, female party membership declined after 1976 and did not begin to increase again until 1987. In the countryside, the downward trend has never been reversed. In the current CCP Central Committee, there are only a dozen female members out of a total of 205. Together with decreasing political participation, discrimination against women in employment has become an increasing problem. The 2010 national census shows that only 62 percent of women between 20 and 60 years old were employed.

XI JINPING AS AN EDUCATED YOUTH

Another important legacy of the CR is the Xi Jinping leadership (Brown 2016). Of the three leaderships after Deng Xiaoping, Jiang Zemin and Zhu Rongji, Hu Jintao and Wen Jiabao, and Xi Jinping and Li Keqiang, only the last one is the CR generation. Though Xi's father is in many ways a victim of the politics of the Mao era, Xi himself does not seem to complain about his experience as an educated youth sent down to a poor village during the CR. In fact Xi is the first formal top Chinese leader since the death of Mao who has defended the Mao era by saying that one should not use the second 30 years of the PRC to denounce the first 30 years (Xinhua 2013). Though the jury is still out, much of Xi's leadership style and policy content reminds one of Mao: anti-corruption, stress on moral education, Mass Line (a policy of communication between the leadership and masses of people at grassroots), constraint on bureaucracy, restriction on official privilege and assertiveness in foreign relations.

Kong Dan, one of the chief *xijiu* and *liandong* leaders (discussed in Chapter 6), but who was also sent to Shaanxi in a village about 58 kilometers away from where Xi was sent, in his interview reveals some of Xi's background (Kong Dan 2015b). Xi stayed in a village for seven years, became a member of the CCP there and the party secretary of the brigade where he was first sent at 15 years of age. Xi claims that every generation of youth has its own circumstances and opportunities and everyone should seek a life and create history under given conditions. Xi's family, especially his father, were victims of the Mao era and the CR. However, Xi takes a positive attitude in his experience and interprets his harsh life in the country as a way of tempering his will and as a way of understanding how the Chinese rural people lived and worked. In his high-profile Chinese New Year visit in 2015 to his rustication place in the North Shaanxi region, he introduced his celebrity singer wife to the people he got to know in the area (*China Daily* 2015). In 2002, Xi wrote an account of his sojourn in the countryside called, "I am a son of the yellow earth."

CONCLUDING REMARKS

The above discussion has only touched the surface of the profound change in Chinese society as a result of the ideas and practice of the CR. Other areas of huge significance have not been discussed. For instance, the improvement of health care in the Mao era in general and during the CR in particular is only mentioned briefly. The critical attitudes that the Chinese have developed toward the authorities is not discussed in depth. Any casual survey on social media will demonstrate that many Chinese today uses the Mao era and especially the CR as a benchmark to evaluate the inequality, corruption and social problems in today's China. If it were not for the official line as well as self-censorship by the Chinese political and intellectual elite, such comparative evaluation would be more pronounced. Finally, by highlighting the positive legacies of the CR, I don't intend to deny that there was tremendous personal suffering experienced by people as high up as Liu Shaoqi and his wife, by people with connections to the West like Nien Cheng and by ordinary people like many school teachers. All I have tried to do is to show how the CR can be constructed for specific political purpose and for a particular conceptualization of ourselves and the world around us.

8

Clashing Views of the Great Leap Forward

INTRODUCTION

What happened during the GLF (1958 to 1961) is still hugely contested. Some facts are established and accepted by historians of all political persuasions: some GLF policies were so radical that they had disastrous consequences (Yang Dali 1996), policies such as the mobilization of neighborhood and village farmers to produce iron and steel to fulfill production quotas, in an attempt to speed up industrialization. It was not only a waste of time and energy but it also destroyed precious resources such as forestry when trees were cut down to make charcoal for iron and steel smelting. It is also generally accepted that grain production declined as a result of these policies, though how much the reduction of grain production was also a result of natural climate conditions such as drought and floods is still debated. Finally, it is also accepted that there was a nationwide shortage of food, that there was a famine and that there were people, mostly rural residents, who died of starvation during the period. Debate occurs in two areas: the death toll of the famine, i.e. how many people actually died of starvation, and who should be held responsible (Riskin 1998).

Those in the scientific community would mostly agree that a "scientific," or at least useful theory or hypothesis is one that makes predictions that can either be proved or falsified. Most theories of social sciences and humanities don't make predictions, or if they do they are unlikely to be proved: note how often China has been predicted to collapse (Chang 2001, Shambaugh 2015). However, regarding the GLF, one prediction can arguably be proved or falsified: if a scholar, a historian, a journalist or a commentator is anti-Communist, anti-Mao or even anti the 1949 Chinese Revolution, he or she, whether Chinese or not, would tend to make or believe claims for the highest possible GLF famine death toll. The other side of the coin of this falsifiable prediction is that if one is of the political left and is sympathetic to the 1949 Chinese Revolution, one tends to be skeptical of the highest number pronounced.

You would think that death toll numbers based on mathematical calculations couldn't just be anybody's guess. But guessing is exactly what has happened with the GLF famine death toll (Riskin 1998). To start with, what is death caused by starvation? If one is sick and elderly one might live longer if the person is well looked after. Lack of nutrition may accelerate the time of death of the elderly and the sick. This has been the case for thousands of years in China and only very recently did the majority of Chinese manage to escape the constant threat of starvation.

What makes the issue of the GLF death toll more contestable is that there was no population census, nor a sample survey, at that time. The most rigorously calculated death toll number by serious scholars such as Coale (1984) and Banister (1987) is based on a mathematical model, primarily, and also based on Chinese demographic publications in the early 1980s. Mathematical models are based on many assumptions, and if any of them are wrong the end results are erroneous. Population censuses and sample marriage and fertility surveys, "scientific" as they may be in the given circumstances, may and can contain errors. The fact is that the population base in China is so large that even a tiny error, an otherwise insignificant omitted category, or missing information, can in fact mean a huge discrepancy in the numbers.

This chapter aims to address these issues. Specifically, it will give concrete examples of how knowledge of GLF is produced by the selection of data or even the fabrication of data. The latest representative work on the GLF by the Chinese journalist Yang Jisheng and a Western historian Frank Dikötter will be discussed in this chapter in contrast with the Chinese scholars Yang Songlin and Sun Jingxian. The clash of views on the GLF is not simply the result of "the Chinese themselves say so," nor "Chinese" versus "foreigners," but of political agenda, political persuasion and the conceptualization of ourselves and the world.

THE POLITICS OF CONSTRUCTING HISTORICAL KNOWLEDGE

History is about the past, but there is no history unless someone writes about it. But who writes history and why? The working class has no history, nor does the Chinese peasantry. They don't have the resources to write history. Why does anyone want to write about the history of the GLF? You must want to prove something or to argue for something. Ilya Somin, professor of law at George Mason University, wants to argue for something: "Who was the biggest mass murderer in the history of the world? ... both Hitler and Stalin were outdone by Mao Zedong. From 1958 to 1962, his Great Leap Forward policy led to the deaths of up to 45 million people—easily making it the biggest episode of mass murder ever recorded" (Somin 2016). Where does he get this figure of 45 million from? From Frank Dikötter, to whom I will return later. Even if one accepts the guess of so many millions, surely the result of a policy failure is not the same as Hitler's planned policy of the Holocaust. Even manslaughter is not the same as murder, both morally and legally. What political point does Somin want to prove by accusing Mao of being a mass murderer, just as Chang and Halliday (2005) do?

Even Dikötter, whom Somin quotes, has to admit that the GLF was in pursuit of "a utopian paradise." Somin (2016) quotes Dikötter, who says "everything was collectivised. People had their work, homes, land, belongings and livelihoods taken from them. In collective canteens, food, distributed by the spoonful according to merit, became a weapon used to force people to follow the party's every dictate." What is prescribed here as historical knowledge of the GLF by Dikötter might be true of one or two places that he was told about, but to make a generalization about the whole of China based on the effect of the GLF on isolated cases is questionable scholarship. Even in the most radical year of 1958, homes in general were not collectivized because villagers still owned and lived in their own homes, nor were belongings collectivized, apart from utensils made of iron and steel that were taken away to fulfill iron and steel production quotas (Gao 1999b). From an administrative point of view, it would be impossible to distribute food by the spoonful according to merit for any lengthy period of time in any place. As a general practice, in the public canteen during that short period of time, food was distributed on a per capita basis, though in some places differences were sometimes made between an adult and a child.

That the GLF resulted in a famine is beyond dispute, and it is one of the black spots for the history of socialist China. However, if one is even slightly sympathetic with the Chinese 1949 Revolution one should look at the disaster in its historical context. To start with, the motivation and intentions were to build a new socialist China and to catch up with industrialization, with naïve enthusiasm. Second, in a pre-industrial and pre-technological breakthrough society with such a precarious ratio of land to population, about 7 percent of the world's arable land to feed almost a quarter of the world's population, famine and starvation had been constant features in China for hundreds of years, if not more. China's history of famine shows that a relatively large-scale famine usually claimed millions of lives (Mallory 1926, Deng Tuo 1937). The most recent famine, a relatively minor one before the GLF, was in 1946, and indeed Dikötter used 1946 famine photos for the front cover of his book on the GLF. Third, famine is not just a Chinese phenomenon: under British rule, India and Ireland also had large-scale famines: "In the last quarter of the nineteenth century, India experienced simultaneously its worst famine ever and its largest grain exports, supplying nearly a fifth of Britain's wheat consumption" (Davis 2001: part iv and chapter 9), and "Under the Raj between 1896 and 1900, more than ten million people died in avoidable famines out of a population of a little more than one-third the size of China's in 1960. A proportionally even greater number of people died from hunger in Ireland in 1845–46 under British rule" (Lin Chun 2015: 16).

Furthermore, as Dreze and Sen (1989) state, without any specific famine, nearly four million people die prematurely in India every year from malnutrition and related problems. Finally, in terms of the historical context, one should remember that the GLF famine was the first and the last large-scale famine in the entire history of the PRC.

By pointing to the historical context I don't mean to say that there was nothing wrong with the GLF or that it shouldn't be criticized, or that there was nothing wrong with Mao. I am arguing, however, that it was a policy failure (Bachman 1991, Teiwes 1984), and a disastrous one at that, but not a policy designed to deliberately murder the Chinese people, like Hitler's Holocaust. I cannot see how anyone can argue otherwise unless one wants to construct the knowledge that there is a constant battle of evil against good, that communism is evil and that Mao was the arche-typical monster of this evil force called communism.

CONCEPTUALIZATION OF THE SOCIALIST ROAD OF COLLECTIVIZATION

It is very difficult to argue that Mao was not the number one person responsible for the GLF disaster since he was the chairman of the CCP and the military commission, the two most powerful positions in the country's system, and also the president of the PRC (a ceremonial position). Furthermore, as I have discussed throughout this book, Mao was the ultimate arbitrator, interpreter and announcer of the narrative of the PRC's direction of development. In other words, Mao held the key to the conceptual direction that dictated the GLF policies. However, to say that Mao held the main positions of responsibility is not to say that Mao alone should be held responsible for the GLF disaster. Nor should Mao be held responsible for everything that happened at grassroots level all over the country. By the same token it is hard to support the claim that Mao knew of the starvation but knowingly went ahead with his personal ambition at the expense of millions of lives, as claimed by Dikötter (2010), Chang and Halliday (2005).

The GLF had its conceptual origin in the future direction of China as well as in the practicum of policymaking after the CCP took over power as a result of the 1949 Revolution. The conceptual origin is related to how China developed socialism and the practicum can be called the governance of "rule of Mandate" (Birney 2014).

Let me start with the conceptualization of socialist collectivization. The land reform program was carried out in the CCP-occupied areas after the surrender of the Japanese in 1945, well before 1949 when the PRC was declared as established and when Chiang Kai-shek took the Nationalist government to Taiwan (Hinton 1972, Cook 2016). Within a year or two of the redistribution of land in what were called "the liberated areas," where the CCP had built their base after battling the Nationalists, there were already signs of disparity between the poor and the rich. The weak and sick households began to sell their land to survive and a new class of "landlords" seemed to be emerging, a familiar scenario during thousands of years of Chinese history. For a party that explicitly claimed to want to build an equal society, this was a concern for the CCP.

More importantly, there was the conceptual issue of the future direction of China in the mid-1950s. One fraction within the CCP leadership represented by Liu Shaoqi, the number two leader in the CCP hierarchy at that time, wanted to consolidate the program of the New Democratic Revolution (Liu 1985: 62), which meant that private ownership of land should be maintained in rural China and private entrepreneurship and patriotic capitalism should be encouraged because such a system would motivate the development of China's economy and the employment of the urban population. Mao, on the other hand, wanted to move to the next stage of socialist development, by which land in rural China would be collectivized and industry nationalized in urban China (Mao 1939).

For Mao the program of the New Democratic Revolution had already been successfully completed by the mid-1950s when colonialists and their compradors, the latter referring to the Chinese capitalists who moved to Hong Kong for instance, were driven out and the feudal system of landlord ownership was overthrown in mainland China by the land reform. For Liu Shaoqi, however, the New Democratic Revolution had only just started as the CCP had only just taken over the mainland.

This difference in conceptualizing the future direction of China is derived from a different understanding of what the CCP took as Marx's "scientific law" of human history: "dialectic materialism." This law of human society, considered to have been discovered by Marx, states that humanity develops from the primitive to the advanced stage through a dynamic relationship between the economic base (such as technology and material production) and the superstructure of the ownership of the means of production (such as the law and the government that maintains such ownership). The dialectic is that when an economic base has developed sufficiently it will lead to a change in the superstructure. On the other hand, the superstructure may either hinder or promote the development of the economic base.

For Liu Shaoqi, China's economic base at that time was not developed enough to change the superstructure of socialist programs of public ownership of the means of production and therefore it would take years of industrialization before China was ready for the next stage. But Mao was more inclined toward the role played by the superstructure in "the law of history." For Mao, a more advanced relationship of the means of production, that is, public ownership of means of production, would bring more rapid economic development. After all, the CCP did not wait until China was fully industrialized to make a supposedly proletarian (working-class) revolution, and the 1949 Revolution succeeded largely due to the role played by the CCP, "the vanguard of revolution," who mobilized the Chinese peasantry, considered backward by orthodox Marxism. In other words, Mao believed that China could march into socialism by skipping the state of capitalism under the correct leadership of the CCP.

Once the direction of collectivization was determined under such conceptualization, how to put the idea into practice mattered. In the hierarchy of the CCP Mao was the ultimate arbitrator, and other comrades in the senior leadership looked up to him for direction. With a long tradition of the hierarchical "rule of mandate" governance practice, which was packaged in the name of Leninist democratic centralism that was the straightjacket on the CCP, every level of leadership looked to the level above for a performance index, but wouldn't look to the level below for an idea of what would be wrong on the ground. Furthermore, the decentralization let loose by Mao led the local authorities to interpret their own policy priorities. On the one hand, everyone seemed to guess what was wanted from a level above in the government hierarchy, and on the other hand, people were motivated to outperform the other to do what they thought was the correct understanding of the situation.

Let us be reminded that one of the reasons for the GLF failure was the establishment of large communes. This organizational structure contributed to the reduction of food production and therefore was a cause of the famine. In a large commune of several thousand households— or even more in some cases, especially a commune that was formed by putting together villages of different lineages, as most of the villages were not that big—it was difficult to manage production activities. It was difficult to supervise, to monitor and to get feedback, even with the best of intentions by everyone. But neither Mao, nor the CCP center in Beijing, had such a design to start with. The CCP resolution on the issue (CCP 1958) of the People's Commune was a resolution in response to what had already happened, as stated by Chen Boda in November 1958 (Yang Shangkun 2001: 297). The resolution states that the size of a commune should be limited to around 6,000 households (this proved to be too big), and any larger ones should not be promoted, that the formation of large communes should be based on *zijue ziyuan* (willingly and voluntarily by the villagers), that the basic production activities and management should not change (*shang dong xia bu dong*) and that the means of production should be collectively owned, not publicly owned.*

It was the same with the phenomenon of public canteens. There was no design from the top to establish public canteens. The practice emerged somewhere and was then promoted, even by leaders like Liu Shaoqi. The practice of setting up village and street stoves making iron and steel was not a policy from the top either, as pointed out by Zhou Enlai (Yang Shangkun 2001: 318).

---

* This is an important distinction: collective ownership means that what is owned historically by the residents of any village cannot be redistributed to anyone outside of that village.

Experiments of all kinds emerged at that time with political passion (Dutton 2016). This passion was reinforced by the previous successes of the CCP leadership, a passion built on a belief that with the correct leadership of the CCP the Chinese masses could achieve anything: the only limitation was one's imagination. This passion in believing in revolutionary change and in China's new destiny was almost religious. It was this semi-religious passion that led to so many policies that are viewed as irrational with hindsight.

When the reality hit them, the CCP leadership, especially Mao himself, quickly moved to address problems arising from having large collective communes. But by the time they realized there were issues it was already too late, partly because some local authorities dragged their feet in reversing their forward policies, as I will discuss. The system that was finalized from the lessons learned from the GLF was complicated and sophisticated, as my brief outline here will show. The highest administrative organ was still called the commune (*gongshe*), under which there were ten or so production brigades (*shengchan da dui*) and under each production brigade there were ten or so production teams (*shengchan xiao dui*). These were the three layers of rural organizations that lasted until the early 1980s. The production team normally consisted of ten to twenty households, depending on the size of the village. For instance, if a village had only ten or fifteen households that village would have only one production team. If a village, like Gao Village (Gao 1999a), had more than 30 households then it was more likely to be divided into two teams. Each team would have a leadership team comprising several people, a team leader, a team accountant and a team women leader. Later, in some villages they sometimes installed a team storeman to look after the store house where the output of the production was kept, and a team work point record keeper.

In this structure of management, a specific amount of land inherited before the 1949 Revolution would be owned by all the members of the village, if the village were the size of a team, and would be managed by that team. The team would share all that was produced on the fixed amount of land. The leadership of the team arranged all of the production activities, and sometimes an ad hoc group was assigned a specific task that required a small group work. In this system, supervision and monitoring was easier and more transparent. Within one team, the contribution of each member to the collective, a man or woman, a child or a disabled person, was recorded by what was called a work point system, and everyone was supposed to do what one could. So the large communes were gone and the principle of "from each according to one's ability and to each according to one's labour" was upheld. At the same time the basic amount of grain would be distributed to everyone on a per capita basis, with a difference between adult and child, irrespective of whether one could work or not, as a basic welfare provision.

What about the "free rider" phenomenon, metaphorically described as the "iron bowl" in Chinese, a bowl with food in it that can never break (irrespective of whether one works for it)? As described in detail in the case study of Gao Village (Gao 1999a), the free rider concern is largely academic when applied to the case of collective agriculture in China. To start with, in a lineage village where everyone was more or less related to each other, the villagers saw basic grain provision for the elderly, the sick and children as morally acceptable. They also accepted the fact that households might have ups and downs, such as more children in a particular household and a sick person in a household one year but not the next. Moreover, there were other means to compensate the households that had contributed more to the team. For instance, these households might be distributed certain amounts of fish from the collective fish pond, or non-grain products such as cotton or peanuts that the households that had contributed less in terms of labor would not have received. The system involved the collaborative participation of all the villagers. It was the first time in Chinese history that the rural collectively managed their affairs.

THE FAILURE OF POLICY PROCESS

It has been argued that Mao pushed the GLF down a slippery slope with two major moves. One was to lecture Liu Shaoqi first, for lingering in the New Democratic period, and then Zhou Enlai for his cautious attitude toward the GLF, accusing leaders like Zhou "as women walking with bound feet," wobbling and slow. Both Liu and Zhou had to adjust their positions to fall into line with Mao. The other major move was the Anti-Rightist Movement in 1957, which, it has been argued, had shut off any opposition to GLF policies from the rational intellectual elite. Both arguments have some merits, and explain the origin and the development of the GLF to a large extent: (1) Mao wanted to end the New Democratic program sooner and to speed up collective farming, and (2) the Anti-Rightist Movement, by creating a climate of Left political correctness, not only silenced opposition but also encouraged those who pushed for radicalism.

However, the two arguments cannot explain all the problems and the scale of the GLF. After all, as we will see shortly, Mao was the one who tried to caution other leaders not to be too radical. To address this issue adequately we need to pay attention to scholars like Bachman (1991) and Teiwes (1984), who try to locate the policy process in the CCP system that led to the disaster of the GLF. As I mentioned above, within the CCP Mao was taken to be a person who not only led but also defined the course of the Chinese Revolution. Other leaders either had to follow him or be demoted in the process of policymaking. In the end, Mao prevailed, and Liu and others, like Deng Xiaoping and Zhou Enlai, not only fell into line with Mao but actively supported the GLF. According to Yang Shangkun's diary entries, in early 1959, Deng Xiaoping (Yang Shangkun 2001: 342), Chen Yun (Yang Shangkun 2001: 349) and Li Fuchun (Yang Shangkun 2001: 339), the three heavyweights in the implementation of the policies, were the ones who insisted on fulfilling the centrally planned industrial production targets. It was Ke Qingshi, the one who was accused of being a puppy dog of Mao by the post-Mao elite, who wanted to slow down (Yang Shangkun 2001: 321).

It was not that those giant figures of the CCP, like Liu Shaoqi, Deng Xiaoping and Zhou Enlai, were stupid, or that they were just afraid of Mao's personal wrath. They were ready to sacrifice their lives when they decided to participate in the Revolution. It was Mao who had given the intellectual narrative for the Revolution for which those CCP leaders were convicted and for which they were willing to experiment for the faster development of a better China. Mao was able to articulate the conceptualization of a socialist country by which China could move forward.

Once they agreed on the conceptualization there was the issue of how to put the theory into practice. The problem was that once the consensus (of the GLF) was reached, however tentatively, everyone would try to pursue their own beliefs. Most of what now seems to be the crazy GLF initiatives did not come from Mao himself. Liu Shaoqi, the second in command, a man with a reputation for being practical, went as far as to say on December 20, 1957 that it would only take China two or three years to overtake Great Britain. Liu also said to the workers in Shijngshan that communism would be realized in their lifetime (Ma Qibing 1991: 148). Even the term "Leap Forward" might be an invention by the person who was initially criticized by Mao for being too cautious, Zhou Enlai (Xie Chuntao 1990: 12). In a talk in Wuhan in July 1963, in the presence of Liu Shaoqi, Deng Xiaoping, Peng Zhen, Kang Sheng, Chen Boda, Wu Lengxi, Yao Qin, Fan Luoyu and Wang Li, Mao said that he saw the term "Great Leap" in newspapers in Beijing in September 1957 when he was with Deng Xiaoping in Moscow and thought the slogan was anti-materialist (Wang Li 2008: 187). Wang further claims that he remembered Wu Lengxi transmitting Mao's criticism of the "Communist Wind" (referring to the political correctness of limiting private space for the development of communism) as early as October in 1957 (Wang Li 2008: 187). Wu Lengxi, editor of the *People's Daily*, in his memoirs, regrets that he did not follow Mao closely enough by tuning down the frenzy in the CCP mouthpiece media outlet that was tremendously influential at that time (Wu Lengxi 1995).

The idea of the People's Commune was first implemented by the Chayashan local authorities in Suiping County of Henan Province in April 1958. When Mao was introduced to the idea by Tan Qilong, the party secretary of Shandong Province, Mao made an offhand remark that the People's Commune sounded good. A journalist picked up the remark and made headline news in the *People's Daily* that "Chairman Mao said People's Commune is good" (Gao 1999a: 123).

The idea of everyone eating together in a canteen was again an experiment initiated by the local authorities. On July 8, 1958, the *People's Daily* published a report that listed eight advantages of setting up a public canteen, including the promotion of work efficiency and liberation of women from the kitchen. The idea was reported to be supported by Liu Shaoqi when he visited Shandong on July 14–18, 1958, when he also suggested that every factory should make their iron and steel instead of relying on external supplies (Ma Qibing 1991: 148). In July 1958, Li Fuchun and Li Xiannian, two leaders in charge of the state's central planning, in their "Outlines for the Second Five Year Plan," stated that it would take no more than two or three years for China to overtake Britain in industry and that increases in agricultural production would be as high as 35 percent. Bo Yibo, another main player in central planning, gave a report on June 17, 1958 titled "Overtaking the UK in Two Years."

The exaggeration of agricultural production, such as 10,000 *jin* (one *jin* equals 0.5 kilos) yield of rice per *mu* of land, so as to boost morale on the one hand and to show performance achievements on the other, was also cooked up by local authorities, encouraged not by Mao but by other senior leaders. The party secretary of Guangdong Province, Tao Zhu, for instance, published an article in the CCP's theoretical journal the *Red Flag* on July 15, 1958 titled "Refuting the Theory that There Was a Limit to the Increase of Grain Production." The then Vice Premier and Foreign Minster Marshal Chen Yi declared that he had seen with his own eyes that in Panyu County of Guangdong Province the yield of one million *jin* of sweet potatoes, 60,000 *jin* of sugar cane and 50,000 *jin* of rice per *mu* (Chen Yi 1958). Tan Zhenglin, the man placed in charge of agriculture, was reported to have said that the amount of grain production that could be produced was only limited to one's imagination (Dong Cunbao 1992: 160).

During the 1962 Seven Thousand People Conference reflecting the failure of the GLF, Tan admitted that he should be held mainly responsible for the "Communist wind". Deng Xiaoping, one of the main leaders responsible for implementing CCP policies, went as far as to stand happily on the top of rice crops to indicate an extraordinary harvest, which in fact was the rice crops assembled from other fields and replanted on the one spot (Rittenberg and Bennet 2001).

In one of his random talks, Mao actually demolished Liu and Deng for going too fast and for being too rash (Lao Tian 2016). The talk, which took place on November 21, 1958 in Wuhan, has not been included in the officially sanctioned selected works of Mao, but can be seen in Mao (1968). To Liu Shaoqi and Peng Zhen, Mao warned sternly that if industrial targets were set too high there might be problems in agriculture to the point of many millions of people dying of hunger. When instructing Deng Xiaoping to replace Wu Zhipu, one of the most radical leaders at that time, to coordinate the draft outline for socialist construction, Mao told Deng that the length of time to complete planned projects should be 15 years instead of ten. The document was later issued as "The Forty Articles Outline on the Construction of Socialism in 15 Years" (Lao Tian 2016).

In 1961, Peng Zhen set up a confidential investigative team to examine CCP Central Committee documents and media reports to find out what was said or reported that led the GLF astray, to be presented at the 1962 conferences attended by 7,000 CCP leaders. During the CR what was called the Changguan Lou Black Meeting (after the Changguan Building where the investigative meetings were held) was presented as evidence of anti-Mao activities by Liu Shaoqi, Deng Xiaoping and Peng Zhen (Song Rufen 2012). Qi Benyu (2016) holds the view that the aim of that investigation was indeed to find faults with Mao, but they failed to find anything.

Driven by a frenzied passion to transform a poor country into a rich socialist China, with a blind arrogance based on the unprecedented good harvests in 1957, the Chinese leadership from the top to the bottom carried out all kinds of experiments, the results of which were disastrous. Whether or not the theoretical direction of socialism in China was too hasty may be debatable, but the policy failure as a result of the policy implementation process released by the dramatic decentralization design meant that the GLF disaster was as logical as it was inevitable.

THE CONTROVERSY ON THE FAMINE DEATH TOLL

As pointed out by Yang Songlin (2013), it is not true that the Chinese wanted to keep the GLF famine a secret. In fact a figure in one of the official publications regarding China's premature deaths in 1959–60 in the "Report of the Damage Caused by Disaster in China 1949–1995" was published by the State Statistics Bureau Publishing House, compiled by the Ministry of Civil Affairs, which is responsible for disaster relief. The report provides the statistics shown in Table 1.

Table 1   The famine situation in 1959–63

Year	No. suffering from malnutrition	No. of children sold	No. of premature deaths
1959	3,020,000	518	17,853
1960	4,740,000	10,688	374,890
1961	30,390,000	666,000	647,010
Total	38,150,000	677,200	1,039,800

Many today would not take this number seriously. In 2011, the CCP Party History Press published the second volume of *The History of the CCP* in which it asserted that the national population in 1960 decreased by ten million from the previous year. *The Seventy Years of the CCP*, edited by Hu Sheng (2010), a veteran CCP official historian, makes the same assertion, and he was awarded the Wu Yuzhang Award and the Guo Moruo Award for Academic Achievements.

The existing research repertoire consists of speculations of a death toll ranging from 10 to 45 million, and sometimes even higher. The population statistics of 1958–61 were released for the first time in the *China Statistical Yearbook* in 1983, according to which the population at the year-end of 1960 and 1961 decreased by ten million and 3.48 million from the previous years respectively. Based on the linear model of population growth in 1960 and 1961, there was -3.05 million and -2.5 million respectively. Following the release of the statistics, Coale (1984) estimates the excess deaths to be 26.8 million in 1958–63. Judith Bannister (1987) estimates that 29.871 million died prematurely in 1958–61.

Other Chinese publications (for a brief survey see Riskin 1998) include Peng (1987), Jin Hui (1993) who asserts that the number of premature deaths in rural China might have reached 40.4 million, and Professor Cao Shuji (2005) at the Department of History at Shanghai Jiaotong University, who concludes that the total number of premature deaths during the GLF was 32.458 million. The most influential Chinese publication toward the end of the last century is probably Jiang Zhenghua, director of the Institute of Demographic Research at Xi'an Jiaotong University, who in a publication concludes that there were about 17 million premature deaths during the period of hardships (Jiang and Li 1988). Jiang was promoted to the office of vice chairman of the Standing Committee of the National People's Congress, most likely as a result of this publication.

The latest Chinese publication known in the West on the subject of the GLF is Yang Jisheng's *Tomb Stone* that has an abridged English version. Yang was a senior journalist at the official Chinese government Xinhua News Agency, and was for many years the deputy chief editor of *yanhuang chunqiu*, a magazine well known for its anti-Mao and anti-Revolution stance, so much so that it was more or less disbanded after Xi Jinping came to power. Yang Jisheng concludes that there were 20.98 million premature deaths and a reduction of 32.2 million births. But as pointed out by Yang Songlin (2013), Yang Jisheng is not consistent and would claim different numbers in his various speeches.

The most celebrated author on the GLF in the West is Frank Dikötter. Among the six books shortlisted for the 2011 Samuel Johnson Prize for Non-Fiction, Dikötter's *Mao's Great Famine* was awarded the British title. Dikötter seems to agree with Becker, putting the the GLF famine death toll at around 45 million. In his *Hungry Ghosts: Mao's Secret Famine*, Jasper Becker comes to this estimate because that was the number given to him by Chen Yizi, the former director of the post-Mao

China's Economic System Reform Institute, who claimed that his institute wrote a report with a conclusion that the famine death toll was 43 million. In a publication titled "Collectivization and China's Agricultural Crisis in 1959–1961," Justin Yifu Lin (1990), once a vice president of the World Bank, an American-trained economist and a legendary defector from Taiwan to mainland China, states that a careful study of the newly released demographic data leads to the conclusion that this crisis resulted in about 30 million excess deaths and about 33 million lost or postponed births in 1958–61.

What are these estimates based on? Some are based on a "the Chinese themselves say so" attitude, like Becker. Commentators and specialists on China are immune to claims by the Chinese who say good things about China. The logic is that of course they would say that. But the same experts may be credulous in response to the Chinese who say things that paint China in bad light. However, the problem with this ethnicity or race judgment is that it fails to recognize that there is no such thing as "the Chinese." Even for the political category of "Chinese" there are different classes and different interests, and they may take different political positions or simply hold different conceptual paradigms. Those who fail to see the Chinese as agents of different political and conceptual positions might be framed within the conceptual paradigm or political necessity that CCP-led China is a totalitarian or authoritarian state, so much so that any differences that can be detected in the system must be either because of a power struggle or dissidents. And they tend to believe the dissidents.

The 1983 Chinese official publication of the population census in fact has a contradiction: in terms of year-end number, a population decrease of ten million is recorded from 1959 to 1960, and 3.48 million from 1960 to 1961, and yet the registered mortality during the period from 1959 to 1961 was no more than 36 million (Yang Songlin 2013). How do you draw a conclusion of 30 million premature deaths during the period if the total registered deaths is 36 million?

Here then comes another dataset that seems to provide an explanation. At the time of the third national population census in 1982, the Chinese State Family Planning Commission (SFPC) also organized a "Retrospective Survey of Women's Marriage and Fertility" on 300,000 women between the ages of 15 and 67 among one million people. The survey was conducted by door-to-door interviews, which is believed to be quite reliable. Each interviewed woman was asked to provide her childbearing and marriage history over the past 41 years since 1940. The SFPC released the results, according to which the actual birth rate is far higher than the "registered birth rate." This fact is confirmed by the 1964 population census: there were 14.31 million four-year-old children (born in 1960) as per the 1964 census. However, there were only 13.92 registered births in 1960.

The fertility sample survey seems to suggest that as many as 40 million people born between 1953 and 1981 were not registered in the household registration system. This means that at least an equal number of deaths occurred during the period. If and when the actual birth rate was higher than the registered birth rate then the apparent contradiction in the 1983 population census can be solved: a solution that potentially explains why there could be a famine death toll of 30 million even though there were only 36 million registered deaths during the period. So the SFPC fertility survey suggests tens of millions of unregistered births, and when they were found to be missing in the later census after the GLF they were assumed to have died during the GLF.

But there is a problem: the fertility survey did not investigate whether the under-registration involved mortality. It is possible that the survey, in the words of Yang Songlin (2013), has "brought the deceased babies back to life" and then to die for the GLF famine figure. Yang Songlin points out that there is a possibility that at least some unregistered births were also unregistered deaths: there were babies who died soon after they were born, as the infant mortality rate was still high then in rural China, before the rural residents had the time or bothered to register their births. If this possibility can be confirmed then it can be argued that the famine death toll based on the SFPC fertility survey is problematic to say the least. That this could be the case is confirmed by the situation in Gao Village: my mother gave birth to 14 children, some of them during the 1950s to the 1960s, but only four survived. And yet none of her children who died young or at birth registered their births or deaths. I myself did not have a registered birth date until I had to travel to Xiamen University to study and a date was made up for that purpose.

Another set of statistics presented by Sun Jingxian (2016) also questions the validity of the estimated famine death tolls derived from the SFPC fertility survey results. Fertility rates calculated on the basis of the SFPC's fertility survey is higher than the census statistics in only two age groups and lower in the others, with a maximum deviation of 125 percent. The credibility of any conclusions drawn from research based on data with so large a deviation and dramatic fluctuation, no matter how scientific the calculation method may be, is questionable (Yang Songlin 2013). It is worth pointing out again that as the Chinese population base is so large, even a seemingly small error can result in a large absolute number.

DISSENTING VOICES AND CLASHING VIEWS

Most dissenting voices that question the famine death toll of 30 million or so, do so through social media for three reasons: (1) the contesting issues of the GLF famine toll were not brought to the attention of most of the Chinese until the 1990s (Riskin 1998), (2) unlike the late 1980s and early 1990s the Chinese authorities have tightened their control on publications and (3) social media that became available only in this century is difficult to control. Mathematician Song Wenbin, in the name of "Yao Qiyuan and Song Xiaoli," published a number of analytical articles on his blog. One of the deciding variables for calculating the number of the famine death toll is what the assumed "normal" mortality rate is: the lower the assumed mortality rate the higher the death toll. Song questions the "normal mortality rate" at eleven per thousand as a benchmark chosen by the mainstream scholars for the GLF period. One basic reason for questioning such a low normal mortality rate is that it is hard to believe that it took China only eight years to reduce its mortality rate from 20 per thousand in the early years of the People's Republic to ten per thousand in 1957, a year before the GLF started, which is the assumed mortality rate for the GLF years from 1958 to 1960, while other Asian and Middle Eastern countries took 27 years to do so (Yang Songlin 2013, Wang Shaoguang 2014).

The tide seems to have turned a little recently. Yang Songlin was able to publish a book-length study of the GLF that is critical of mainstream scholars. In addressing the death toll numbers, Yang specifically tackles the Chen Yizi assertion of 43 million. Yang states that he has interviewed Dr. Wang Xiaoqiang, who was the executive director of China's Economic System Reform Institute when Chen Yizi was the director. Wang denied there was ever a project of investigation on the GLF at the institute (Yang Songlin 2013). Wang explained that such a project would require a huge amount of funding and take many scholars to work on it for a long time, which could not possibly be operated by the institute at that time. So the "the Chinese say so" claim of 43 million death toll made by Becker has yet to be corroborated.

Sun Jingxian, a professor of mathematics, was one of the first to be taken seriously by officials in China in questioning the mainstream scholarship when he managed to publish "A Study on China's Population Variance in the 1960s" in the *Journal of Marxism Studies* of the Chinese Academy of Social Sciences (CASS), a very official journal. In this study Sun argues that there had been about seven million unregistered deaths before 1957. These deaths were registered later in 1959–61 during the implementation of the Regulations on Household Registration, which caused a statistical inflation of seven million deaths around 1960. Sun's estimate of the famine death toll is several million, not tens of millions. Sun argues that the ten million negative growth in 1960 and 3.48 million negative growth in 1961 published in the 1982 census are not proof of a famine death toll of more than tens of millions.

Sun first draws the reader's attention to the anomalies over a longer period, in the sense that the year-end population number or growth rate is either too high or too low given the assumed birth and death rates. The lower growth was recorded not only in the year of 1960, 1961 and 1962, but also in the year of 1963, 1964 and even 1967 and 1981. According to the statistics in the published census from 1956 to 1959, China's population anomalously increased by 11.92 million people, and from 1960 to 1964 the population anomalously decreased with a total of 26.44 million. From 1968 to 1979 there was an anomalous increase of 15.57 million people. Sun then points out an astonishing coincidence: the number of the anomalous increase of the two periods is roughly the same as the anomalous decrease between 1960 and 1962. Sun therefore argues that the 1960 to 1962 anomalous decrease is related to the anomalous increase of both the period before and the period after. For Sun, most researchers don't see the connection but focus on the anomalous decrease in the GLF period in isolation, and therefore claim that the anomalous decrease was the result of the GLF famine. Nobody has noticed the roughly similar sets of statistics: 26.45 million of anomalous increase during the two periods, one before and one after the GLF, and the 26.4 million decrease during the GLF consequence period, as shown in Figure 1 (the vertical coordinate indicate accumulated figures of anomalous population changes).

Sun suggests that the explanation for such coincidence lies in the fact that the registration system failed to record the population accurately

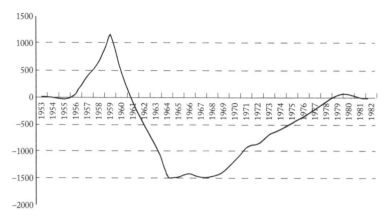

Figure 1 Accumulated figures for China's year-end anomalous population changes, 1954–82 (unit: 10,000)

due to the specific domestic pattern of migration at that time. The population data published in 1983 by the National Bureau of Statistics is based on house registration data collected by the Public Security Bureau. Though household registration started in 1950, 87 percent of China's population was not registered until 1953 as the system only started in the cities. Though some efforts were made, including the 1955 "Directives on Establishing a Permanent Household Registration System," for many years during the 1950s Chinese population data were sketchy at best. In January 1958, the PRC Household Registration Statute was issued to set up a complete household registration system, but the onset of the GLF and emergence of the commune system postponed a systematic setup.

In an ideal situation, the actual population is the same as the household registration collected population. But an ideal situation did not exist, and one reason for this is the inbound and outbound migration between urban and rural sectors, as seen in Table 2, that prevented accurate registration from taking place.

Based on data in Table 2, in the four years from 1956 to 1959, China's household registered urban population increased by 40.86 million. Of this growth, only 10.76 million was accounted for by natural population growth (taking into account births and deaths). This left 30.1 million unaccounted for, which in turn means that 30.1 million individuals migrated from the countryside to urban areas from 1956 to 1959.

China's rural population increased by 34.74 million, but the household registration population only increased by 16.56 million, leaving a discrepancy of 18.18 million. Linking this to the historical fact of the large-scale rural-to-urban migration that occurred during this period, Sun concludes that this 18.18 million represents the net figure of rural-to-urban migrants that got cancelled from their rural household registration.

Table 2 Urban population changes, 1956–9

Year	Year-end household registration population	Natural population growth rate (‰)	Natural population growth	Household registration population growth	Net household registration population in-migration
1955	8,285				
1956	9,185	30.44	266	900	634
1957	9,949	36.01	345	764	419
1958	10,721	24.33	251	772	521
1959	12,371	18.51	214	1,650	1,436

Note: From 1958 to 1960 more than ten million rural people moved to urban centers every year (unit: 10,000)

Sun further cites a 1959 rural population census in Shandong Province, the only province that had taken one, which discovered that 1.52 million household registrations should be cancelled because of double registration. According to this rate, Sun estimates that it corresponds roughly to the 18 million discrepancy for the whole of China (Sun Jingxian 2013, 2016).

China's migration patterns underwent a major shift, changing fundamentally from rural-to-urban migration to urban-to-rural migration. The significant reduction in urban population began in the second half of 1960, but mainly occurred in the three years from 1961 to 1963, and China's urban household registered population dropped by 14.27 million, despite a natural population growth of 8.98 million. Taking into consideration natural population growth, China's urban household registered population fell by 23.25 million during this period.

Yang Jisheng responds to Sun by saying that there cannot be an unregistered population since daily provisions and even the education of children or nurseries were based on household registration. But this response ignores two crucial facts. The first is that the household registration system could not be effectively enforced during the GLF as the system was not complete. The second is that household registration could be effectively enforceable in the urban sector but not in the rural sector, as the rural sector did not have to depend on the government for daily necessities. Returnees mostly returned to their own villages and therefore were accepted without questions being asked. In fact many returnees not only did not reregister, but also refused to because they wanted to believe that their return to the villages was only temporary. This pattern is confirmed in my study of Gao Village. Returnee Gao Renchang's family of four for a long time wanted to and fought to get back to the city of Jingdezhen, even though Gao Village accepted them without question (Gao 1999a). In fact as early as in 1995 Yang Zihui (1995) argues that the anomalous decrease of population during 1959–61 is related to the issue of unregistered households. But nobody paid any attention to that.

Another dataset confirms the technical problems related to the missing population during the GLF period: the 1982 SFPC fertility sample survey mentioned above has the number of 14,307,196 born in 1960. However, in the 1990 sample survey the number of people born in 1960 is said to be 14,443,119. In the 2000 sample survey, the population born in 1960 increased again to 14,684,726. So after 40 years the number of living people born in 1960 has not decreased, as it naturally should do as a result of death and migration, but increased (Yang Songlin 2013).

CONSTRUCTION OF THE GREAT LEAP FORWARD

Like Becker's *Mao's Secret Famine*, Dikötter also names the GLF as *Mao's Great Famine*. According to them, Mao owns the famine. A monster has to be pinned down to construct the GLF for consuming the Communist evil. The celebrated author Jung Chang endorses Dikötter in the latter's book blurb by declaring that it was very impressive scholarship based on "the access to Communist Party archives that has long been denied to all but the most loyal historians," "meticulously researched and brilliantly written" and most authoritative.

Instead of analyzing policy and organizational failures such as overly large communes that led to supervision failure, information failure such as the difficulty of knowing what was actually happening on the ground in time to address the problems before it was too late, and mass movement actions driven by political passion for experimentation, Dikötter focuses on isolated facts during the GLF, such as some houses being dismantled for the purpose of collecting fertile soil in some places, and violence against villagers by some local official thugs. Dikötter (2010: xiii–xiv) goes to great lengths to describe them so as to construct a sense to the reader that this was a nationwide phenomenon that happened everywhere: "we can infer that between 1958 and 1962 by a rough approximation 6 to 8 percent of the victims were tortured to death or summarily killed—amounting to at least 2.5 million people. ... Up to 40 percent of all housing was turned into rubble, as homes were pulled down to create fertiliser." Referring to the 2.5 million proposed by Dikötter as simply killed, Aaron Leonard (2017), a freelance journalist, states: "Yet a closer read reveals it as fallacious, as artful writing full of extrapolation and conjecture."

Dikötter's detailed description may be vivid, but his way of extending particular cases to generalize the whole of China in *statistical* terms is no different from the CCP itself in its method of *dianxing diaocha* (typical case study), like that of the landlord Liu Wencai (Dutton 2016), that was "studied" as a typical landlord class in pre-1949 China to illustrate the theory of class struggle. Liu Wencai did not do all the bad things that he was accused of having done. But to the typical case study method of the CCP, that was only an irrelevant detail, because for political purposes the point was to construct a typical landlord to prove a class struggle theory. For Dikötter, it does not matter whether what he describes happened in other places of China: what matters is the construction of a typical GLF.

Dikötter argues that there is enough archival evidence, from a sufficiently large and diverse range of party units, to confirm that the figure of 43 to 46 million premature deaths proposed by Chen Yizi is in all likelihood a reliable estimate. Dikötter bases his estimate on what he claims to have found in the archives that only he has access to. We have to remember that even though a case study of one place can be insightful and useful, and even if it can be confirmed, to deduce a total mathematical number in a country as large and diverse as China is a different matter. We also need to realize that not everything bad about China said by a Chinese must be true, especially in the case of a number announced by Chen Yizi who actually defected to the West. A Chinese person can be politically and ideologically motivated and can also follow conceptual paradigms, as well as being motivated by pragmatic personal reasons.

Interestingly, as reported by Snow (1971: 411), the origin of the commune was interpreted in the West at that time as being the result of "intraparty seizure of power by the left wing in China during the months June to November 1957," and Liu Shaoqi was identified as the "mentor" of this left group (Donald Zagoria 1973). "And yet, when I asked a Very High Official the direct question, who did the final 'push' that launched the communes, his answer was, 'the peasant masses started them. The Party followed'" (Snow 1971: 418). Regarding weather and climate conditions, Zhou Enlai told Snow that there were "the worst series of disasters since the nineteenth century" (Snow 1971: 586). Nearly 40 percent of China's farmland was reported afflicted by prolonged drought, unprecedented floods in the northeast, hailstorms in the south and other natural calamities (Snow 1971: 111).

Snow, who popularized Mao in his in his book *Red Star over China* (1937), could be said to be a biased witness and a partial reporter in this case. But "In general, it appears that the indications of hunger and hardship did not approach the kinds of qualitative evidence of mass famine that have accompanied other famines of comparable (if not equal) scale, including earlier famines in China" (Riskin 1998: 120). In its 1961 secret report on the rural situation in China, the CIA does not seem to support the wildest claims either when it summarizes: "Widespread famine does not seem to appear at hand, but in many provinces many people are at a bare subsistence diet and bitterest suffering lies imme-diately before June when the first 1961 crops will be harvested" (CIA 1961: 3). It is also interesting to see how the CIA interpret the cause and course of the GLF: "As a result of two successive years of poor harvests, the withdrawal of the Soviet technicians, and the dislocation created by the 'Leap Forward' the country's leaders have been forced sharply to slow down the pace of the country's economic development program" (CIA 1961: 1).

Of course, one should not and would not take the CIA as a reliable witness. But if anything one would expect the CIA to say the worst about China since the GLF happened during the height of the Cold War, with which the CIA was closely engaged. The CIA summary is remarkable in many ways. First, it mentions the Soviet withdrawal as one of the reasons for the slowdown of China's economy, as claimed by the Chinese government. Second, it admits to not having seen widespread famine when the report was written in April 1961. Finally, it points out "poor harvests" and "dislocation"—the latter is exactly the source of explana-tion offered by Sun Jingxian for the population discrepancies in the 1983 registered population report. Yet 30 million people are supposed to have died of starvation "without anyone knowing at that time that a famine took place" (Patnaik 2002, 2011). It is worth noting that Hong Kong at that time was an "open" ground for the KMT authorities in Taiwan and Western countries to gather information about mainland China.

One of the most astonishing and supposedly most condemning indictments of Mao discovered by Dikötter (2010: xiii, 33, 68, 70, 134) is that Mao was willing to let half of the Chinese population die for the sake of a utopia. Dikötter's discovery is supposedly demonstrated by Mao's remarks: "When there is not enough to eat people starve to death. It is better to let half of the people die so that the other half can eat their fill." Dikötter then declares that Mao and other leaders knew what was happening in the countryside as a result of the GLF. But as Warren Sun—a highly respected Australian scholar of elite Chinese politics, who, together with another reputable Australian scholar, Frederick C. Teiwes, published respectable works on Chinese politics in the field—points out, Dikötter's claim is either a deliberate fraud or an indication of Dikötter's incompetence in reading the original text in Chinese. Mao's remark was an earthly metaphor that is typical of him, made in the context of urging the Chinese leadership to reduce the number of planned projects so that resources were not so thinly spread (Sun 2013). In other words, Mao was trying to do exactly the opposite of what Dikötter claims Mao was doing: to cool down the GLF fever. As a trained historian, Dikötter admits that "Since the data present a whole range of problems, from lack of internal consistency to the under-registration of births and deaths and exclusion of the armed forces, different authors have tinkered with this or that variable either to lower or to heighten the number," referring to the famine death toll, and that "this book has been written with relatively 'soft' materials" (2010: 324).

However, for the majority of the consumers of GLF knowledge, Dikötter can get away with what he calls "soft materials" so long as the story is right, though serious scholars would not let him get away with this so easily. An Oxford-educated scholar, Anthony Garnaut, condemns Dikötter for "using archival anecdotes stripped of geographic, temporal, and institutional context" (2013: 233), and for drawing "generalizations from fragmentary evidence"—the descriptive flourish is seen as the author's poetic summary of archival reports in his personal collection (2013: 233). "The juxtaposition and sampling techniques used by Dikötter fall short of academic best practice" (2013: 234), and Garnaut details how Dikötter could be accused of being a plagiarist

(2013: 234). So why would Dikötter take such a fraudulent approach? Because Dikötter has to build "the moral dimension of totalitarianism evil" (2013: 236).

CONTRADICTORY CONSTRUCTION
OF THE GLF BY YANG JISHENG

For his award-winning book *Tombstone*, published in Hong Kong in Chinese, the first edition of which appeared in 2008, Yang Jisheng is highly acclaimed in the West after an abridged English version appeared in 2010. Introduced by Edward Friedman, once a member of the Concerned Asian Scholars, and Roderick MacFarquhar, a veteran scholar on China, Yang was praised for his courageous work on the GLF. But Yang Jisheng's work is full of contradictions, at least in the Chinese version, as I will point out shortly.

Dikötter was aware of Yang's work but does not like it, for obvious reasons: Yang does not have a sustained story that portrays Mao as total-itarian evil. In the Chinese version, Yang (2008: 811) admits that up to the 1959 Lushan Conference it was Mao who made all the remarks that were realistic given the situation at that time, and that it was in 1961 that Mao felt that he was cheated by the local government officials when he realized there was a high famine death toll. Mao then sent Tian Jiaying, Hu Qiaomu and Chen Boda (three of his closest secretaries) separately to Zhejiang, Hunan and Sichuan to investigate and assess the situation. Liu Shaoqi, Zhou Enlai, Zhu De and Deng Xiaoping also separately went to Hunan, Sichuan and Beijing to investigate. In the English version, Yang only admits indirectly that Beijing did not realize the seri-ousness of the situation until the end of 1960, when Yang describes the reaction of Premier Zhou Enlai to the Xinyang incident (the worst-hit area with the highest famine death toll): "I am responsible for such an incident in Xinyang, not a single person reported it to us, and the central government knew nothing about it" (Yang Jisheng 2010: 60).

Radical GLF policies did not last long. As Yang admits, as early as May to July 1959, various kinds of contracting-out practices (the so-called responsibility reform that was supposed to be the main content of post-Mao reform) were already being carried out (Yang Jisheng 2008: 823). In many places county and provincial leaders turned a blind eye to these practices even though these measures were still considered politi-cally incorrect. What also merits observation is that Zeng Xisheng, the provincial head of Anhui—another one of the worst-hit provinces—who was the most radical in carrying out rash GLF policies, was also the one who explicitly supported the contracting-out system (2008: 824). After the Lushan Conference the central government and various provincial governments were still very critical of the contracting-out or responsibility measures, and other CCP leaders were more harsh in their criticism of the practice than Mao himself (2008: 825). Only toward the end of 1960 when Mao and other leaders realized the seriousness of the situation did Beijing allow the contracting-out measures officially to go ahead (2008: 825). Yang's presentation here, unlike that of Dikötter, confirms the argument that the GLF was a policy failure, and some of those who were mostly responsible for the failure tried to make a 180 degree change after it was already too late.

Yang Jisheng was a devoted Communist or else he would not have become a senior CCP journalist. What has made him a fierce fighter for "journalist integrity," as he claims to be in his late life, in writing about the "truth" of the GLF? Yang says that he became critical of the CCP regime during the CR when big posters exposed the official privilege of party officials (Yang 2008: 11). He then began to examine the GLF critically—linked to the fact that his father was starved to death—whereas before he had defended GLF policies.

Let us step back a little. Let us say that it is true that Yang's father died of starvation. But did Yang know of any people other than his father in his hometown village who died of starvation at that time? Did he witness other deaths or mass graves? In my village study I describe how hungry my family and I were, but there was no death from starvation. If the figure of 30 million famine deaths were true, one in every 20 Chinese at that time was starved to death; famine of this scale must have left physical evidence. Yang Jisheng (2008: 15) mentions that Felix Greene, in his *Curtain of Ignorance* (1964), and Edgar Snow did not record seeing any sign of mass starvation because they were deceived by the Chinese. But what was he doing when he was a journalist who had access to top-level information and who also still had relatives in rural China at that time?

Like Dikötter, Yang Jisheng makes the general claim that "The basic reason why tens of millions of people in China starved to death was totalitarianism" (2008: 17). If that was the case one has to explain what caused famines in China before 1949, like the ones in 1946, 1942, etc., to explain the famine in British-ruled India and to explain the fact that the

GLF famine was the first and the last large-scale famine in the whole history of the PRC.

Yang's own evidence, like that presented above, that the leaderships debated and experimented with the responsibility system even as early as 1959, in fact repudiates his own conceptual framework of totalitarianism. Here is another piece of evidence presented by Yang himself: Yang observes that while other provinces began curbing the Exaggeration Wind after the second Zhengzhou Conference (February 27 to March 5, 1959), Li Jingquan's (the head of Sichuan Province, the largest grain-producing province and another of those worst hit) unyielding stance was exemplified in his refusal to pass the letter from Mao to production team cadres. On April 29, 1959, Mao wrote an "internal party communique" on agricultural production that was "practical and realistic" (2008: 205). Is it not extraordinary that a provincial leader could refuse to deliver a letter as he was instructed to from the very top, from Mao?

There are several points that need to be made here. First, it is clear that Mao already wanted to reduce the collective organization structure to the smallest possible for management and accountability. The second point is that Mao did not trust that middle-level government officials would carry out the spirit of his instruction and therefore addressed his letter directly to the grassroots production team cadres. The third point is that exactly as Mao had anticipated, local leaders like Li did not want to carry out Mao's instruction, and "on May 7, 1959, the Central Committee repeated the order to transmit Mao's memo to the Production team immediately. Li ignored it" (Yang Jisheng 2008: 206). When it did reach some local leaders, Li even "ordered the internal memo recalled" (2008: 206).

Zeng Xisheng, the party secretary of another badly hit province, Anhui, acted more or less the same way. During what is known as the Seven Thousand Participants Conference in 1962, Zeng confessed that he was resisting Mao's instruction by having Mao's letter quickly recalled within a month of it being sent (Li Jianshu 2016).

Mao's non-totalitarian decentralization model, which proved to be vital for the success of the post-Mao reforms, was also demonstrated by the Seven Thousand Participants Conference in 1962. The conference was originally intended to get the party secretaries of the six Central Bureaus* and provincial leaders to work out policies to deal with the

---

* Beijing divided China into six large districts and each district is a bureau that administrates several provinces.

aftermath of the GLF. Given that those top leaders found it hard to come up with something good enough, one of the bureau heads, Tao Zhu, suggested enlarging the meeting to include every prefectural leader (*diwei*), upon which Mao decided to make the conference even larger to include all the county party secretaries. Hence a conference on January 11, 1962 with 7,000 delegates. According to Li Jianshu (2016), there were no opening ceremonies and all the reports and speeches were distributed to the delegates before they were delivered. But there was an unspoken tension among the top leaders at the conference: the central leaders like Liu Shaoqi, Deng Xiaoping, Zhou Enlai, Chen Yun and Li Xianian wanted the conference to be focused on containing decentralization (*fandui fensan zhuyi*), but local leaders like Ke Qingshi, Tao Zhu, Wang Renzhong and Peng Zhen would not agree. Everyone was unhappy but nobody knew what to do. Prompted by a letter sent by Ma Sai, the deputy party secretary of Bangbu city, Mao decided to prolong the meeting for the delegates so they could vent their anger and grievance (*chuqi*).

Clearly, the consensus on the GLF was broken by mid-1959 and Mao wanted more feedback from the bottom. Therefore, Yang's totalitarianism explanation is not sustainable. A more sophisticated and convincing thesis is to return to the Foucauldian conceptualization of discourse and governmentality. The Chinese—including Deng Xiaoping, Zeng Xisheng, Li Jingquan and Yang Jisheng himself—in the Mao era had a certain set of values and beliefs, and they carried out their work under the circumstances in accordance with their values and beliefs they held at that time.

Though Yang has put together some interesting information on the background of the GLF, his conclusions and assumptions are being widely challenged inside China, both on social media and increasingly in formal publications. When the news appeared that Yang won the 2016 Louis M. Lyons Award for Conscience and Integrity in Journalism, a group of professors in Shandong University presented a protest. Many flaws have been pointed out by dissenting voices, and we will now turn to one example.

A claim made by Yang Jisheng is that the famine death toll in Sichuan Province alone was ten million. Yang adopts this claim from Liao Bokang, former chairman of the Chinese People's Political Consultative Conference Sichuan Provincial Committee, then secretary of the Youth League Chongqing Committee during the GLF. The basis on which Liao made the claim was that a footnote in a document issued by the party's Sichuan Committee shows that Sichuan's population at the end of 1960 was 62.36 million while the State Statistics Bureau's population yearbook shows that the number in 1957 was 72.157 million, and therefore there must be at least ten million deaths. The trouble with this assertion is that even if there was indeed a footnote to that effect in a document in existence, it does not fit in with the PRC's Population Statistical Data, which shows that Sichuan's population in 1960 was 68.54 million, or according to the figure from another publication, *China's Population*, which Yang Jisheng quoted in his *Tombstone*, of 68.97 million. Both figures are bigger than Liao Bokang's number by more than six million (Yang Songlin 2015).

CHINA AS AN EPISTEMOLOGICAL METHOD:
DEBATES ON THE GREAT LEAP FORWARD INSIDE CHINA

In the name of "the first international conference on the evolution of China's land system" a public debate took place in July 2014 at the Central University of Science and Technology in Wuhan, where an important rural studies center is headed by Professor He Xuefeng. Some major participants involved in the GLF debates participated, including Sun Jingxian, Yang Songlin and Yang Jisheng. It was called international because some Western scholars were invited and several of the invitees attended. According to one participant of the conference, Yang Jisheng took the floor first and told the audience of his indignation because, according to him, Sun Jingxian was allowed to publish his attack on him while he was not allowed a response. When Sun Jingxian took the floor he reported his research and conclusions on the GLF and declared that Yang Jisheng, Cao Shuji, Jin Hui and others all commit errors in their estimates when they conclude there was a GLF famine death toll of 30 million (Xuan Wen 2017). Sun also addressed a major criticism of his own research based on the claim of under-registration or double registration, which says that Sun cannot be correct since China imposed very strict *hukou* (household) registration, without which children could not even be enrolled into schools. Sun's explanation, as mentioned earlier in this chapter, is that missing registration or double registration happened at a time when the *hukou* system regulations could not be fully enforced and when there was huge migration during the GLF. Sun also pointed out the fact that the rural sector did not rely on government ration tickets for food and welfare provisions, and therefore *hukou* registration only restricted their movement to the urban sector but did not impact their livelihood when they returned to the country, facts of which can be confirmed in Luo Pinghan (2003).

Sun then proceeded to point out specific cases of how Yang Jisheng misleadingly presents numbers and information in *Tombstone*, examples of which include the famine death toll in specific areas such as Fuling, Tongwei, Huining, Dingxi, Jingning, Xihaigu, Nanyang, Xuchang and Fengyang, presented by Yang as recorded in local annals or gazetteers. When he checked the references, Sun states, the numbers presented by Yang in places like Changshou, Lishui and Gaoyou could not be found. When there are numbers recorded in other places the numbers are the actual total deaths but are presented by Yang Jisheng as the famine death toll. Sun also addressed Yang's accusation of Zhou Enlai, who according to the account in the *Tombstone* had organized an investigation into the GLF famine death toll in 1961, and who, when he realized the death toll was as high as tens of millions, ordered the destruction of the report. Sun states, however, when he checked a publication by Zhou Boping, one of the three people listed by Yang to have participated in the investigation, and the official *Biography of Zhou Enlai* and *Zhou Enlai Chronicle* there was no evidence of such an event. Finally, Sun addressed Yang's indignation of not being allowed to respond. Sun claimed this was not the case because in his email to Sun, the editor of the *Journal of the Chinese Social Sciences* explained that he had suggested to Yang that they would publish a response, but that the length of the article should be limited to 3,000 words, a suggestion to which Yang did not respond. It would be inconceivable that Sun would make such a claim in public in front of Yang if it were not true. According to Sun, Yang declined to respond to Sun even though the conference had been arranged in order for this to take place (Sun 2016).

However, in the journal *yanhuang chunqiu* Yang's colleague Hong Zhenkuai ran an article in support of Yang Jisheng and criticized Sun for his work. In his response Sun Jingxian (2014) published a piece, with two relevant datasets on Sichuan Province, as shown in Table 3.

Hong Zhenkuai argues that the second dataset (which shows a death rate of 46.97 percent, 53.97 percent and 29.42 percent in 1959, 1960 and 1961 respectively) is reliable evidence of the GLF famine death toll in Sichuan, whereas Sun believes the first dataset (which shows 19.22 percent, 47.78 percent and 28.01 percent in 1959, 1960 and 1961 respec-

Table 3 Two sets of mortality data of Sichuan Province from 1958–62

Year	First dataset		Second dataset		Discrepancy in number of deaths
	Death rate	Number of deaths	Death rate	Number of deaths	
1958	17.37	126.0	25.17	178.2	52.2
1959	19.22	140.9	46.97	328.2	187.3
1960	47.78	339.8	53.97	364.7	24.9
1961	28.01	186.0	29.42	192.4	6.4
1962	14.61	94.6	14.62	94.6	0

Note: Death rate = ‰, unit = 10,000 persons

tively) is closer to reality. The second dataset is from the *Sichuan Volume of Chinese Population*, in which it is stated clearly that between 1950 and 1956 there was no comprehensive and therefore accurate registration system. Sun agrees with the stated rationale and points out a crucial factor that Hong does not take into account: the number of deaths counted in 1959 and 1960 include the number of people who actually died before 1958 but were not registered as such. They were then counted as deaths during the 1958–60 period. Taking this crucial factor into consideration, the China Statistics Bureau and the Chinese Public Security made adjustments for the population statistics for Sichuan, hence the first dataset. On the other hand, Sun points out, when local authorities write up their annals and gazetteers they do not made the same adjustments, hence the second dataset.

Sun then takes up Hong's example of Daxian District in Sichuan Province, which according to Hong was one of the 18 districts most seriously affected by the famine. From what Sun can find, there was a phenomenon of edema or hydropsy disease during the second half of 1959. They recorded the consequences of starvation resulting in illness and set up clinics in 61 of the total 218 production brigades, with 220 medical teams involving 1,337 personnel, and treated 52,451 people.

In Table 4, which shows data from the Dazhu County Gazetteer, the second column shows the numbers of people who were said to have edema or hydropsy, column three shows the numbers of those who were recorded as cured and the last column contains the number of deaths in each year from these two conditions.

According to this, the number of people who died in this area of Sichuan—the province worst hit by edema or hydropsy—was 3,130, one in 207 people in four years. But if the famine death toll were assumed to be more 30 million nationally, that would be one in 20 people who died. If the famine death rate in the worst-hit area in one of the worst-hit provinces (for this very reason rescue measures were organized and therefore there is a record) was one in every 207 people, how is it possible to have a national famine death rate of one in every 20 people?

Table 4   Edema in Dazhu County, 1959–62

Year	Number of patients	Number of healed patients	Death toll
1959	10,400	9,708	692
1960	22,040	20,981	1,066
1961	17,000	15,814	1,186
1962	6,233	5,948	186
Total	55,673	52,451	3,130

In 1983, when the Chinese population census was published—the publication of which led to the studies of demographic change by Banister and Coale, as discussed above—Li Chengrui was the director of the State Statistics Bureau. It is not surprising that many would accuse Li of being responsible for the accepted wisdom that the GLF cost at least 30 million lives. But Li himself rejected that accusation. In his preface to Sun Jingxian's planned book *Restore the Truth to History*, Li (2015) declares that Sun made three important contributions on the issue of the GLF: (1) an exposure of a monstrous lie of 30 million famine death toll, (2) an in-depth study of whether there was a reduction of ten million from 1959 to the year-end of 1960 and (3) important ideas about population movements during the GLF period. Li thinks that Sun's demographic movement does explain the so-called millions of missing people. Those movements are: from 1956 to 1960, about 30,100,000 rural residents moved to the urban sector, some of whom did not cancel their rural registration, and as a result of which by the end of 1959 there were 11,620,000 who were cancelled from the population statistics during 1960–1 when household registration was reinforced. From the second half of 1960, about 20 million people were repatriated to the rural sector. Of these people some cancelled their urban registration but did not register in the rural sector, though they worked and lived in their own villages, a phenomenon that led to 12,900,000 being unaccounted for. Sun also points out that there was the phenomenon of

unregistered deaths from 1953 to 1959, to which the household registration reinforcement period added 6,750,000 deaths during 1960–1. Li
then summarizes Sun's calculation as this: the 1960 year-end population
did not reduce by ten million as compared with 1959, but increased by
3,700,000. But compared with the growth rate from 1955 to 1957, with
an annual growth of 11,510,000, there was a reduction of 7,800,000
people, according to a linear model of population growth.

Li then addresses the issue of his role in the population census and
his own assessment of not only the death toll but also other scholars. Li
points out that during the Florence 12th Conference by the International
Demography Sciences there were scholars who were critical of Coale's
linear model estimation of death toll. After the Florence conference
Li called more Chinese scholars to get into the study of the subject,
but hardly anyone responded. Jiang Zhenghua was eventually asked to
carry out the project, after which he concluded that the famine death
toll was within in the range of 17 million. Jiang's project was evaluated
when experts and scholars from the Population Census Office of the
State Council, China Population Association, Xi'an Jiaotong University,
the State Statistics Bureau, the Ministry of Public Security, the SFPC,
the Chinese Academy of Social Sciences, the People's University and
the Chinese Institute of Applied Mathematical Science had a joint
workshop on Jiang's research. The experts basically affirmed Jiang's
research and made comments for revision, the final version of which was
first published in the journal of Xi'an Jiaotong University. However, the
State Bureau of Statistics took the attitude that research on the topic is
too large and too complicated and that Jiang's research was not endorsed
as official but as a personal academic pursuit. Li then asserts that in his
own publication in 1996 that he intended to point out that the linear
model account of population loss by Coale has a technical error and
the assumed population loss should be 22 million, not 27 million as
calculated by Coale. But Li declared that his 22 million number was
aimed to correct Coale's technical error, and was not his own estimate of
the actual famine death toll.

CONCLUSION

The estimation that the number of premature deaths exceeded 30
million in 1959–61 was not totally groundless because there is a big dent
in the registered population at year-end, but despite the fact that the dis-

crepancies between the pre-1982 figures of registered population growth and of normal population growth are obvious, neither the minister for Public Security nor the State Statistics Bureau under the leadership of Li Chengrui provided, or has ever been able to provide, an explanation for the dent. Hence the famine death toll was given as the obvious explanation. But Professor Sun now provides an alternative account: the increase in the registered population before 1960 was by far in excess of actual population growth, while the registered population growth in 1960–4 was excessively lower than the actual growth. Such contradictions were gradually eradicated, as it took 15–16 years for the lost *hukou* to be restored after 1965.

The discussion in this chapter shows that the estimation of the GLF famine death toll ranges from several million to 50 million. It is interesting to note that most Chinese writers tend to increase the numbers of their estimates as the years go by. It is also interesting that many Chinese writers tend to dismiss or discount weather and climate factors in contributing to the decline of crop production, even though it was one of the official Chinese explanations, and even though there is documentary evidence of the effects, as seen in for instance Liu Yingqiu (2005), National Prevention of Flood and Drought and Nanjing Hydrological Institute (1997), and Feng Peizhi et al. (1985).

It is often cited as evidence to condemn Mao that Liu Shaoqi said the GLF disaster was 30 percent natural disaster and 70 percent man-made. In spite of the fact that Liu's remark is taken out of context, in that he was talking about the specific area he investigated around his hometown, even 30 percent natural disaster is a huge factor that needs to be taken into consideration. Yang Shangkun, in his January 1, 1961 diary entry states that the food crisis was mainly caused by especially severe weather conditions (*teda zaihai*) and only 20 percent of the country was affected by work mistakes (Yang Shangkun 2001: 630).

The crux of the matter lies in the politics of the production and consumption of knowledge. When the Chinese began to be more and more involved in global capitalism, an increasingly critical construction of Mao, the Mao era and of Chinese socialism was made by the Chinese intellectual elite. It is therefore not a coincidence that people like Sun Jingxian (2011) were able to publish dissenting scholarship in official outlets, even though these dissenting voices have been going on for a long time in social media such as Wuyouzhixiang, a pro-Mao website that has been shut down. Since Xi Jinping came into power, the pendulum has swung from the extreme right toward the left. Xi's well-known remark that one should not use the second 30 years of the history of the PRC to denigrate its first 30 years, though itself an attempt at depoliticizing the debates on socialism versus capitalism, may actually herald emerging debates on the GLF inside China.

9
National Interest and Transnational Interest: The Political and Intellectual Elite in the West

INTRODUCTION

On his personal blog, Emeritus Professor Stein Ringen of the University of Oxford, put forward three rules in dealing with what he calls dictatorial China (Ringen 2016a):

> First, we should engage with China on all levels. That is in our own interest. ... Second, we should speak out in clear language against China's breach of human rights and rule of law ... Third, we should speak out in clear language against China's policies of aggression, in particular against neighbors ... If "we" follow these rules, will we be punished? I doubt it. Certainly not if we stand together and do not allow China to divide and rule.

Quoting Ringen here is an attempt to draw our attention to two themes that run through this chapter: (1) that academics in the West, with exceptions of course, have their national interest in mind when they construct China, and (2) they draw a line between "us" and "them," with the Western "us" clearly in contrast to the Chinese "them."

The Chinese government spokespersons are fond of repeating the cliché that the US, the most developed country, and China, the most populous developing country, should cooperate and complement each other to achieve a win-win situation. That was agreed and everyone was happy when the blood and sweat of the Chinese migrant workers churned out endless supplies of cheap goods for Western consumers. However, when the Chinese, having in general observed the rules of the WTO which had largely been drawn up by the West, seem to have caught up with the competition and want to upgrade their production chain, the "The Chinese win twice" alarm bell starts to ring.

This chapter presents evidence and analysis of how the Western intellectual elite produces knowledge of China for the consumption of either their perceived national interest, or transnational interest. It needs to be pointed out that for the Western elite in general, national and transnational interest are very often one and the same. Some in the Chinese elite might conceptualize that Chinese national and transnational interests are one and the same, but more often than not Chinese national and transnational interests are not one and the same because China is still a developing country.

China is a developing country not only because her per capita income is low (about 20 percent of that of the US) but also it is still making a living at the lower value end of the production chain. One striking piece of evidence is that of the 100 largest transnational companies in 2016, there are only five from the developing countries, two from China, one from Malaysia, two from Mexico and one from Brazil (UNCTAD 2016). Almost none of the world's 500 biggest high-technology and global brand companies, or those of the global service industries, are from developing countries. Of the 2,500 largest research funding companies China has a share of only 5.8 percent, whereas Sweden, Switzerland and Holland, with a combined population of only 35 million, have a share of 8.3 percent, higher than China with a population of 1.3 billion (Nolan 2017: 20). Because of the financial, military and technological dominance of the West, and especially because of the West's dominance on the production of knowledge, the national interest and transnational interest of most Western countries are often one and the same.

The West, led by the US, has to maintain an assertive posture, particularly on political issues around the world. Americans' widespread belief that theirs is a special country, an "indispensable nation" as stated by former Secretary of State Madeleine Albright, is a powerful God-given narrative in US policy. "So how can we play that stabilizing role, deter conflict among these potentially competing countries and at the same time maintain our economic advantage in the region? I think that's essentially the geopolitical problem" (Navarro 2016). The US led the way in crafting numerous multilateral institutions, and most of those served America quite well.

To serve the geopolitical interest of the West, the Western political and intellectual elite tout the value of democracy to the countries they want to target while blatantly turn a blind eye to crimes committed by the US and its allies, as documented by Noam Chomsky whose relevant publications are too numerous to cite. One can think of the US alliance with Saudi Arabia, the various covert interventions of the 1950s and 1960s in Guatemala, Iran, Laos, Chile; the Vietnam War; the invasion of Granada in 1985; Panama in 1989 that removed Manuel Noriega; the various arms deals that made up the Iran-Contra Affair; the invasion of Iraq in 2003; the "promiscuous" use of drone strikes in Yemen and Afghanistan during Obama's first term (Karabell 2017).

This chapter argues that even in a genuine pursuit of the knowledge of China, there is no innocent "objective" China to be discovered by the Western intellectual elite. As soon as one uses personal experiences and/or conceptual frameworks, not to speak of political/geopolitical positions, to approach China, one is adopting a perspective. For example, even the seemingly innocent linguistic issue of simplifying Chinese characters can easily descend into mad political football: the conceptualization of the Cold War against communism frames the simplification of Chinese characters in mainland China as the purposeful destruction of Chinese traditional culture (Gao 2000).

The conceptualization of China in terms of Orientalism is another example, as demonstrated by the supposed Deng Xiaoping saying "to get rich is glorious" (MacFarquhar 2016). The phrase was popularized by Orville Schell in his 1984 book *To Get Rich is Glorious: China in the '80s.* But Schell never actually attributed the words to Deng, telling the *LA Times*'s Evelyn Iritani in 2004 that it merely "grew out of the zeitgeist" of China's economic reforms. The zeitgeist of China's economic reform is to develop market capitalism, which is no more vulgar and exotic than that in the West. But for many in the West, the Oriental Chinese care only about money and are unable to develop without the generous help of the West. Robert Boxwell (2016), director of the Consultancy Opera Advisors, tells us that, "By making too many concessions to China, the West has given 'wings to a tiger'," and that "Thanks to Western investment and markets, China now has the world's second largest economy and largest military, yet doesn't seem to quite like the rules that got it there. The West helped transform a China that is massively stronger than a generation ago and appears to be less interested in human rights than ever." It is hard to see a more contemptuous attitude toward the Chinese in general and working-class Chinese in particular.

THE WESTERN INTELLECTUAL ELITE
AND NATIONAL INTEREST

In traditional China the scholar-gentry class was supposed to be well read in classics and then become government officials by succeeding in paper examinations. This ideal scenario was violently interrupted by the constant political movements of targeting intellectuals that had Mao's ear. However, as I discussed in the previous chapters, the Chinese intellectual and political elite have accomplished the mission of becoming one elite class, running China together. Similarly in the West, especially in the US, the development of think tanks, foundations, NGOs and business consultancies has led to an increasing marriage between the political and intellectual.

I will point out one example to demonstrate how the Western intellectual elite is embedded with their national interest. Elizabeth Economy is the C. V. Starr senior fellow and director for Asia studies at the Council on Foreign Relations, and has published widely on both Chinese domestic and foreign policy. One of her books on China's environmental challenges (Economy 2004) not only has a Japanese edition (2005) and a Chinese edition (2011), but also won her many honors including being named one of the top 50 sustainability books in 2008 by the University of Cambridge, the 2005 International Convention on Asia Scholars Award for the best social sciences book published on Asia, and being listed as one of the top ten books of 2004 by *The Globalist* as well as one of the best business books of 2010 by Booz Allen Hamilton's *strategy+business* magazine. She has published articles in scholarly journals including *Foreign Affairs*, *Harvard Business Review* and *Foreign Policy*, and op-eds in the *New York Times*, *Washington Post* and *Wall Street Journal*, among others. Economy is a frequent guest on nationally broadcast television and radio programs, has testified before Congress on numerous occasions, and regularly consults for US government agencies and companies. She writes about topics involving China on the Council on Foreign Relations' Asia Program blog, *Asia Unbound*, which is syndicated by Forbes.com, and authors a monthly column on China's environment for *The Diplomat*. Economy serves on the board of managers of Swarthmore College and the board of trustees of the Asia Foundation. She is also on the advisory council of Network 20/20 and the science advisory council of the Stockholm Environment Forum. She is a member of the World Economic Forum's

(WEF) Global Agenda Council on the US and served as a member and then vice chair of WEF's Global Agenda Council on the Future of China from 2008 to 2014. Economy has also served on the board of the China-US Center for Sustainable Development. She has taught undergraduate and graduate-level courses at Columbia University, Johns Hopkins University's Paul H. Nitze School of Advanced International Studies and the University of Washington's Jackson School of International Studies. She is an accomplished scholar by any standard, but she is more than that. As her testimonial at the US–China Economic and Security Review Commission on the economic aspects of the "rebalance" to Asia in March 2016 shows, she is working for the national interest of the US (Economy 2016).

This is not in any way to imply that Economy's scholarship is not solid. On the contrary, it is her solid scholarship that serves the interest of the US. Solid, and even rigorous, scholarship does not mean it is geopolitically neutral. Economy worries that if the Chinese Dalian Wanda buys out AMC theaters, the movie chain will not show a film about Tibet. She worries that the Committee on Foreign Investment in the United States's review of Chinese investment may not be tough enough to protect US political and security interests. There is nothing remarkable about an intellectual elite working for the interest of a nation that employs him or her. However, there are two points that need to be made: (1) national interests may and do clash—what does a scholar do when that happens? (2) because of historical developments the intellectual elite serving the national interest of the US in particular and the West in general are at the same time largely serving the interests of the transnational capital.

On the other side of the Atlantic, Professor Ringen (2016a) argues that the two decades between Deng Xiaoping and Xi Jinping were the golden years for the People's Republic, meaning in the China under the leadership of Jiang Zemin and Hu Jintao there was a hope of liberalization that would bring freedom to China. Under the leadership of Xi Jinping, Ringen argues that China's economic growth has slowed to a trickle and the country has turned to aggression in its neighborhood. Ringen asserts that Xi is reverting to ideology and "ideology is a dangerous force" because "ideologies explain history and destiny in a way that seems truthful to all who are entrapped in them. They become belief-systems and make people, both leaders and the led, believers." What is Xi's ideology, according to Ringen? "China Dream," which is about the great nation of China but not the Chinese people. The irony is that Ringen seems unaware that by making these assertions he himself is being ideological.

The Brookings Institute, a supposedly private, non-partisan and non-profit think tank, has 20 research centers, 90 professorial-level researchers and three overseas centers of which one is at the Beijing Tsinghua University. This is a superb example of how the US-led West dominates the agenda for international geopolitics. This is a prestigious institution where politicians and government officials retire to be research fellows, and where the US government recruits its officials, for example, former Assistant Secretary of State Susan Rice and Ben Bernanke, former chair of the US Reserve Bank. The fact that it gets funding from governments with mixed human rights records, such as the United Arab Emirates, as well as from Norway and Denmark is evidence of its geopolitical position. By the same token one should not be surprised at how Western scholarship allocates little effort to exposing the 1965 Indonesian Massacre. In contrast to what they say about the black book of communism, the mainstream "international community" says as little as possible about the massacre in Indonesia. Professor Wieringa points out that the massacre remains of little interest in Australia. This looks strange since Australia is not only the closest neighbor but also very much involved. In despair, Wieringa (2016) pleads that "Archives from the CIA and all countries that supported the Suharto regime must be opened. Universities all over the country must be encouraged to teach and research the history of the post-October 1 massacres and/or set up departments of genocide studies."

DESPOT, DICTATOR AND AUTHORITARIANISM

In Western scholarship, as well as in the eyes of Chinese neoliberals, China can never be a normal country without Western-style democracy. Emperors in traditional China were despots and Mao was a dictator. The two decades under the collective leadership of Jiang Zemin and Hu Jingtao were authoritarian, but now Xi Jinping is back to being a dictator again (so asserts Ringen). "The authoritarian rules of the game that have held sway since the beginning of the modern reform era" are "representing a break with post-1978 practices" (Minzner 2016). Veteran China-watcher Willy Lam (2016) noted in a recent column that the ascendance of Xi Jinping constitutes a body blow to the institutional reforms that Deng introduced in order to prevent the return of Maoist norms.

Nathan Attrill (2016) at the prestigious Australian National University announces that "The nation that had stood up in 1949 was, at the time of Mao's death, a much poorer and weaker society following decades of failed economic policies and constant social mobilisation." This is asserted in spite of the available data and information that demonstrate otherwise, as one of the respondents on the website says:

> Rubbish. In 1949, when Mao took power, average life expectancy was 41 years old. Literacy was below 15 percent. Electricity availability zero outside a few cities. By 1979, before Deng Xiaoping's economic reforms, literacy rate was in the 80s, which means 100 percent of young people. Electricity coverage almost everywhere, even in the poorest rural areas. The railways, roads, dams and electricity networks that would make reform and opening possible, were all Mao's work. And that barely scratches the surface. Attrill (2016)

But facts should never get in the way of a conceptual framework which states that only the capitalist market economy is on the right side of history. Along similar lines of the Chinese leadership turning into a dictatorship, the veteran China-watcher Andrew Nathan (2016) asserts that Xi "wants to reform the universities, not in order to create Western-style academic freedom [what a surprise] but to bring academics and students to heel (including those studying abroad)."

Recent developments in China do present evidence that the Chinese state is tightening its grip on how the Chinese should conceptualize the CCP, China and the world, because as China faces a new international climate of economic recession, the current model of development is being questioned. The credibility of the CCP is at risk as corruption rots its core. The issue of whether state-owned enterprises and collective rural land should be privatized all need to be addressed urgently. Under these circumstances, facing demands from different vested interest groups from all directions, the Chinese leadership feels that it is losing control if something is not done. All evidence on the ground is that there is some tightening of control here, for example on the education front and with anti-corruption, but some loosening of control elsewhere, like in the fields of finance and trade. There is no evidence that Xi wants to be a dictator or to develop a personality cult.

For instance, at tertiary education institutions, contrary to what Nathan says, there is much reform in Chinese universities that cannot neatly be described as either the pursuit of academic freedom or bringing academics and students to heel, as observed by Professor Daniel Bell, a liberal academic who has been working in China for many years, first in Beijing Tsinghua and now on the Qingdao Campus of Shandong University. For Bell it is obvious that in Chinese academia that there are many efforts to promote scientific innovation and liberal arts education, to forge links with outside institutions and to promote the teaching of Chinese classics (in a critical way): all this is happening in Chinese universities notwithstanding increased censorship (Bell 2017, personal communication).

All indications are that the current Chinese leadership is somehow still trying to find a way for China to move forward, which is neither the total left of the past Mao era, nor the total right of the West. A good example is shown by its ambiguity toward religion. China is widely condemned for its suppression of religious freedom, with recent media reports of Chinese authorities taking down crosses on church roofs in Zhejiang Province. But according to one articulate source (anonymous 2017, personal communication) who has been working with Christians in China for almost 40 years, and has written and spoken widely on the subject, the removal of crosses in Zhejiang has stopped and many have gone back up. Even Party Secretary Xia Baolong (under whose leadership the crosses were removed) has been removed from office and given an unimportant position in Beijing. As confirmed by this source who works on the ground with religion in China, Christianity is growing all over the country, generally with the government's acquiescence, if not approval. One notable example is that the Amity Printing Press in Nanjing continues to print copies of the Bible for the growing Christian community in China (and around the world), and is now the largest printer of Bibles in the world. Party members are not allowed to join a religion, but many do and some openly argue that they should be allowed.

The Chinese "feeling the stone to cross the river" approach to finding a conceptual framework is clumsy. They attempt to rescue some values from both traditional Chinese tradition and the immediate revolutionary past. The attempt to rescue some traditional Chinese values to construct a conceptualization of development is shown not only in Xi's visit to Qufu, the hometown of Confucius, but also the putting up of a Confucius statue on the iconic Tiananmen Square, but then removing it quietly without explanation a few months later (Li Yang 2011). The attempt to rescue some values from China's revolutionary discourse is shown by Xi's invocation of Mao's "Talks at the Yan'an Forum on Literature and Art" in explaining why cultural and media workers must display "Party character" and serve as the Party's "throat and tongue," and has used the resolution that Mao wrote for the Party's 1929 Gutian Conference to emphasize the importance of Party control of the army (Nathan 2016). But it is far from clear that Xi will succeed in building up a conceptual framework that can unite the Chinese together in spirit. The jury is still out, not for whether Xi is a dictator, but for what China's future direction is.

CONSTRUCTING CHINA: THE CASE OF ZHOU YOUGUANG

When Zhou Youguang, an economist and linguist, died in 2017 it was global news (Associated Press 2017), and he was hailed as the father of the Romanization system of Mandarin Chinese. Why does the media want to produce a piece of knowledge framing Zhou as the father of Romanization when in fact he was not (Li Xuzhi 2017)? My speculation is that there are two reasons: one is that Zhou was Western educated, first at Shanghai's St. John's University, then in the US—he even worked for some time as a banker on Wall Street. The second reason is that he had been vocally anti-Communist and anti-Chinese government. "In his later years, he became a scathing critic of the ruling Communist Party and an advocate for political reform, making him persona non grata at official events" (Associated Press 2017).

It is true that the Associated Press does not make an assertion regarding Zhou being the father of Romanization without sources. In fact it is based on what the Chinese say themselves (Zhou Suzi 2012). It was reported as such in the *Peoples' Daily*, the *Central TV News* and all the other major news outlets in China. But a simple check on the Chinese Language and Characters website, in the section that outlines the Chronicle of the Formulation of the Pinyin Proposal, makes it clear that in February 1952, when the Language Reform Committee was set up and when the Romanization, called *pinyin* in Chinese (literally meaning "spell the sound"), program was on the agenda the committee membership did not even include Zhou. The Committee, chaired by Wu Yuzhang, encouraged by Mao, called for applications of *pinyin* proposals, and by 1955 more than 650 proposals had been received. In February

1952, a *pinyin* proposal committee was set up and the membership did include Zhou, but as the last in the list.

What made Zhou known was his publication "What is Nationalist Form?" that strongly supports the Romanization of Chinese, in which Zhou argues that there is no unchangeable national form, and that all important written languages have been formed cross-nationally and that written symbols can be international. In other words, Zhou strongly argues for the use of Latin letters to spell the sounds of Chinese, when there was a lot opposition. In this sense Zhou made an important contribution. But Zhou, a relatively minor scholar at that time in any field, let alone linguistics, was not the power behind the decision to go ahead, nor the technical innovation for the Romanization program.

In fact it was Mao's speech that finally decided the outcome of the debate on national form. Zhou's publication is a general exposition on the issue and does not include a *pinyin* proposal. After many meetings and consultations, with the involvement of Mao and Zhou Enlai on the decision on Latinization, and after receiving 4,300 submissions between 1956 and 1957, two *pinyin* drafts emerged to be the most acceptable, one drafted by Wang Li, Lu Zhiwei and Li Jingxi, and one by Ding Xilin, Lin Handa, Wei Que and Li Jingxi. Zhou had not drafted a single proposal.

In 1956 a review committee on *pinyin* was set up headed by Guo Moruo, a committee that passed the first draft of the proposal to work on in November 1956, which was then passed by the first plenary of the Chinese National People's Congress in 1958. Zhou was arguably an important member of those who designed the *pinyin* program because of his one publication and his subsequent participation, but Wang Li, Lu Zhiwei and Li Jingxi made far greater contributions to the final product. Zhou Yougunag was lucky enough to live the longest, dying at the age of 111, and as such claimed the credit.

Mao himself played a significant role in getting the program of Latinization started. As early as August 1949, Mao received a letter from Wu Yuzhang, who suggested the Latin spelling of the Chinese sound. Mao passed Wu's letter to Guo Moruo, Mao Dun and Ma Shulun, who also supported the idea, and at that point the Committee of Language Reform was set up. Wu was then asked to chair the committee. In January 1956, after Wu Yuzhang's speech on Chinese language reform, Mao said he agreed with Wu Yuzhang's proposal of language reform, and to use Latin letters. Commenting on some professors' complaints about using foreign letters to spell Chinese, a language that according to their complaint was the best in the world, Mao said satirically that if Latin were invented by the Chinese there would not have been any complaint (Wang Jun 1995).

In fact the Latinization of Chinese sounds was started by Western missionaries, and the earliest Chinese who worked along those lines was Lu Gangzhang (1854–1928). The first practical Latinization of Chinese sounds was initiated in the 1930s by Qu Qiubai, Wu Yuzhang, Lin Boqu and Xiao San, with Soviet sinologist Alexandr Dragunnov as well as Guo Zhisheng, and aimed at raising the literacy of the 100,000 Chinese workers in the Soviet Far East. The chief propagator and person in direct charge of the post-1949 *pinyin* program was Wu Yuzhang (Huang Zubin 1978).

So why did a minor member of the Chinese elite become a public figure of interest for both the Chinese and Western media? Zhou became a public intellectual because of his neoliberal views and his outspoken criticism of not only the CCP but also Mao. In his 2012 interview with *Kaifang*, a tabloid magazine in Hong Kong, Zhou asserts that Lenin was a spy for Germany which provided Lenin with 50 million marks, that nobody in the West wants to study Marx because Marxism is of no value (Zhou was trained as an economist) and that Boris Yeltsin is to be admired because of his contribution to the collapse of the Soviet Union. Zhou also claims that Mao had no modern knowledge whatsoever, and that according to Hong Kongers, mainland China was lucky in that Mao died early and had no son to take over (Zhou Suzi 2012).

WESTERN MEDIA AND ACADEMICS

The media not only set the agenda so as to construct news for consumption (Lippmann 1922, Gans 1979, Zhang Guoliang et al. 2012), but also frame stories so as to promote certain conceptualizations of the world for consumption (Gitlin 1980, Pan and Kosicki 1993, Herman and Chomsky 1988). The story of Zhou Youguang is an example: the aim was to promote Zhou as a credible witness and commentator on the construction of contemporary China. Another example is the removal of crosses by the CCP authorities in Zhejiang mentioned earlier. When the forceful removal was taking place, it was headline news; but when the crosses were put back, the media was silent.

For the media it is not what happens that matters but whether what happens fits an agenda. By reporting the forceful removal of crosses the agenda and the general conceptual knowledge of the Communist suppression of religion was reproduced and reconsumed, while the complex reality of the situation was not of any concern. As a result the dynamics within society cannot be part of an understanding of China, and the CCP is understood as a monolith of suppression. So when certain dynamics finally bring change to the surface, what is seen as sudden change always takes China experts by surprise, whereas the understanding of China by the general public in the West is years if not decades behind.

Here is an example from personal experience. In 2009, I took a group of Australian high-school principals and academic leaders to China for a study tour. On the first day of the tour I took the group to the famous Shanghai Nanjing Road Mall for a walk. One of the group, an articulate teacher of slight left-wing persuasion, who even had some idea of Mao's concept of "mass line," looked around and behind. When I asked what he was looking for his answer took me back a little. He was trying to see whether the Chinese police were following him. After a couple of days in Shanghai, he commented that China was freer than Australia. I was equally taken back by his second comment, which was made after his observation that the supposed illegal street pedlars would run away when they saw the police approaching and then came back again when the police disappeared. This Australian friend of mine is not a "bogan" or "redneck," but a very articulate and informed educator. His understanding of China as a police state is as misperceived as his understanding of a China that is freer than Australia, even though a concession might be given that he was a little ironic in both remarks.

The average person in the West gets information about China from the media; and the media sets the agenda and frames stories about China in ways that are predetermined by geopolitics or by its conceptualization of China. Very often, though not all the time, Western academics collaborate with or support the media either due to geopolitical or conceptual conviction. In his questioning of the legitimacy of the Australia-China Relations Institute at the University of Technology Sydney, Leibold (2017) at La Trobe University, in a piece titled "The Australia-China Relations Institute Doesn't Belong at UTS" states that:

> Last month eight of Australia's top journalists visited China for a week as guests of the Australia-China Relations Institute (ACRI) at

the University of Technology Sydney (UTS). They were greeted by top Communist Party officials and toured some of China's new infrastructure projects. Some (but not all) returned to Australia singing the praises of Chinese President Xi Jinping's showcase "One Belt, One Road" (OBOR) initiative and the opportunities for Australian businesses.

The framed message is that the ACRI is pro-China and has connections with the Chinese authorities which brainwashed some journalists to say good things about China. What is left unsaid is that some of these journalists had not been to China for years and some for decades until this visit. Surely they would have something to say that could be different from what they had thought China would be after so many years of change.

At exactly the same time, Nick McKenzie and Chris Ulhmann (2017) claim that "Chinese Donations [to Australian political parties] could Compromise," and that "billionaires linked to Communist Party offered cash to our political parties but with strings attached." Never mind the fact that "the Chinese" referred to is an Australian citizen, Leibold's commentary is in coordination with an Australian media agenda that the Chinese CCP government ideology has infiltrated Australia, that Chinese suppression of dissidents reached beyond its border and that Chinese donations to political parties undermines Australian democracy, when the Australian ABC flagship program the *Four Corners* broadcast its "Power and Influence" along those lines.

Professorial Fellow at the University of Canberra, Michelle Grattan (2017), in a piece titled "Chinese Influence Compromises the Integrity of Our Politics," asks, "And why would former trade minister Andrew Robb not see a problem in walking straight from parliament into a highly lucrative position with a Chinese company?" Why indeed, when it is a "Chinese" company. Grattan further states that the Chinese company "Landbridge's acquisition of the Port of Darwin was highly controversial, despite being given the OK by the defence department." Grattan conveniently chooses to leave out the fact the purchase was also cleared by the Australian Security Intelligence Organisation. Why is this legal and security-cleared acquisition a worry for Grattan? Well, she admits, "the Americans are [certainly] angry."

To back up its claims that Chinese activities are "damaging Australia's political system," and "harm Australia's national security and political stability," the *Four Corners* broadcast on June 5, 2017 interviewed a CIA officer, Peter Jenkins, director of the pro-US Australian Strategic Institute, and Professor John Fitzgerald, a highly respected historian on China who, as acknowledged on the program, was the chief representative in Beijing for the Ford Foundation from 2008 to 2013, an American institution that is one of the most influential soft power organizations in the world. The *Four Corner* reporter, Nick McCkenzie, says "Back in his [referring to the businessman Chau Chak Wing who is an Australian citizen] homeland China, he was also a member of a communist party advisory group known as a people's political consultative conference or CPPCC." Professor Rory Medcalf claims that Chinese businessmen want "to demonstrate that they're being good members of the party."

It is true that any organization in China is under the control of the CCP, as China in reality is a party state. However, both of these statements miss the subtlety and the dynamics of the system. There is a stipulation that 60 percent of the membership of the People's Political Consultative Conference must be non-CCP members. There should not be any need to point out that not everyone in China is a member of the CCP, but there is a need to point out that the number of Christians in China are more than the number of the CCP members. The *Four Corners* program does not say whether these accused businessmen are actually members of the CCP. The irony is that while the Australian businessman is reported as "Chinese," Feng Chongyi at UTS, featured in the program for his being detained and interrogated by the Chinese authorities in China, is referred to as an "Australian professor" though Feng is apparently a member of the CCP and holds a Chinese passport. Of course Feng can be called an Australian professor since he works at an Australian university and has Australian resident status. The point is that by selecting some "facts" while leaving out other "facts" a story is purposefully framed for a specific conceptualization.

What matters is not what one does but who does it. Australians of Chinese ethnic origin are still Chinese whereas migrants from Israel, or of Jewish origin, or from Britain, Italy, Greece, Germany or the US, are not necessarily identified as such. Yes, the Chinese authorities want to counter what they understand as the Western dominance of what is right and what is wrong. But the Chinese are crude, high-handed and clumsy when they try to push their agenda and try to promote their "soft power." But the main issue is not that the Chinese may push too blatantly or too covertly, but that the Chinese have no legitimacy in doing this kind of thing at all, as they are on the wrong side of history. Above all, the conceptualization of the "Chinese" is that they are the Other no matter what. They were the Other racially or culturally in past centuries (Gao 2017), and they are now the Other politically. There is no moral ground for the "Chinese" to say anything positive about China.

Here lies the profound dilemma for the Chinese political and intellectual elite: a conundrum caught in-between national and transnational interests. They are defensive of the Chinese state because only the Chinese state can provide them with the basis of their very existence. On the other hand, they want to join global capital and be part of the transnational system. The West will accept them if they act as dissidents against the Chinese state. For the Western political and intellectual elite the dilemma is even more unsettling, even though there is no contradiction between their national and transnational interests. On the one hand, they would like their transnational companies to make profits out of the Chinese market, and even hope to incorporate the Chinese into their system. This is demonstrated by the fact that "More than 50 percent of Chinese exports are produced by foreign-funded factories. Foreign firms account for 70 percent of high-tech exports" (McGregor 2017). But on the other hand, they are afraid that the Chinese would outperform their transnational capitals because there is "now the real threat: Chinese techno-nationalism" (McGregor 2017). Their fear becomes more acute when they see that the Communist-run Other threatens the moral high ground of their conceptualization of the world because Chinese authoritarian capitalism is incompatible with the existing system (McGregor 2017).

Apart from the scaremongering Cold War rhetoric, the media does not seem to have the vision to see that in the long run it is all for the interest of the capital, which has only one color: profit. The Chinese capitalists, Communist or not, are part of global capital. How else can you explain the fact that firmly avowed anti-Communist conservative politicians, like those in the Australian Liberal Party, accept highly paid jobs in companies that have links with CCP, if it is true? The very existence of the Western political system is to serve the interest of capitalism, increasingly of a transnational nature; hence the politician-to-private-industry revolving doors, cushy appointments and influential positions for political buddies. Is the giant mining company BHP an Australian company for instance? The capitalists of Chinese origin are just trying to copy the practice of institutionalized and legitimized political bribery in the form of political donations and lobbying for their business interests.

A CRITIQUE OF THE LEFT IN THE WEST

Fredric Jameson, one of the most important figures of the Left in the West, states that Western political philosophy since 1968 has shifted from the politics of power to that of identity (Balunovi 2016). This is interesting because it is supposedly against identity politics, such as indigenous identity, minority identity, Black identity or gay/lesbian identity that many voters of the so-called marginalized classes revolted against the Western political and intellectual elite in the Brexit referendum and the recent US presidential election. To address the problem of working-class interest Jameson suggests a program for the Left in the West: full employment and minimum wages globally. Jameson admits that the greatest obstacle for such a counter-shift is that global capital is transnational. Therefore nationalism is not a solution because the problems are transnational. But at the same time Jameson thinks there is a need for a powerful state in time of economic crisis. This is the blind spot that Jameson fails to detect: national and transnational interests are very often one and the same for Western developed countries. How are you going to have full employment in the West when Western transnationals move their factories to countries like China where they can maximize their profit? Surely the very reason that Western transnationals move out of their own nation states is to avoid the costs derived from measures such as minimum wages to protect the living standards of the working class, which are higher than the middle class or even the elite in countries like China.

Jameson blames, rightly I think, the Western Left for not thinking beyond national borders and for being "even more provincial than the right" (Balunovi 2016). Jameson wishes that there would emerge a new media to counter what he considers the dominance of the Right, and also thinks that "The slogan of democracy is not something I am very comfortable with, mainly due to American foreign policy and this is why I don't think it is the best slogan for the left" (Balunovi 2016). Therefore he refers to Stuart Hall's concept of discursive struggle for the political Left. Again I think Jameson is right on the money.

But how do Western academics fight a discursive struggle when their very existence is in an environment in which their national interest is identical with their transnational interest? Jameson is desperately looking for an alternative, and thinks that "The left was exhausted from its previous experiments—Stalinism, defeats like those of Allende, the disappearance of the Soviet Union itself and the defection of the various social democratic parties by the momentary ('discursive') triumph of free-market rhetoric … [A] few years ago I would be talking about Venezuela or Brazil—I guess I can't do this anymore" (Balunovi 2016).

Perhaps without realizing it the fundamental problem with Jameson is that his imagining of the future is too centered on the West. He wants a global movement like minimum wages for workers all over the world as a solution to protect the interest of the working class in the West, but ignores the fact that third world countries can and have been developing their own models. When Jameson talks about the failure of the Left and the failure of the socialist state he doesn't even mention Mao or China. Hence the Left, like the Right in the West, continues to attack China for human rights abuses and for the absence of democracy, in complete harmony with US foreign policy.

As for the discursive struggle, attempts have been made, though not necessary by the political Left, to fight what is considered to be the epistemological hegemony of the American-dominated Anglophone academia that privileges the disciplines as the sources of universal theory (Jackson 2003). However, deconstructionist attempts representing a counter-current of thought in social science—aimed at problematizing the production of knowledge that privileges "the West" as the dominant legitimate source of knowing—gained very little ground in Chinese studies, in spite of progress made in fields such as anthropology, postcolonial studies and cultural studies, and in spite of "post-positivist" approaches such as critical theory, post-structuralism, thick description, the linguistic turn, the interpretive turn and the practice turn. As Dutton concludes, important as it is, the invocation of language is neither direct nor effective enough to challenge "the dominant positivist social science 'stories'" (Dutton, 2002: 502). In the words of Tani Barlow (1997: 1), "academic scholarship and popular knowledge about East Asia had remained almost unbearably static."

The main reason for this state of affairs is that unless one takes a class conflict stand, it is hard for a producer of knowledge to navigate the contradictory conceptualizations and practices that exist between national and transnational interests. The construction and consumption of knowledge about China are highly contingent on where a person is from culturally and politically. Australia, where I write from, is a good example. According to Garnaut (2015), former Australian Prime Minister Tony Abbott told the visiting German Chancellor Angela Merkel that Australia's China policy was motivated by both "fear" and "greed." According to a 2016 Lowy Institute Poll, 86 percent of Australians cite China's human rights record and 73 percent cite China's system of government as having a negative influence on their attitudes toward China (Oliver 2016: 4). But as pointed out by O'Neil, who cites William Blum (2006), since the end of World War II the US has attempted to overthrow more than 50 foreign governments, most of them democratically elected, dropped bombs on more than 30 countries, attempted to suppress a populist or nationalist movement in more than 20 countries and grossly interfered in democratic elections in more than 30 countries. There would be outrage in "the international community" if China did any one of these acts.

CONCLUSION

Production of knowledge of China does not tell "the truth, the whole truth and nothing but the truth" because that can never be the case. For instance, there is a myth propagated by both the Nationalists and the Communists in China, repeated even today (though in some cases because of ignorance), that Sun Yat-sen was a *boshi* (PhD) when actually he practiced as medical doctor in Hawaii. The propaganda regarding Sun plays on the English title "Dr." that conventionally refers to both a PhD degree and a medical professional. The purpose of the propaganda is to uphold the "truth" that as the Father of the Republic Sun must be seen as very knowledgeable, not just as a medical doctor.

Likewise there are "facts" that are consistently presented in the field of China studies in the West. One is that Deng said "to get rich is glorious," when actually it is a myth repeated many times without citation or reference by journalists and academics (MacFarquhar 2016, Webster 2015) that it is accepted as fact. The purpose of upholding this myth is twofold: to affirm the neoliberal conceptualization that greed is the motivation and only reason for China's development, and also to affirm the conceptualization of Orientalism in that the little man Deng was likable but nevertheless vulgar.

Another "fact" is that Li Zhisui was Mao's personal physician, whereas during the Mao era there was no such concept of "personal doctor," an idea that is very Western and still alien to the Chinese today. Dr. Li was one of the medical personnel, albeit a very qualified one, working in a clinic on the CCP and Chinese State leadership compound (Qi Benyu 2016). The purpose of propping up this truth is that what Dr. Li Zhisui says about Mao must be true since he was an insiders' insider whereas in fact the *Private Life of Chairman Mao* (Li Zhisui 1994) was doctored by his US mentors (Gao 2008). Still another "fact" is that Li Rui was Mao's secretary, whereas Li was actually just a part-time correspondent secretary for about a year. Li had no inside knowledge of elite politics except what happened at Lushan in August 1959, which was related to himself. In fact by April 1959 Li was already out of favor with Mao (Yang Shangkun 2001: 375).

All these "facts" are repeated in the West to serve some particular conceptual knowledge framework. The "to get rich is glorious" truth kills two birds with one philosophical stone: one economic rationalist bird is that personal greed is the reason behind the economic take-off in the post-Mao era, and that before greed was allowed to play its role Mao era China was poor and backward. The second bird is the Orientalist one, in that the Chinese are vulgar and all they want is money. The Li Zhisui and Li Rui truths both serve the conceptual framework that the Communist Revolution was a disaster facilitated by Mao, who was a vicious monster; and such conceptual knowledge is supported and validated by the testimonies of two trusted and articulated professionals who were very close to Mao, the so-called insider knowledge.

As discussed elsewhere in this book, Li Rui is one of those who popularized the Mao persona when he wrote a biography of the young Mao. In fact, Li Rui was the one, according to one recently revealed version of events, who confessed to Mao and got his colleagues into trouble during the fatal Lushan Conference in 1959. If Li Zhisui were really Mao's personal physician he betrayed his profession by writing a book detailing the private life of his patient. But once you accept the conceptualization that Mao was a monster and that the CCP was evil then not only there is no moral dilemma, but the fabrication of facts is morally justified.

For the political and intellectual elite in the West, national and transnational interest can and very often are one and the same. The dilemma for the Left in the West is: can they work against their own national interest? For their Chinese counterparts, the situation is equally frustrating. During the Mao era they were coerced or stunned into following the line of discourse that advocated that their national interest was often in contradiction with the dominant capitalist transnational interest. But the post-Mao mainstream Chinese political and intellectual elite has become increasingly transnational. However, because of Western dominance, Chinese national interest and transnational interest are not always one and the same either in imagination or in reality. Hence their split personality.

10

Geopolitics and National Interest I: China's Foreign Policy and Domestic Politics

President Trump's appointment as secretary of state, Rex Tillerson, paid his first visit to China only after he had consulted the US's closest Asian allies, Japan and South Korea. But that was not good enough for Washington's elite strategists. Denyer (2017) declares that "In China debut, Tillerson appears to hand Beijing a diplomatic victory." What did Tillerson do wrong? He accepted the Chinese formula of "mutual respect." Ely Ratner, who is the Maurice R. Greenberg senior fellow in China studies at the Council on Foreign Relations and used to work as deputy national security advisor to Vice President Joe Biden, took to Twitter to call it a "big mistake and missed opportunity" by Tillerson for parroting Chinese government "platitudes and propaganda" (Ratner 2017). To these defenders of American interests, China's characterization of the US–China relationship in terms of mutual respect portends US decline and accommodation, and Tillerson buys into this dangerous narrative, which not only encourages Chinese assertiveness but also raises doubts in the region about the future of US leadership in Asia. In other words, US dominance in Asia runs counter to the conceptualization of mutual respect in the Sino–US relationship. For Ratner, terms like "mutual respect" and "nonconfrontation" are code in Beijing for US accommodation of a Chinese sphere of influence in Asia, requiring that the US back off and respect China's demands over issues including Taiwan and Tibet.

On the other hand, Orlins (2017), president of the National Committee on US–China Relations since 2005, suggests that mutual respect is good for peace and prosperity, as shown by the Sino–US relationship cemented by the 1972 Shanghai Communiqué in which the

US acknowledged that "Chinese on both sides of the Taiwan Strait agree there is one China, that Taiwan is a part of China, and that the United States does not challenge that position." One example Orlins lists as a benefit is the evolution of Taiwan into a democracy, and the fact that investors like him have made huge amounts of money from both sides of the Taiwan Strait. Orlins admits that China won US respect by fighting the Soviet Union and fighting the US in Vietnam. Because of that China was already on the international stage. According to Orlins, China, but not other countries, was able to bargain with the US because it was already out of the capitalist system and the US could not control the Chinese elite. What Orlins fails to mention is that this was true only then but not now. Thanks to Deng Xiaoping China has got into the capitalist system again, and whether the US can control the Chinese elite, totally and thoroughly, today depends on the direction of the Xi Jinping leadership. The jury is still out.

Clearly, whether one conceptualizes international relations as coexistence, mutual respect and cooperation in areas of climate change and peace, or as a law of the jungle overwhelmed by the dominant powers who dictate the so-called "rule-based international community," predetermines one's constructing of China's foreign policies. If one's conceptualization is the latter then China cannot be but assertive and aggressive as a later developer from a weaker position when the "rule-based international community" was already established; whatever China does is breaking the status quo. This is well understood by some in the American elite:

> the United States, because we've been the preeminent power in the world since World War II, basically thinks you deter by showing your capability and making it clear to the opponent that they cannot prevail and that the cost of trying is going to be so high our opponents are going to decide it's not even worth going down that road. ... dominance is a key aspect of this. Now when the Chinese look at deterrence, they've usually been the weaker party; ... they think obscurity and non-transparency will deter us because we're not sure what China can do. ... the weak fear transparency, and the strong flout their power. (Navarro 2016)

This conceptualization of international relations is based on two major assumptions: (1) a nation state is like a person that acts rationally and

(2) there is no societal change within the nation state that may impact its international relations. But a nation state is not one person acting rationally. There are different interest groups pulling and pushing from all directions. Due to the internal dynamics in China the country is at least half in the global capitalist system, and much of its elite has a split personality of being Chinese and transnational at the same time. The Chinese political and intellectual elite is not one single personality but divided by representatives of different class interests. China's foreign policy is driven by the combined desire for and understanding of national interest and transnational interest. On the one hand, leaders of both the Mao era and post-Mao era wanted to preserve and defend what they considered to be the national interest. On the other hand, some of them work for but also in many ways are constrained by transnational interest.

AN OPEN OR CLOSED CHINA? CONSTRUCTING CHINA'S DOMESTIC AND FOREIGN POLICIES

The post-Mao era is nicknamed *gaige kaifang* (reform and open) by the Chinese political and intellectual elite. It is true that China has in many ways become a more open society, and many reform policies have been implemented. However, the term *gaige kaifang* is also a political construction. For instance, the dismantling of the collective farming system, a change that has resulted in household farming, is not really a policy of reform but of restoration (to a degree), reverting to a system that is 2,000 years old. While it is true that post-Mao China has been open to investment and business from outside the mainland and from transnational capitalists, China was not an entirely isolated entity in the Mao era. China under Mao participated in the Korean and Vietnam wars against the West, and supported anti-colonial and anti-imperialist nationalism in Africa, Asia and Latin America, in so-called Third World countries. By design, China did not "liberate" Hong Kong so that China could use it as a window on to the Western world of trade, business and technology. China held the annual Guangzhou Trade Fairs to do with business with those who could come and who were given permission from their own countries. And as mentioned previously, as soon as the US released its grip on China with Nixon's 1972 visit, Beijing started importing Western industrial technology.

The *gaige kaifang* construction of China usually fails to admit that there were restrictions on the outside world entering China. For instance, Beijing very much wanted the so-called overseas Chinese to visit China, but almost all the regimes in the East and South Asia regions forbade their citizens from traveling there. Even the fact that Zhou Enlai announced a policy of not recognizing dual citizenship so as to ease the anti-Communist fear did not improve the situation much. During the Cold War, the Western capitalism bloc placed very stringent financial, scientific, technological, economic and trade sanctions against China, like those against Cuba until recently. For the same reason, China was excluded from the international arena and was not even a member of the United Nations until 1971 when the US under Nixon and Kissinger decided to play the China card against the former Soviet Union.

There are two obvious points regarding the issue of when and how China has been open. One point is that in order to drive the narrative home that Maoist China was closed and remained a pariah state, the facts regarding how Beijing and Mao tried to open China are omitted in describing China's foreign policy. Such efforts include China's connection to a vast number of countries other than the developed West, Beijing's eventual success of getting into the United Nations and Mao's initiatives, like ping pong diplomacy, to get the US to open up to China. The other point is that evidence of China's not being open are selected and highlighted without the proper historical and transnational context. What is contained in these two points is an attempt to produce the kind of knowledge that narrates how wrong, how irrational or even how evil the Mao regime was. This line of production of knowledge is pursued for the purpose of anti-communism and of narrating not only how superior the West is but how Western superiority is the norm.

This chapter and Chapter 11, by focusing on China's foreign policies as they are manifested in China's border disputes, will attempt at demonstrating the two points mentioned above. This chapter will discuss China's land dispute with its neighbors, and is largely a review of the two most authoritative studies, one by Neville Maxwell (2014) and one by Eric Hyer (2015),* whereas Chapter 11 will discuss the issues surrounding China's maritime dispute on the SCS.

---

* Much of the information and discussion in the rest of this chapter appears in Mobo Gao "The Tree May Prefer Calm But the Wind Will Not Subside" *China Quarterly*, March 2018, volume 233, pp. 230–42.

CHINA'S LAND DISPUTES WITH ITS NEIGHBORS:
THE BURDEN OF HISTORY

During the August 2017 border conflict between India and China, Jerome Cohen and Peter Dutton observe (2017):

> For the past month, there has been a tense stand-off between China and India in the tri-border Himalayan region that includes Bhutan. Troubles began when China resumed building a road on the Doklam Plateau [called the Donglang region by the Chinese], which is disputed between Bhutan and China. India, because of its own security interests and as Bhutan's security guarantor, stepped in to defend the position of the kingdom. China now claims India has invaded "its" territory. Tensions are high, and more than a few commentators have suggested this may be the most serious Sino-Indian border crisis since their 1962 war.

An understanding of China's historical behavior in dealing with its neighbors in border settlements is an important way of understanding China's foreign policies. China is one of the few countries that has borders with so many countries—mostly small, but including two giant neighbors in India and Russia. To see how China has dealt with these small countries, as well as its larger neighbors, is helpful in assessing its behavior. Another important point is that as China is still a nation state in the making (see Chapter 2 for discussion of this issue), its foreign policies and international relationships are largely consumed by border issues. Finally, China, being labeled as a dictatorial Communist state, previously and again now (Ringen 2016b), has often been perceived as unpredictable and lacking transparency in its behavior. A review of China's approach to its land border disputes may surprise readers who hold such a view.

But first we need to review China's historical legacies, or the burden of history. No country's foreign policies can be discussed without referring to its history. For better or worse the burden of history for China is especially acute, not because of the fact that China has a very long recorded history but because of how the last Chinese dynasty, the Qing Dynasty, found itself in the world. In more than 2,000 years of history, as dynasties emerged and then disappeared, the territories of China became larger or smaller from time to time. However, the history of the Qing

Dynasty was different in two important ways: (1) it was so strong during its height that it created one of the largest territorial empire in China's history, and (2) when the dynasty came to its end China was carved up by Western imperialism and colonialism.

When Western influence arrived in China during the eighteenth and nineteenth centuries the Chinese not only had to take up the challenge of different cultures and technology but also different conceptualizations of existence, such as clear delimited boundaries of nation states. This legacy of history had left two related and interacting issues: (1) efforts to build up the Chinese nation state and (2) how to deal with the aftermath of colonialism. The conundrum of the Chinese nation state is not only derived from the fact that there were so many ethnic groups in what is called territorial China, but also from the fact that the last dynasty, the Qing Dynasty run by the Manchus, left a large but disintegrating territory. The issue of a huge land mass inherited from the Manchus, who were invaders from the north, is further complicated by the fact that Western colonialism had encroached on bits and pieces that were considered part of China, like Taiwan by the Japanese, Hong Kong by the British, large areas ceded to expansionist Russia and so on. This is what Hyer calls "a dual legacy of pre-nineteen-century regional hegemony followed by a colonial domination by the West" (2015: 22).

Many of China's border areas were not geographically delimited by accurate surveys or treaties, and in the words of Hyer, "The boundary disputes between China and its neighbours are one legacy of the age of imperialism: imposed boundaries that may ignore 'historical customary' divisions or boundaries that were never clearly delimited and often never demarcated" (2015: 34–5). In the case of Sino-Indian territorial disputes, for instance, from the Chinese point of view there is no reason why China should accept the so-called "McMahon Line" drawn up by British colonialists on behalf of India. So when the Chinese make a claim based on late Qing Dynasty territories, some of which were lost to colonialism, China is likely to be seen to be irredentist. However, the Chinese may ask: where should China draw a line of concession? Surely, no country would agree that whatever was taken is unrecoverable and that no questions should be asked. Even if one would be willing to do that, what was taken in many cases was not clearly delimited in the first place. The question remains: how is it possible to reconcile the consequences of the so-called "hundred years of humiliation" delivered by imperialism and colonialism with a geographical reality on the ground that was not clearly delimited to start with? This burden of history is the question on the minds of all those who have run the Chinese state since the end of the Qing Dynasty, Communist or not.

STRATEGICALLY DEFENSIVE BUT TACTICALLY CONCESSIONAL

The PRC, irrespective of who are in power, Mao or Deng for instance, acts strategically when it deals with its border disputes. For instance, the PRC left Hong Kong alone when it could literally have taken it over in 1949. Strategically it was good for China to let Britain run Hong Kong, as by doing so the PRC could more or less hijack a major Western country into being less hostile to the new government. At the same time it could use Hong Kong as a window to deal with the West in trade, information, intelligence and technology. But when the Chinese realized that it was not easy to settle the Taiwan issue, especially during the time of the US Reagan administration, Beijing started to prepare for the settlement of Hong Kong with the formula "one country two systems" as a model to solve the Taiwan issue.

In border disputes China is ready to compromise and has not been an aggressor, in contrast to the common perception and assumption that China is aggressive and a threatening Communist bully. The assumption, or axiom, that underlies Western political and strategic thinking about the problems of Asia is that the designs of Communist China are militant and aggressive. Sometimes this is summed up in the unexplained and unthinking phrase "the threat from China," for example in a leading article in *The Times* on June 18, 1970 (Maxwell 2014). Paul Hasluck, as pointed out by Maxwell, then Australia's minister for external affairs, said that "the fear of China is the dominant element in much that happens in Asia" (Maxwell 2014: 3–4). In 2015, former Australian Prime Minister Tony Abbott said that Australian attitudes toward China can be summed up in two words: fear and greed (Garnaut 2015). Nearly a half century after Hasluck the basic fear of China has not changed, even though China has never threatened Australia in any way. Why?

After examining the settlements of border disputes that China had with Russia, Korea, Burma, Nepal, Pakistan, Afghanistan, Mongolia, Laos and Vietnam, Maxwell concludes that "the PRC's record in dealing with the always delicate and potentially explosive issues of territorial ownership is good, and but for the blemish of its aggression against

Vietnam [1979] might be considered exemplary" (Maxwell 2014: 44). And as Maxwell points out, Deng Xiaoping's invasion of Vietnam was not about territorial dispute.

China has had territorial land disputes with 14 countries and has settled all of them, with the exception of India and India's semi-satellite Bhutan. The reason why China could not settle disputes with Bhutan is most likely because of India, as observed by Hyer: "We can safely assume that the basic reason it took so long to even initiate negotiations for a Sino-Bhutanese boundary treaty is India's domination of Bhutan's foreign affairs" (2015: 104–5). Hyer's conclusion is confirmed by what is unfolding in front of our eyes, as summed up by Cohen and Dutton in the quotation above. Maxwell goes even further by saying that the reason why the Sino-India border dispute remains unsettled is that the Indian government under Nehru was not only inflexible and rigid but also arrogant and deceitful, and that the 1962 war has made subsequent reconciliation emotionally difficult for India. For Maxwell, India simply refuses to negotiate with anyone.

China's strategy in dealing with territorial disputes has been consistent, a consistency even shared with the KMT government. While maintaining a Qing Dynasty China as an overall framework, China is willing to come to a compromised agreement on the basis of existing arrangements. The ROC led by Chiang Kai-shek agreed to Outer Mongolian independence, and the PRC under Mao did not try to reverse that. China did not try to claim back the territories ceded to Russia in the nineteenth century, and settled disputes not only with Russia but also with the states that came into existence after the collapse of the former Soviet Union. In fact China under Mao even agreed to negotiate with India on the basis of what is termed the McMahon Line. In order to maintain its overall security China is willing to give concessions in order to achieve an overall strategic goal. This is confirmed by Kissinger's assessment of China being a *weiqi* (or *go*) player (Kissinger 2014). Kissinger stresses that China does not engage in trickery and is willing to forego pettiness: "trickery sacrifices structure to temporary benefit. Reality is the cement of international order even among opponents: pettiness is the foe for permanence" (Kissinger 1979: 746–7).

The overall Chinese approach to border disputes with its neighbors is guided by the conceptualization of "seek what both sides have in common while leaving the differences aside." This non-belligerent approach has a deep Chinese philosophical source according to which long-term benefits should take priority over short-term gains. According to this historical conceptualization of human affairs, what is considered right and wrong, what one is passionate about and what makes one's emotions boil, are always time- and space-specific. What is considered as honor and integrity is also historical. Putting differences aside for future generations to solve is the best way to avoid wars.

Examples of Chinese compromise include: "The Chinese were much more conciliatory and flexible … China had given up its claims to larger areas while Burma had made only minor concessions to offset China's transfer of the Namwan Assigned Tract" (Maxwell 2014: 78). In another case, "Nepal gained about three hundred square miles and China received about fifty-six square miles of the disputed territory" (Hyer 2015: 89). In yet other cases, "The boundary settlement generally corresponded to Pakistan's initial claims" (2015: 112), and "China accepted almost all of the Mongolian claims," settling the boundary dispute in a way "highly favourable to Mongolia" (2015: 174).

China took the approach of shelving the dispute on Diaoyu/Senkaku Island to establish a diplomatic relationship with Japan, although beginning in 2010, Tokyo has claimed that the while Beijing was willing to sidestep the issue, "Japan never recognized the existence of an issue to be solved on the territorial sovereignty over the Senkaku Islands" (Hyer 2015: 183). Whatever might have been the case, sidestepping the issue made it possible to establish the normalization of diplomatic relations between China and Japan which has benefited not only the people of those two countries, but also the whole world. Equally, the normalization of relations between China and the US was a win-win for both countries and for the world, while the Taiwan issue was considered to be a small difference, as understood at that time before the democracy thesis was brought to play: it was a regional dispute and an internal Chinese one that could be left to the parties involved. The approach taken by Zhou Enlai/Mao and Kissinger/Nixon was to put their differences aside while seeking to reach a mutually beneficial goal.

Hyer states that "Beijing has been much more pragmatic in approaching territorial and boundary disputes than many had assumed" (2015: 7). By quoting (Fravel 2005), Hyer states that "In fact, China obtained less than 30 percent of the territory it claimed in the already concluded settlements, and is seeking only 24 percent of the disputed territory in its outstanding disputes with India and Bhutan" (Hyer 2015: 7). The Chinese agreed to the "claims and settlements [that] exclude the vast territories that Chinese believe were historically part of imperial China before being carved off by imperial powers, and Beijing has not insisted on the far-reaching historical claims it initially asserted" (Hyer 2015: 7–8).

The Chinese 1962 war with India was not Chinese aggression "bent on occupying more disputed territory but rather sought a boundary settlement and launched the invasion in a desperate attempt to force India back to the negotiating table" (Hyer 2015: 56). Though the Chinese always claim that all the treaties and agreements signed during what they call "the hundred years of humiliation" were unequal and therefore China would not in principle accept or be bound by them, this rhetoric of the moral high ground does not mean the Chinese would not bend on historical reality. Thus the Chinese waited until 1979, when the lease of 99 years of the New Territory expired to recover Hong Kong. By the same token, despite the Chinese claim that the territory ceded to Russia was taken by unequal treaties, they actually negotiated disputes based on the existing borders. It was "the Soviets [who] changed their position to argue that the 1689 treaty was unequal whereas subsequent treaties were equal" (2015: 133), because the 1689 treaty was in China's favor as the Qing Dynasty was strong then whereas subsequent treaties were signed when the Chinese state was weak. "Beijing insisted that it sought only Russian recognition of this historical fact in principle, and not any major readjustment of the current boundary. Moscow rejected this assertion and responded inflexibly" (2015: 138).

CONSTRUCTING CHINA'S FOREIGN POLICY IN THE WESTERN MEDIA

How the Western media constructs PRC foreign policies is best illustrated by its report of the Hong Kong handover. The last governor of Hong Kong, Chris Patten, pushed for the last-minute change of the status quo before the handover of Hong Kong to the PRC in 1997, and "the governor won the plaudits of the Western Press. The instinctive assumption, applied whenever the PRC comes into conflict with another government, that Beijing must be in the wrong, came into play" (Maxwell 2014: 272). This "two whateverism" instinct seems irresistible: whatever China does must be wrong and whatever the other side has in conflict with China must be right. In the case of Patten, as pointed out by Maxwell, there were influential media friends like Jonathan

Dimbleby to support him (Maxwell 2014: 272). The other factor that favored Patten is both the context of the Tiananmen event under the full scrutiny of the international media, which happened to be gathered in Beijing to cover the Gorbachev visit, and the context of the subsequent collapse of the former Soviet Union. Within these contexts "the international community" thought that a little push by the last governor in Hong Kong would lead to the death of the Communist regime in China.

HOW CHINA'S DOMESTIC POLITICS IMPACTS ON ITS FOREIGN POLICIES

While the Chinese government under different leadership has some consistency in strategically defending the territorial legacy of the Qing Dynasty, but is also willing to allow tactical concessions, there are differences in foreign policy decisions as the result of domestic politics. In the territorial dispute with Vietnam in the SCS, for instance, it needs to be pointed out that Vietnam, in its time of fighting with the US, with China's support, did not raise a territorial dispute with China. Equally, had Mao been alive, it would have been very unlikely that China would have invaded Vietnam in 1979.

China's invasion of Vietnam in the name of "teaching a lesson" is one of the landmarks of post-Mao China under Deng turning toward capitalism. In fact Deng could be interpreted as learning a lesson, immediately after his visit to the US, about catching up with US capitalism. When in the Mao era China's domestic politics was guided by the theory of class struggle, the disputes with Vietnam could be interpreted as internal contractions among the people. Once the theory of class was thrown out of the window, these kinds of disputes became contradictions between different nation states of different ethnic identities.

Regarding the Diaoyu/Senkaku Islands disputes, the continuity of different Chinese governments is amply demonstrated by the fact that both the PRC and the ROC in Taiwan claim the islands, and that the ROC "passed legislation in 1970 allowing oil exploration in waters surrounding Taiwan that include the Senkakus, and Chinese from Taiwan landed on the islands and planted the ROC flag" (Hyer 2015: 182). Since the 1990s, the rise of mainland Chinese nationalism matches Japan's "more muscular foreign policy" and China has a "more rigid policy towards the Senkaku Islands" (2015: 192). In other words, both Japanese and Chinese nationalism was on the rise. But why?

Japan's "more intransigent policy" (Hyer 2015: 192) was due to "the conservative turn in Japan" and the dispute was "a symbol of Japan's concern over a rising China." But what is the explanation of China's rise of popular nationalism (Gries 2004)? The standard explanation often offered in the media and many scholarly writings is that the Chinese power holders want to divert the Chinese people's discontent from domestic oppression to external targets so that the CCP maintains legitimacy in holding on to power. There is *prima facie* evidence, like TV programs demonizing the Japanese in the genre of narrating the Japanese invasion and occupation of China. While this explanation seems plausible, it may not be the only or even the most important reason. To attribute the massive production of anti-Japanese invasion TV to state-manipulated propaganda is outdated. China is a far more diverse and complex society now and the media is vastly commercialized (Zhao Yuezhi 2008, Xie Baohui 2014). Even with the increasing political pressure of censorship, the capitalist logic in the Chinese media market, as documented by Xie Baohui and Zhao Yuezhi, still works in China.

The bitter legacy of Japanese imperialism during World War II is still emotionally strong among the Chinese population in two related ways. One is that the Chinese don't feel they actually defeated Japan, but that the Americans and Russians did. The other is that the Chinese feel that although they suffered most from the Japanese invasion they did not get to punish the Japanese: they did not get any war compensation and do not even get a sincere formal apology. This sense of the Japanese going unpunished was accelerated by the Cold War. For the convenience of the Cold War the US not only preserved the Japanese emperor system but also let many war criminals go unpunished. The current Japanese Prime Minister Abe's grandfather was accused of being a war criminal. Eventually he was not only let off the hook but also became one of the post-war prime ministers. One can understand the depth of the emotion if one thinks of how the victims of the German Holocaust are being hunted down as evil doers even today, something that is supported without hesitation in the West.

But there is something else that is even more profoundly complex: Chinese domestic politics. As already discussed, during the entire period of the Mao era the philosophical guidance for Chinese politics was dominated by the theory and practice of class struggle as understood and implemented largely by Mao. Within this narrative, blame for the brutality and horror, including the Nanjing Massacre, can be firmly attributed to the capitalist imperial system. The Chinese could have a good relationship with the people of Japan, who were exploited and used by the ruling class. Once this conceptual paradigm is abandoned, ethnic identity is the target. Just as with Xinjiang and Tibet, once the state depoliticizes society any tensions and conflicts of interest are interpreted through the framework of ethnicity (Wang Hui 2006, 2011, 2014).

CONCLUSION

One overall conclusion that can be drawn from the above discussion is that China has not been aggressive in its foreign policies or irredentist in border disputes. In its land dispute with its neighbors China has exercised restraint and has been ready to make concessions so as to achieve strategic security.

However, this overall conclusion does not exclude variation in foreign policy as the result of domestic politics—politics not necessarily in terms of the elite fraction but in terms of a conceptual paradigm. I have argued, for instance, that the relationship between Japan and China worsened after the class category of Japanese people was replaced with the identity category of ethnicity, coinciding with the fear of the rise of China. Hyer's statement that "China's policy was only marginally affected, if at all, by domestic politics or elite factionalism" (2015: 265) is therefore partially true. China's way of dealing with its neighbors in border settlements may not have been affected much by elite politics, but domestic politics in ideological orientation does affect foreign policies and border issues. As another example, the issue of the border along the Amur and Ussuri rivers was put aside when China and the Soviet Union were ideological friends (Maxwell 2014), but flared up when China's domestic politics was most radical in the late 1960s.

Finally, China's foreign policy of strategic defense and tactical concessions should be understood against the background of how other powers treat China. Hyer would argue, for instance, that China's approach to shelve the Diaoyu/Senkaku Island disputes with Japan is based on its strategy of obtaining a secure international environment, and to seek Japan's assistance in capital and technology. This might well be the case. But we need to probe further: surely China would have wanted to have a better relationship with Japan sooner. But why 1971? If Japan was not willing, nothing would and could have happened, no matter how hard China tried. Japan was willing to come to the table because the

US changed its position with Kissinger's secret visit to China and the announcement of the Shanghai Communiqué.

In other words, how China acts toward the rest of the world also depends how the rest of the world acts toward China. According to the legendary documentary maker and journalist John Pilger (2016), "The Coming War with China" has been the design of the US for some years. Headlines like "It is High Time to Outmaneuver Beijing in the South China Sea" (Babbage 2016) and "Taiwan, Trump, and the Pacific Defense Grid: Towards Deterrence in Depth" (Timperlake and Laird 2016) appear here and there from time to time. "The tree may prefer calm but the wind will not subside." The US military-industrial complex has the ability to "summon the wind and call for rain" to change the course of history. As Michael McDevitt, senior fellow in strategic studies at the CNA Corporation, admits, the US has not only set the agenda of condemning China's actions in the SCS but also was "indirectly" responsible for "Manila's decision to go to the Permanent Court of Arbitration over Chinese claims and actions in the SCS" (McDevitt 2017).

Geopolitics and National Interest II: The South China Sea Disputes

INTRODUCTION

The rise of China on, or the return of China to, the international stage is a phenomenon of unprecedented significance that induces anxiety and even fear globally. In the words of one seasoned China specialist, the reality is that China, in a different way to any other country in the world, is the most alien to a world largely Westernized for hundreds of years, and thus its "threat" is bigger than that of Russia (part of European history since its birth) or Islam, also part of Mediterranean history since its birth. China exists on another dimension that was put off for years and now won't simply go away (Sisci 2016).

It is under such circumstances that a Chinese naval vessel shadowing the USNS *Bowditch* in the SCS recovered an oceanographic glider that had been launched by the US ship. The devices used by the US Navy were supposed to collect scientific data, such as salinity, temperature and current flow. The incident occurred about 70 nautical miles off Subic Bay, well within the exclusive economic zone (EEZ) of the Philippines. While the Chinese vessel's recovery of the drone was supposedly unlawful according to Bateman (2016), the legality of the research activities by the USNS *Bowditch* are also open to question. Marine scientific research in an EEZ is under the jurisdiction of the coastal state and should only be undertaken there with approval. It's unlikely that approval for this research was even sought from and given by the Philippines.

With the unexpected 2016 election victory of Donald Trump as the president of the US, the relationship between China and the US—arguably the most important international relationship in today's world—has been dragged into uncharted territory. With a president who not only has no experience in politics and diplomacy, but also seems extremely wayward regarding norms and precedence, 2017 onwards will likely be full of surprises, some of which might be nasty.

The PRC's rejection of the Hague Tribunal ruling in 2016 that China's claim of historical ownership of SCS waters within the dash lines is not valid, and that all the physical features above water within the area are not islands but rocks that are uninhabitable, is predictable. But why did the issue flare up in 2016? As Hyer (2015) makes clear, PRC claims over the SCS is not PRC expansionism or China becoming more aggressive when it has already become economically and militarily powerful. The Chinese Premier Zhou Enlai declared the sovereignty of the PRC over the SCS as far back as in August 1951, inheriting previous claims by the ROC. In fact the acceleration of tensions that led to the Hague ruling had much to do with international geopolitics in general and the US's "Pivot to Asia" in particular.

THE SOUTH CHINA SEA

China occupied Woody Island (Yongxing Dao) in the Paracel group after the evacuation of Nationalist troops in 1950. In 1974 Chinese forces occupied the remaining islands in the Parcel group held by the collapsing South Vietnamese. All these claims and enforcement of them were in fact inherited from the ROC: in 1935 the Nationalist government's China Map Verification Committee declared sovereignty over 132 islands, reefs and shoals in the SCS. In 1947 the committee published a map that included a U-shaped line (eleven dashed lines) encompassing the entire SCS. From the Chinese point of view, as Hyer quotes the Chinese position from a scholar Chen Jie: "Initially taking advantage of China's turbulent domestic policies and its preoccupation with superpower threats, regional countries have occupied China's islands and reefs, carved up its sea areas, and looted its marine recourses. Beijing does not view establishing a foothold in the South China Sea as constituting territorial gains but minimizing territorial losses" (Hyer 2015: 240).

As Hyer convincingly shows, the SCS has become a hot spot for dispute not only because of the potentially rich energy resources, but because of the anxiety caused by the rise of China. From the late 1940s to the late 1970s when the Cold War was hot, the influence of the US on the one side and the Soviet Union on the other had maintained a sort of equilibrium in the area. However, with the end of the Vietnam War, the retreat of the Americans and the Russians seems to have left an opportunity for Chinese dominance that many fear. According to

Hyer, in spite of the fact that the Chinese National Peoples' Congress promulgated a "Law of the People's Republic of China on the Territorial Sea and Contiguous Zone" in 1992, which asserted China's claims on Dongsha (the Pratas), Xisha (the Paracel), Zhongsha (the Macclesfield Bank) and Nansha (the Spratly) islands, "it is unlikely that Beijing will block a settlement if other parties are all willing to compromise or participate in a joint development agreement while putting off settlement of the sovereignty question" (Hyer 2015: 246), because "China's vigilance is not unlike the behavior of the other disputants, however, and does not necessarily foreshadow aggressive action to assert control over all of the South China Sea" (2015: 250). Writing before the 2016 Hague Arbitration Ruling, Hyer argues that the fact that, "Following Deng Xiaoping's decision to shelve the controversy and pursue cooperative development, China did not unilaterally pursue oil or other resource development in disputed areas of the South China Sea whereas other states did, especially Malaysia and Vietnam" (2015: 252), is encouraging and "the voice of pragmatism won out. China has not elevated the SCS to a 'core interest'" (2015: 255). Hyer seems in agreement with the veteran Fravel (2010) that as China has and will take a compromise position between history and reality, a middle way between "axiomatic" and "calculated" policies (May 1962), "if nothing occurs to threaten Beijing's security interests in the South China Sea, the status quo could continue indefinitely" (Hyer 2015: 259). But that is a big if.

WHAT IS THE BASIS FOR THE CHINESE CLAIMS?

As Figure 2 shows, there are extensive overlapping claims over the physical features within the dash line, and the overlapping becomes more intensive around Spratly Island. What is the basis for the Chinese claims when the chart clearly shows that Spratly Island is so far away from China? As Austin (2016) points out, to the Chinese both Spratly and Parcel islands are Chinese territory that were stolen by Japan in a long and brutal war just months before Japan invaded Hainan Island in 1939. This core belief has nothing to do with the discovery of offshore oil, or even a conceptualization of "maritime expansion, second island chain, 'one belt one road,' or revision of world order, including law of the sea" (Austin 2016).

The Chinese point out that the Philippines' claim to some of the Spratly Islands only arose between the mid to late 1970s when it enjoyed

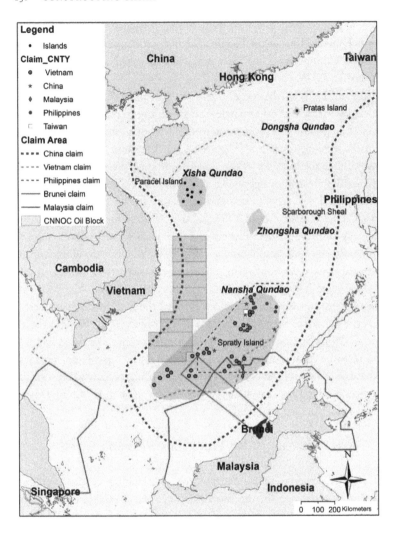

Figure 2 Conflicting claims of the SCS

a strong military alliance with the US and when China was busy with its domestic politics. The Chinese believe their recent reclamations of and fortifications of the reefs they have occupied since the 1980s are the least they can do to protect their claims without resorting to evicting the Philippines by military force from the islands it has occupied. From the Chinese perspective they are exercising restraint. It is the US and its allies who want to escalate tension in the area. The US-Philippines joint military exercise, with the participation of Australian forces, in addition to two Japanese warships and a submarine that happened to be visiting the Philippines in a goodwill tour at the time, is, to the Chinese, provocative and a push for militarization.

For other observers, "China's claims, it seems, are as valid—if not more so—than many of the other claimant states" (Blaxland 2016). In fact the Hague 2016 ruling has put the Taiwan authorities into a very difficult position, especially for the political fraction that pushes for Taiwanese independence. Under the Treaty of Peace, signed between Japan and the ROC on April 28, 1952, the Spratly and Parcel islands have been returned to the ROC, and by extension China is the rightful owner, whichever China it might be, since the US, Japan, Australia and all ten countries in the Association of Southeast Asian Nations abide by the one China policy: that Taiwan is a part of China. If Taiwan cuts itself off from China—not just from the ROC, but from even China in the abstract—it weakens its claim over the sovereignty of the SCS, a position that is hard to see as legitimate by the citizens of a nation state. Under such circumstances China is still willing to negotiate with each claimant in a peaceful manner. Michael Pascoe (2016) rightly asks this question: "Which came first: (a) the US 'pivot to Asia' (AKA 'encircling China') or (b) China increasing its forward defense stance in the South China Sea by building artificial islands?" The answer, according to Pascoe, is (a).

What seems to be ironic is that China's claim of not wanting to militarize the area was used by the Hague Tribunal to deny China's claim over sovereignty. Because China had repeatedly emphasized the non-military nature of its actions and had stated at the highest level that it would not militarize its presence in the Spratlys, China's activities are deemed not to be military in nature. Accordingly, the tribunal concluded that Article 298 did not pose an obstacle to its jurisdiction of denying China's sovereignty.

According to Article 298(b), disputes concerning military activities, including military activities by government vessels and aircraft engaged in non-commercial service, should be excluded from the jurisdiction of a court or tribunal under Article 297, paragraph 2 or 3. In other words, had China used military forces in the area the tribunal would not have the right to make a ruling.

THE VIETNAMESE CLAIMS

When, on September 4, 1958 the Chinese Premier Zhou Enlai declared that China's decision regarding the 12 nautical miles of China's territorial waters included the two archipelagos Paracel and Spratly, on September 14, 1958 Pham Van Dong representing the Democratic Republic of Vietnam (North Vietnam) sent a Diplomatic Note to China stating that:

> We would like to inform you that the Government of the Democratic Republic of Vietnam has noted and support the September 4, 1958 declaration by the People's Republic of China regarding territorial waters of China. The government of the Democratic Republic of Vietnam respects this decision and will direct the proper government agencies to respect absolutely the 12 nautical mile territorial waters of China in all dealings with the People's Republic of China on the sea (Vietnamnet 2011).

Vietnam later tried to vitiate its actions by arguing that the diplomatic note was sent under complicated circumstances of war against Western colonialism and because North Vietnam then was supporting its "comrades" (Vietnamnet 2011). "Hanoi seems, at this time [1956], to have supported the claim of the Chinese People's Republic" (Tønneson 2006: 52–3).

THE PHILIPPINE CLAIMS

A reader's response to Hugh White (2016) points out the problems with the claims by the Philippines:

> Professor White's assertion that allegedly "China seized Scarborough Shoals, which lie quite close to Manila, from the Philippines in 2012" is seriously flawed and thus has no merit. If he cares to revisit the 1898 Treaty of Paris, the 1900 Treaty of Washington and the 1930 Convention between the United States and Great Britain, he will discover that they described the western limit of the Philippine territory as 118 degrees East longitude. But as the map shows, China's islands and reefs in the Spratly, Paracel, Pratas, Zhongsha, which include the Macclesfield bank and Huangyan Dao (Scarborough shoal) are all due West of that 118 degrees East longitude. It was the corrupt President Ferdinand Marcos who annexed 8 features in the Spratly on 11 June 1978, using Presidential Decree 1596, under the pretext they were terra nullius, which had no basis under any law.

THE INTERNATIONAL ORDER AND THE SCS

The website Quora published a map with US military bases surrounding China and then asks a question: "Why is China Building Islands So Close to US Military Bases?" There are answers from the US, India and China. Some of the respondents are not sure whether the question is a satire. One reader asks "Are you kidding to ask this question?" and one simply states "What a stupid question!" One respondent wants to know what is meant by "close." One points out a fact that it is quite astonishing to reflect on: since the US has military bases everywhere in the world, anywhere is close to its military bases. One Indian respondent ponders why Australians want to live close to US military bases in Australia. "If you really want to know the answer, the Chinese want to grow vegetables on these artificial islands," one says. Finally someone has a map with all the US military bases in Europe and Asia, with Russia at the top of the map, and the words "Russia wants war!" and "Look how close they put their country to our bases."

To the Chinese, the whole episode of the Hague Permanent Court of Arbitration (PCA) ruling on the SCS was the result of a US-designed and US-sponsored scheme to "pivot Asia," targeting the rising China, as Figure 3 demonstrates. Inexperienced in how to play the game, the rules of which have been set by Western powers, China did not want to participate in the process of the PCA in the first place: a mistake on China's part according to some experts.

That the US is somehow behind the PCA is admitted by Michael McDevitt, senior fellow in strategic studies at the CNA Corporation, for instance, who states that the US has not only set the agenda of condemning China's actions in the SCS but was also "indirectly" responsible for "Manila's decision to go to the Permanent Court of Arbitration over Chinese claims and actions in the SCS" (McDevitt 2017), though he does not specify what "indirectly" means.

In the words of Saches (2017), today's China offers a rude awakening for Americans who believe that the US and the US alone should dominate the world. Each time the US has had a rival for global leadership, they have aimed to eliminate rivalry and to subordinate the rival to US power. The first example was with the former Soviet Union: pushing NATO eastwards toward Russian borders by incorporating the Eastern European and Baltic countries into the US-led military alliance, and then incorporating Ukraine and Georgia as well. The second

Figure 3 "The Truth Behind Philippine's Stance Over South China Sea Disputes," People's Daily, China @ PDChina

example was its wars to overthrow, or try to overthrow, several hostile governments in the Middle East, including Afghanistan, Iraq, Libya and Syria.

Starting with President Ronald Reagan, the US foreign policy establishment went to work to counter Japan. It began accusing Japan of unfair trade practices, currency manipulation, unfair state aid to Japan's businesses and other exaggerated or flat-out false claims of nefarious behavior. The US began to impose new trade barriers and forced Japan to agree to "voluntary" export restraints to limit its booming exports to the US. Then, in 1985, the US struck harder, insisting that Japan massively revalue (strengthen) the yen in a manner that would leave Japan far less competitive with the US. The yen doubled in strength, from 260 yen per dollar in 1985 to 130 yen per dollar in 1990. Japan had been pushed by the US to price itself out of the world market. By the early 1990s, Japan's export growth collapsed and Japan entered two decades of stagnation. On many occasions after 1990, Saches (2017) asked senior Japanese officials why Japan didn't devalue the yen to restart growth. The most convincing answer was that the US wouldn't let Japan do it.

Now comes China. American primacists are beside themselves that China seems to have the audacity to poke its nose into "the American century." Rather than let China catch up, the primacists say, the US should badger and harass China economically, engage the Chinese in a new arms race and even undermine the one China policy that has been the basis of US–China bilateral relations, so that China ends up in economic retreat, retracing the steps of the British Empire, the Soviet Union and Japan (Saches 2017).

Regarding the SCS dispute, Sourabh Gupta (2017a, 2017b) thinks the Hague ruling was "harsh" and "reckless" in its total condemnation of China, and that China has a case regarding its historical rights to the SCS islands (Gupta 2016). Gupta also argues that it is within China's rights to construct artificial islands on the high-tide features that it administers in the SCS, as well as on those submerged features that lie within the territorial sea of a high-tide feature that it administers or claims. Such construction is not an "illegal taking of disputed international territories"—much less a violation of the undisputed territorial sovereignty of a neighboring state "akin to Russia's taking [of] Crimea" (Gupta 2015).

A BRIEF HISTORICAL REVIEW

Like the land disputes that China had with its neighbors until the Western concept of the nation state was imposed by Western colonialism, China had no clear boundary claims over the SCS islands. Even until "the 1930s the dispute over the Spratlys and Paracels had been mainly a Franco-Japanese affair, with a weak and war torn China as the third party. From 1945 to 1956 the main dispute had been between France on the one side and the two Chinese regimes on the other" (Tønneson, 2006: 48).

After the surrender of the Japanese to the allies at the end of World War II in 1946, the ROC soldiers led by Chiang Kai-shek, aided by US warships, traveled all over the SCS. They not only recorded all the islands/rocks with a Chinese name but were garrisoned on Taiping, the only island that is habitable. That was when the eleven-dash line was drawn with the assistance of the US Navy. When the eleven-dash line claim was made and printed in an ROC map in 1947 there were only two nation states in the region, the ROC and the Philippines—and the rest were still colonies of Western powers. As Tan (2016) points out, none of the colonial powers like Spain, the US, Britain, Holland or France disputed China's sovereignty over the Pratas, Paracel and Spratly islands, or the Macclesfield Bank and Scarborough Shoal (Huangyan Dao) territories. In the 1887 Sino-Franco Convention, France agreed that all the isles east of the treaty delimitation line were assigned to China. In the 1898 Treaty of Paris, signed when Spain handed the Philippines as a colony to the US, Article III described the western limit of the Philippines as 118 degrees east longitude. China's claims are all located west of that point. The Philippines wanted to annex the Spratlys in 1933. On 20 August that year, US Secretary of State Cordell Hull wrote that the islands of the Philippine group which the US acquired from Spain by the treaty of 1898, were only those within the limits described in Article III (Tian Shaohui 2016), and it may be observed that no mention has been found of Spain having exercised sovereignty over, or having laid claim to, any of these (Spratly) islands.

Note that the claim over the SCS by the PRC not only overlaps that made by the ROC, but is also narrower with a nine-dash line. Under such historically complex circumstances it is understandable that no matter how much the US wants to, it is hard for it to make a stand against China over the control of territory, or sovereignty over islets and rocks that generate rights over adjacent seas and sea beds. Instead, the US, its allies and the "international community" constantly tout the approach that the PRC's claims and its assertive activities, such as creating artificial islands by digging and piling up sand, threatens freedom of navigation. But as pointed out by Freeman (2016), given the kind of commercial shipping in the SCS freedom of navigation has never been threatened or compromised there. In fact, China is the country that wants to maintain freedom of navigation most as it is the main sea route for ships to leave China.

In fact China is not the first nor the only country that has been creating land by dredging sand in disputed area; Vietnam was creating artificial islands for years before China started and already has forces stationed on some of the islands it claims, but that are also claimed by both China and the Philippines. China is just catching up. Japan interfered with Taiwanese fishing in what Japan claims to be its EEZ, supposedly generated by its possession of Okinotorishima, originally a pair of mushroom-shaped rocks, of king-size bed dimensions, sticking a few meters above the water at high tide. But Japan has built an

8,000 square meter platform on top of them to claim 400,000 square kilometers of EEZ—impressive engineering that didn't make the front pages in the Western media (Clemens Stubbe Østergaard 2016, personal communication).

As the insider China observer Sydney Rittenberg (2016, personal communication) points out, China is not making new claims but enforcing claims that have long been in existence. Rittenberg argues that the Hague ruling on China's sovereignty claims is not a legally binding document, but an opinion. Reading statements from US "Secretary Ash Carter and Admiral Harry Harris ... what really sticks in their craw is the diminishing, and probable loss, of US dominance in that part of the Pacific, not issues of sovereignty" (Rittenberg 2016, personal communication). It is the US that has stoked tensions by giving other nations around China the backing they need to aggressively pursue territorial interests. It is the US that has maintained military bases and assets with nuclear strike capacity within range of Chinese civilian centers. It is the US that has initiated a "pivot to Asia" whereby 60 percent of US naval and aerial units will be positioned in the Asia Pacific theater by the end of the decade.

This kind of double standard by the "international community" can only be understood in terms of the geopolitics of US dominance in Asia and the Western dominance of the world. Underlying this geopolitics of Western dominance is the fear of China, whether it's the "yellow peril" fear of China during the second half of the nineteenth and first half of the twentieth century when there was a White Australian policy (Gao 2017), or exclusion of the Chinese in the US and Canada, or the "red under the bed" during the second half of the twentieth century, or the rise of China during the twenty-first century. The fear has always been there when China has been seen as different, whether the difference is conceptualized racially, culturally or politically, and the fear has been there even when China is seen to become the same.

But is the fear justified? As evidence from the rigorous research by Maxwell (2014) and Hyer (2015) discussed in Chapter 10 demonstrates, China has always been ready to make tactical concessions. This is confirmed and clearly stated by Chas W. Freeman, Jr. (2017), a former US ambassador to China, in his comment on current situation:

> China waited a decade to respond to multiple seizures of disputed islands and reefs in the South China Sea by other claimants. The

Philippines began the process of creating facts in the sea in 1978, Vietnam followed in 1982, and Malaysia did the same in 1983. In 1988, China intervened to halt the further expansion of Vietnamese holdings. Since then China has established an unejectable presence of its own on seven artificially enlarged land features in the South China Sea. It has not attempted to dislodge other claimants from any of the four dozen outposts they have planted in Chinese-claimed territories. China has been careful not to provoke military confrontations with them or with the U.S. Navy, despite the latter's swaggering assertiveness. A similar pattern of restraint has been evident in the Senkaku Islands (钓鱼岛), which China considers to be part of Taiwan and Japan asserts are part of Okinawa. There, China seeks to present an active challenge to Japanese efforts to foreclose discussion of the two sides' dispute over sovereignty. It has done so with lightly armed Coast Guard vessels rather than with the PLA's naval warfare arm. Japan has been equally cautious. China negotiated the reunification of both Hong Kong and Macau, although it could have used force, as India did in Goa, to achieve reintegration. China has negotiated generous settlements and demarcations of its land borders with Afghanistan, Kazakhstan, Kyrgyzstan, Nepal, Pakistan, Russia, Tajikistan, and Vietnam. China's borders with the former British empire in Bhutan, India, and Myanmar remain formally unsettled but for the most part peaceful.

THE HAGUE RULING AND TAIWAN'S CONUNDRUM

Regarding the 2016 Hague Ruling, Wang Jiangyu argues that "While the Tribunal's own legitimacy seems to be unquestionable, whether it had jurisdiction over the dispute is debatable. Most likely it has, but China's certain arguments against the jurisdiction are worthy of discussion. However, the final award's interpretation and application of certain provisions of UNCLOS [United Nations Convention on the Law of the Sea] are problematic and possibly erroneous" (Wang Jiangyu 2017: 185).

It is important to point out the sovereignty exception to the compulsory dispute settlement of UNCLOS. That is, it is widely agreed that the convention does not govern sovereignty-related issues. Accordingly, the questions of sovereignty and related rights over land territory are outside the subject matter of an UNCLOS court or tribunal (Wang Jiangyu 2017: 190).

China's claim over the SCS is indicated by its declared nine-dash line on its map. But officially, China has never made it clear what it wants by maintaining the nine-dash line. There are three possible interpretations of China's nine-dash line claim: (1) the nine-dash line aims only to indicate the lands over which China claims sovereignty, (2) the nine-dash line is intended to be a national boundary between China and its neighbors and (3) the nine-dash line is intended to indicate China's historic claim. While China keeps a strategic "ambiguity" without official clarification, "It can then be reasonably concluded that the nine-dash line represents China's claims over all the lands within the line, plus historic rights within the nine-dash line—under Article 14 of its 1998 law on the EEZ and the continental shelf—in respect of fishing, navigation, and exploration and exploitation of resources" (Wang Jiangyu 2017: 203).

From the point of view of Taiwan, the Hague ruling on the ROC's (Taiwan's) Taiping Island as a "rock" very "unfortunately" damages the whole ruling and puts Taiwan in a very difficult position: China's SCS claims are primarily derived from the ROC's assertions over the years. As Freeman (2015) narrates:

In 1945, in accordance with the Cairo and Potsdam Declarations and with American help, the armed forces of the ROC government at Nanjing accepted the surrender of the Japanese garrisons in Taiwan, including the Paracel and Spratly Islands. Nanjing then declared both archipelagos to be part of Guangdong Province. In 1946 it established garrisons on both Woody (Yongxing) Island in the Paracels and Taiping Island in the Spratlys.

As one reader's response to Freeman says:

In practice, as some in the region recall, long before the United States turned against them as part of its "pivot to Asia" in 2010, America had supported China's claims in the Paracels and Spratlys. The U.S. Navy facilitated China's replacement of Japan's military presence in both island groups in 1945 because it considered that they were either part of Taiwan, as Japan had declared, or—in the words of the Cairo Declaration—among other "territories Japan [had] stolen from the Chinese" to "be restored to the Republic of China." From 1969 to 1971, the United States operated a radar station in the Spratlys at Taiping Island, under the flag of the Republic of China.

Clearly Taiwan's adherence to its SCS claims strengthens China's legal position. Even worse for the Taiwan independence advocates, Taiwan's claim over the SCS islands, just like its claim over the Diaoyu/Senkaku islands, reinforces the one China narrative. In other words, Taiwan's claims over these islands weakens its position of separate sovereignty. This is a huge conundrum for Taiwan's aspiration of independence: Taiwan cannot afford to abandon its long-held claim over these islands because the very legitimacy of a sovereignty is to protect its territory. That is why the independence-advocating Democratic Progressive Party government under Tsai Yin-wen had to defend its sovereignty over the islands it occupies by rejecting the UNCLOS ruling. But by doing so it places itself firmly into the one China framework.

CONCLUSION: THE POLITICALLY CORRECT CONSTRUCTING OF CHINA OVER THE SOUTH CHINA SEA ISSUE

By citing evidence from think tanks like the Asia Maritime Transparency Initiative at the Centre for Strategic and International Studies and Australia's Lowy Institute, and media outlets such as *Fox News*, *Breitbart* and the *Washington Times*, Valencia (2017) points out that Western think tanks tend to exaggerate the China threat in order to get the Trump administration to construct a China that presents an imminent risk to US national interests. According to Valencia, "academic analysts themselves push US-slanted research," and the figure of more than US$5 trillion in trade that transits the SCS is cited as evidence of China's claim over the SCS threatening international trade while not to pointing out that most of the trade goes to China. Valencia is right in observing that the Western media follow the US's clever conflation of freedom of commercial navigation with the freedom to undertake provocative military intelligence, surveillance and reconnaissance activities. The media constructing of China over the issue of SCS is not just (mis)constructing, as Valencia titles his paper. In fact this is a consistent practice in the politically correct construction of China on the basis of geopolitics and from the point of view of the perceived Western national interest. As also pointed out by Valencia, the Western media uses legal ambiguities to evade a regime governed by scientific consent while choosing not to point out the fact that the ocean is for peaceful purposes as required by UNCLOS, and that intrusive and controversial practices threatening the use of force is prohibited by the UN charter. But to justify aggressiveness against China one has to construct an aggressive China.

Bibliography

Allan, Sarah (2015), *Buried Ideas: Legends of Abdication and Ideal Government in Early Chinese Bamboo-Slip Manuscripts*, New York: State University of New York Press.

AFP (2016), "The 'Panama Papers' Law Firm Has More Offices in China Than in Any Other Country," www.businessinsider.com/panama-law-firm-lots-of-china-offices-2016-4?IR=T, accessed April 7, 2016.

Ali, Tariq (2010), "The Nobel War Prize," *London Review of Books*, December 11, www.lrb.co.uk/blog/2010/12/11/tariq-ali/the-nobel-war-prize/, accessed February 4, 2011.

Amin, Samir (1994), *Re-Reading the Postwar Period: An Intellectual Itinerary*, Translated by Michael Wolfers. New York: Monthly Review Press, 1994.

Amin, Samir (2013), "The Implosion of Global Capitalism the Challenge for the Radical Left," ebookbrowse.com/the-implosion-of-global-capitalism-the-challenge-for-the-radical-left-samir-amin-pdf-d323242072, accessed January 14, 2013.

Anand, D. (2009), "Strategic Hypocrisy: the British Imperial Scripting of Tibet's Geopolitical Identity," *The Journal of Asian Studies*, 68 (1), pp. 227–52.

Anderson, Benedict (1991), *Imagined Communities: Reflection on the Origins and Spread of Nationalism*, London: Verso.

Andreas, Joel (2009), *The Rise of the Red Engineers: The Cultural Revolution and the Origins of China's New Class*, Stanford, CA: Stanford University Press.

Ang, Ien (2001), *On Not Speaking Chinese: Living Between Asia and the West*, London and New York: Routledge.

Aron, Leonard (2017), "Review of Frank Dikötter, *Mao's Great Famine*," *Logos: A Journal of Modern Society & Culture*, http://logosjournal.com/2011/fall_leonard/, accessed September 14, 2017.

Associated Press (2017), "Chinese Linguist Zhou Youguang Dies at 111," www.wsj.com/articles/chinese-linguist-zhou-youguang-dies-at-111-1484409638, accessed September 14, 2017.

Attrill, Nathan (2016), "China's Leadership Model Goes Back to the Future," www.eastasiaforum.org/2016/04/20/chinas-leadership-model-goes-back-to-the-future/, accessed February 28, 2018.

Austin Greg (2016), "Avoiding Groupthink on China: What we Know and Don't Know About China's Foreign and Military Policies," *The Diplomat*, http://thediplomat.com/2016/10/avoiding-groupthink-on-china/, accessed July 27, 2017.

Ba Jin (1991), 随想录 (Random Thoughts), Beijing: Sanlian Chubanshe.

Babbage, Ross (2016), "It is High Time to Outmaneuver Beijing in the South China Sea," *War on the Rocks*, https://tinyurl.com/yabxlfo6, accessed December 30, 2016.

Bachman, David M. (1991), *Bureaucracy, Economy, and Leadership in China: The Institutional Origins of the Great Leap Forward*, Cambridge and New York: Cambridge University Press.

Balunovic, Filip (2016), "Fredric Jameson: People Are Saying 'This is a New Fascism' and My Answer is – Not Yet!" www.criticatac.ro/lefteast/fredric-jameson-fascism-not-yet-there/ accessed June 7, 2017.

Bannister, Judith (1987), *China's Changing Population*, Stanford, CA: Stanford University Press.

Barlow, Tani (1997), "On Colonial Modernity," in *Formation of Colonial Identity in East Asia*, Durham, NC and London: Duke University Press, pp. 1–20.

Barnouin, Barbara and Yu Changgen (2006), *Zhou Enlai: A Political Life*, Hong Kong: The Chinese University of Hong Kong Press.

Bateman, Sam (2016), "South China Sea Dramas Distract from Bigger Problems," https://tinyurl.com/y8old2wj, accessed January 2, 2017.

Baum, R. and A. Shevchenko (1999), "The State of the State," in R. Macfarquhar and M. Goldman eds., *The Paradox of China's Post-Mao Reforms*, Harvard, MA: Harvard University Press, pp. 333–60.

Beijing Youth (2013), http://finance.sina.com.cn/china/20131031/031017172171.shtml, accessed April 6, 2016.

Bell, Daniel (2015), *The China Model: Political Meritocracy and the Limits of Democracy*, Princeton, NJ: Princeton University Press.

Bell, Matthew (2013), "The Manchus Ruled China into the 20th Century, But their Language is Nearly Extinct," *PRI's the World* www.pri.org/stories/2013–12–03/manchus-ruled-china-20th-century-their-language-almost-extinct, accessed January 15, 2017.

Benton Gregory and Lin Chun, eds. (2009), *Was Mao Really a Monster?* London: Routledge.

Bian Qin (2016), "'伤痕文学' 话语框架竟是美国策划的" (The American Designed Literature of the Wounded), 海疆在线, http://bbs.tianya.cn/post-333-854210-1.shtml, accessed September 14, 2017.

Birney, Mayling (2014), "Decentralisation and Veiled Corruption under China's 'Rule of Mandates'," *World Development*, 53, pp. 55–67.

Blainey, Geoffrey (1963), *The Rush that Never Ended*, Melbourne: Melbourne University Press.

Blaxland, John (2016), "Ideas for Australia: Australia Boosts Defences, But Must Pick Its Fights Carefully in a Time of Tensions and Uncertainties," *The Conversation*, April 22, 2016, http://theconversation.com/ideas-for-australia-australia-boosts-defences-but-must-pick-its-fights-carefully-in-a-time-of-tensions-and-uncertainties-56123, accessed September 14, 2017.

Blum, William (2006), *Rogue State: A Guide to the World's Only Superpower*, London: Zed Books.

Bo Yibo (1949), "关于一九五〇年度全国财政收支概算草案的报告" (Report on the 1950 Year Budget), www.zg1929.com/baike/index.php?doc-view-1672.

Bourdieu, P. (1986), "The forms of capital," in J. Richardson (ed.), *Handbook of Theory and Research for the Sociology of Education*, New York: Greenwood, pp. 241–58.

Boxwell, Robert (2016), "By Making Too Many Concessions to China, the West Has Given 'Wings to a Tiger'," *South China Morning Post*, April 5, 2016, www.scmp.com/comment/insight-opinion/article/1933643/making-too-many-concessions-china-west-has-given-wings-tiger, accessed June 4, 2017.

Bramall, Chris (1993), *In Praise of Maoist Economic Planning: Living Standards and Economic Development in Sichuan since 1931*, Oxford: Clarendon Press.

Brown, Kerry (2016), *CEO, China: The Rise of Xi Jinping*, London and New York: I.B.Tauris.

Buckley, Chris (2017), "China's Foreign Minister Castigates Canadian Reporter for Rights Question" *New York Times*, www.nytimes.com/2016/06/03/world/asia/canada-china-wang-yi.html?_r=0, accessed September 14, 2017.

Bulag, Uradyn (2002), *The Mongols at China's Edge: History and the Politics of National Unit*, New York: Rowman and Littlefield.

Byron John and Robert Pack (1992), *The Claws of the Dragon: Kang Sheng—the Evil Genius Behind Mao—and His Legacy of Terror in People's China*, New York: Simon & Schuster.

Callahan, William (2004), *Contingent States: Greater China and Transnational Relations*, Minneapolis: University of Minnesota Press.

Callahan, William (2005), "Nationalism, Civilization and Transnational Relations: The Discourse of Greater China," *Journal of Contemporary China*, 14 (43), pp. 269–89.

Cang Ming (2017), "新中国的民族识别的背景"(Background of the Nationality Identification in the New China), lecture power points, personal communication.

Cao Shuji (2005), "1959~1961年中国的人口死亡及其成因" (Mortality of China's Population and Its Causes from 1959 to 1961), 中国人口科学 (Chinese Demographic Science), No. 1, pp. 14–27.

CCP (1958), 中共中央关于在农村建立人民公社问题的决议 (The CCP Central Committee Resolution on the Issue of the Establishment of the People's Commune, August, 1958), http://cpc.people.com.cn/GB/64184/64186/66665/4493238.html, accessed October 9, 2017.

Chakrabarty, Bidyut (2014), *Communism in India: Events, Processes and Ideologies*, Oxford: Oxford University Press.

Chan Anita, Stanley Rosen, and Jonathan Unger (1980), "Students and Class Warfare: The Social Roots of the Red Guard Conflict in Guangzhou (Canton)," *The China Quarterly*, 83, pp. 397–446.

Chan, Anita, Stanley Rosen, and Jonathan Unger (eds.) (1985), *On Socialist Democracy and the Chinese Legal System: The Li Yizhe Debates*, Armonk, NY: M. E. Sharpe.

Chang, Gordon (2001), *The Coming Collapse of China*, New York: Random House.

Chang, Jung (1991), *Wild Swans: Three Daughters of China*. London: HarperCollins.

Chang, Jung and Jon Halliday (2005), *Mao the Untold Story*, London: Cape.

Chen, X. (1995), *Occidentalism: A Theory of Counter-Discourse in Post-Mao China*, Oxford: Oxford University Press. Chen Boda (1943), "评蒋介石《中国之命运》" (On Chiang Kai-shek's China's Destiny), *Jiefang Ribao*.

Chen T'a (Da) (1923), *Chinese Migrations, With Special Reference to Labour Conditions*, Washington: Washington Government Printing Office.

Chen Weisong (2017), "刘晓波其人其事" (Liu Xiaobo and Things About Him), http://news.china.com.cn/txt/2010–10/26/content_21202476.htm, accessed September 14, 2017.

Chen Yi (1958), "Guangdong Panyu xian fangwen ji" (Travel Notes from Panyu County in Guangdong Province), *People's Daily*, September 26.

Chen Yinque (1997), 唐代政治史述论稿 (On the History of Tang Politics), Shanghai: Shanghai Antique.

Chen Yinque (2004), 隋唐制度渊源略论稿 (On the Origin of the Sui-tang System), Beijing: Sanlian Shudian.

Chen Yushan (1979), "一份血写的报告" (A Report Written in Blood), http://blog.renren.com/share/241763025/12459631368, accessed September 14, 2017. *China Daily* (2015), "President Xi's New Year Visit Marks Village Homecoming," http://usa.chinadaily.com.cn/china/2015–02/14/content_195 91417.htm, accessed February 27, 2018.

China Statistics Year Book (1994), Chief Editor Zhang Sai, Beijing: China Statistics Press.

Chomsky, Noam (2017), "Trump's First 100 Days Are Undermining Our Prospects for Survival," www.truth-out.org/opinion/item/40011-noam-chomsky-trump-s-first-100-days-are-undermining-our-prospects-for-survival, accessed March 30, 2017.

Chou Niu (2016), 王长江给共产党捅了娄子 (Wang Changjiang Makes Blunders for the CCP), http://blog.sina.com.cn/s/blog_b4b4ea3c0102xe1d.html, accessed August 16, 2017.

Chow, Rey (1998), "King Kong in Hong Kong: Watching the 'Handover' from the USA," *Social Text* 55 (Summer).

Chun Ming (2016), "党史专家甄别'周惠谈李锐' 及其李锐夜闯美庐真假" (CCP History Expert Checks the Validity of Zhou Hui's Talk About Li Rui and the Claim of Li Rui's Visit of Mao at the Latter's Residence to Make a Confession), www.360doc.com/content/16/0511/01/12776403_558101498.shtml, accessed August 18, 2017.

CIA (1961), "The Economic Situation in Communist China," https://tinyurl.com/y9lldhbr, accessed April 8, 2017.

Clark, Paul (2008), *The Chinese Cultural Revolution: A History*, Cambridge: Cambridge University Press.

Coale, Ansley J. (1984), *Rapid Population Change in China, 1952–1982*, Washington, DC: National Academy Press.

Cohen, Jerome and Peter Dutton (2017), "How India Border Stand-off Gives China a Chance to Burnish Its Global Image," *South China Morning Post*, Insight Opinion, July 21, 2017, www.scmp.com/comment/insight-opinion/article/2103432/how-india-border-stand-gives-china-chance-burnish-its-global, accessed July 22, 2017.

Cole, Michael (2017), *Convergence or Conflict in the Taiwan Strait: The Illusion of Peace*, London and New York: Routledge.

Cook, Alexander (ed.) (2014), *Mao's Little Red Book: A Global History*, Cambridge: Cambridge University Press.

Cook, Isabel (2016), "Land Reform in Ten Mile Inn," www.isabelcrook.com/ pursuits/ 10mileinn/, accessed December 2, 2016.

Cooper, Ramo Joshua (2004), *The Beijing Consensus*, London: The Foreign Policy Center.

Cope, Zak (2012), *Divided World Divided Class: Global Political Economy and the Stratification of Labour Under Capitalism*, Kersplebedeb.

Coppel, C. A. (1982), "The Position of the Chinese in Indonesia, the Philippines and Malaysia," in *The Chinese in Indonesia, the Philippines and Malaysia*, 2nd edition, London: Minority Rights Group Report, No. 10, pp. 2–9.

Crossley, Pamela Kyle (1999), A *Translucent Mirror: History and Identity in Qing Imperial Ideology*, Berkeley and Los Angeles: University of California Press.

Cui Weiyuan (2008), "China's Village Doctors Take Great Strides," *Bulletin of the World Health Organization*, 86 (12), pp. 914–15.

Cui Zhiyuan (1996), "Anshan Xianfa He Hou Futezhuyi" (The Angang Constitution and Post-Fordism), *Dushu* (*Reading*), 1.

Dai Jaifang (1994), 走向毁灭：文革文化部长于会泳沉浮录 (Towards Ruin: The Rise and Fall of the Minister of Culture of the Cultural Revolution), Beijing: Guangming ribao chubanshe.

Davis, M. (2001), *Late Victorian Holocausts: El Nino, Famines and the Making of the Third World*, London: Verso.

Deng Rong (1967), "邓榕对邓小平的揭发" (Exposure of Deng Xiaoping by Deng Rong), 新北大公社02621支队编《彻底清算邓小平在无产阶级文化大革命中的滔天罪行》 (To Thoroughly Clear Up the Monstrous Crimes of Deng Xiaoping During the Cultural Revolution Compiled by the New Peking University Commune), April 1967.

Deng Tuo (1937), 中国救荒史 (A History of the Chinese Famine Rescue), Beijing: Shangwu Chubanshe.

Deng Xiaoping (1980), "Answers to the Italian Journalist Oriana Fallaci," August 21 and 23, in Deng Xiaoping, *Selected Works*, vol. 2 (1975 to 1982), Beijing: Renmin Chubanshe.

Denyer, Simon (2017), "In China Debut, Tillerson Appears to Hand Beijing a Diplomatic Victory," *Washington Post*, https://tinyurl.com/y7vsxn4q, accessed March 20, 2017.

Dikötter, Frank (2010), *Mao's Secret Famine: The History of China's Most Devastating Catastrophe, 1958–62*, London: Bloomsbury.

Dikötter, Frank (2016), "The Silent Revolution: Decollectivization from Below During the Cultural Revolution," *The China Quarterly*, 227, pp. 796–811.

Dirlik, Arif (1996), "Chinese History and the Question of Orientalism," *History and Theory*, 35 (4), pp. 96–118.

Dirlik, Arif (2016), 'Beijing Consensus: Who Recognizes, Whom and to What End?" www.chinaelections.org/uploadfile/200909/20090918025246335.pdf, accessed September 14, 2017.

Dong Cunbao (1992), 谭政林外传 (An Unofficial Biography of Tan Zhenglin), Beijing: Zuojia Chubanshe.

Douw, Leo (1999), "The Chinese Sojourner Discourse," in Leo Douw, Chen Huang, and Michael R. Godley, *Qiaoxiang Ties: Interdisciplinary Approaches to Cultural Capitalism in South China*, London and New York: Kegan Paul International in Association with IIAS, Leiden and Amsterdam, pp. 22–44.

Dreze, J. and A. Sen (1989), *Hunger and Public Action*, Oxford: Clarendon Press.

Drezner, D. (2013), "The System Worked: Global Economic Governance During the Great Recession," *World Politics*, 66, pp. 123–64.

Du Guang (2007), "送别包遵信 推进新启蒙--曾经沧海" (Farewell Bao Zunxin, Push for Xin Qimeng: The Past Years), www.360doc.com/content/071130/08/16239_859121.html, accessed June 15, 2009.

Dutton, Michael (2002), "Lead Us Not into Translation: Notes Toward a Theoretical Foundation for Asian Studies," *Nepantla: Views From South*, 3 (3), pp. 495–537.

Dutton, Michael (2016), "Cultural Revolution as Method," *The China Quarterly*, 227, pp. 718–33.

Economy, Elizabeth (2004), *The River Runs Black: The Environmental Challenge to China's Future*, 2nd edition, Ithaca, NY: Cornell University Press.

Economy, Elizabeth (2016), "A 'Gut Check' on U.S.-China Policy," *Forbes Asia*, April 5, www.forbes.com/sites/elizabetheconomy/2016/04/05/a-gut-check-on-u-s-china-policy/#edf8ac7709fd, accessed May 8, 2017.

Elliott, Mark (2001), *The Manchu Way: The Eight Banners and Ethnic Identity in Late Imperial China*, Stanford, CA: Stanford University Press.

Esherick, W. Joseph (2006), "How the Qing Became China," in Joseph Esherick, Hansan Kayali, and Eric Van Young (eds.), *Empire to Nation: Historical Perspective on the Making of the Modern World*, London: Rowan Littlefield Publishers.

Fallows, James (2011), "Liu Xaiobo and the '300 Years' Problem," *The Atlantic*, October 21.

Fan Gang (2005), "腐败的经济学原理" (The Economic Principles of Corruption), *Development*, 10, pp. 14–15.

Fan Weizhen (2002), 李白的身世、婚姻与家庭--兼质疑郭沫若等的李白论 (Li Bai's Family Background and Marriage), Haerbin: Heilongjiang Renmin Chubanshe.

Fei Xiaotong (1980), "关于我国民族的识别问题" (Issues on China's Nationality Identification), 中国社会科学 *(Zhongguo Shehui Kexue)*, No 1.

Fen Peizhi, et al. (1985), 中国主要气象灾害分析, 1951–1980 (An Analysis of the Main Climate Factor on China's Disaster), Beijing: Qixiang Chubanshe.

Fields, Belden (1984), "French Maoism," *Social Text*, 9/10, pp. 148–77.

Fish, Eric (2015), "Has China Discovered a Better Political System than Democracy?" *The Atlantic*, www.theatlantic.com/international/archive/2015/10/china-politics-communism-democracy/412663/, accessed September 16, 2017.

Fravel, M. Taylor (2005), "Regime Insecurity and International Cooperation: Explaining China's Compromise in Territorial Disputes," *International Security*, 30 (2), pp. 46–83.

Fravel, M. Taylor (2010), "International Relations Theory and Chia's Rise: Assessing China's Potential for Territorial Expansion," *International Studies Review*, 12 (4), pp. 505–32.

Freeman. W. Chas (2015), "Diplomacy on the Rocks: China and Other Claimants in the South China Sea," chasfreeman.net/diplomacy-on-the-rocks-china-and-other-claimants-in-the-south-china-sea/, accessed August 14, 2017.

Freeman, W. Chas (2016), "Remarks to East Bay Citizens for Peace, the Barrington Congregational Church, and the American Friends Service Committee," Rhode Island, chasfreeman.net/the-end-of-the-american-empire/, accessed August 11, 2017.

Freeman, W. Chas (2017), "Thinking About War with China," remarks at a discussion of "Avoiding War with China" at the Elliott School of International Affairs, the George Washington University, chasfreeman.net/thinking-about-war-with-china/, accessed August 13, 2017.

Friedersdorf, Conor (2017), "Is 'the Five Eyes Alliance' Conspiring to Spy on You?" *The Atlantic*, www.theatlantic.com/politics/archive/2013/06/is-the-five-eyes-alliance-conspiring-to-spy-on-you/277190/, accessed September 16, 2017.

Fukuyama, Francis (2014), *Political Order and Political Decay: From the Industrial Revolution to the Present Day*, New York: Farrar, Straus and Giroux.

Fuxingwang (2016), "贺卫方, 不要信口开河" (He Weifang: Please Don't Spout Off the Mouth), www.mzfxw.com/e/action/ShowInfo.php?classid=12&id=60972, accessed September 20, 2017.

Gan Yang (2007), 通三统 (The Combination of the Three Traditions), Beijing: Sanxian Shudian.

Gans, H. J. (1979), *Deciding What's News*, New York: Pantheon.

Gao, C. F. Mobo (1994), "Maoist Discourse and a Critique of the Present Assessment of the Cultural Revolution," *Bulletin of Concerned Asian Scholars*, 26 (3), pp. 3–21.

Gao, C. F. Mobo (1998), "Chinese Reality and Writings by Chinese Expatriates," *Bulletin of Concerned Asian Scholars*, 30 (3), pp. 61–68.

Gao, C. F. Mobo (1999a), *Gao Village: Rural Life in Modern China*, London: Hurst & Co.

Gao, C. F. Mobo (1999b), "Manufacturing of Truth and Culture of the Elite," *Journal of Contemporary Asia (Manila)*, 29 (3), pp. 309–27.

Gao, C. F. Mobo (2002), "Debating the Cultural Revolution: Do We Only Know What We Believe?" *Critical Asian Studies*, 34 (4), pp. 419–34.

Gao, C. F. Mobo (2003), "启程: 一个农村孩子关于七十年代的记忆", 七十年代, 北岛, 李陀主编, 香港: 牛津大学出版社, 2008, 801–92页 (Start on a Journey: Memories of a Child from Rural China), in Bei Dao Li Tuo (ed.), *The Seventies*, Hong Kong: Oxford University Press, 2008, pp. 81–92.

Gao, C. F. Mobo (2006), 關于「文化大革命」的記憶、思考和爭論: 解讀「浩劫」話語 (Memories of the Cultural Revolution: Deconstructing the Holocaust Discourse), in Song Geng (ed.), *Globalization and Chineseness: Postcolonial Readings of Contemporary Culture*, Hong Kong: Hong Kong University Press, pp. 247–60.

Gao, C. F. Mobo (2008), *The Battle for China's Past: Mao and the Cultural Revolution*, London: Pluto.

Gao, C. F. Mobo (2015), "The Cultural Revolution: Class, Culture and Revolution," in Guo Yingjie (ed.), *Handbook of Class and Class Stratification in China*, Cheltenham: Edward Elgar, pp. 44–58.

Gao, C. F. Mobo (2017), "Sojourners or Settlers: A Critique of the Cultural Perspective on 19th Century Chinese Migrants to the British Colonies," *Asian Studies Review*, 41 (3), pp. 389–404.

Gao Hua (2000), 红太阳是怎么升起的：延安整风运动的来龙去脉 (How Did the Red Sun Rise: The Cause and Effect of the Yan'an Rectification Movement), Hong Kong: 香港中文大学出版社.

Gao Hua (2008), "中国要前进 毛泽东是绕不过去的," (China Cannot Skip Mao Zedong to March Forward), news.ifeng.com/history/2/shidian/ 200809/ 0921_2666_795589.shtml, accessed 16 September 2017.

Gao Hua (2011), 高华答凤凰周刊问 (Gao Hua Interview with Fenghuang Weekly), http://blog.sina.com.cn/s/blog_627b3e5f0102dzoj.html, accessed May 28, 2017.

Gao Wenqian (2007), *Zhou Enlai, the Last Perfect Revolutionary: A Biography*, translated by Peter Rand and Lawrence R. Sullivan, New York: PublicAffairs.

Garnaut, Anthony (2013), "Hard Facts and Half-truths: The New Archival History of China's Great Famine," *China Information*, 27 (2), pp. 223–46.

Garnaut, J. (2015), "'Fear and Greed' Drive Australia's China Policy, Tony Abbott Tells Angela Merkel," *Sydney Morning Herald*, April 16. www.smh.com.au/ action/printArticle?id=98462086, accessed June 9, 2015.

Garside, Juliet and David Pegg (2016), "Panama Papers Reveal Offshore Secrets of China's Red Nobility," *The Guardian*, April 6.

Ge Zhaoguang (1998), 七世纪前中国的知识、思想与信仰世界—中国思想史第一卷 (Thinking and Believes in Pre-Seventh-Century China: History of Chinese Thought, Volume One), Shanghai: Fudan University Press.

Ge Zhaoguang (2006), 古代中国文化讲义 (Lecture Notes of Ancient Chinese Culture), Shanghai: Fudan University Press.

Geir Lundestad (2010), "China Made Peace Prize Decision for Us, Says Nobel Judge," *The Guardian*, October 28.

Gellner, Ernest (1983), *Nations and Nationalism*, Ithaca, NY: Cornell University Press.

Gitlin, T. (1980), *The Whole World is Watching: Mass Media in the Making and Unmaking of the New Left*, Berkeley: University of California Press.

Gladney, Dru (1994), "Representing Nationality in China: Refiguring Majority/ Minority Identities," *Journal of Asian Studies*, 53 (1), pp. 92–123.

Gladney, Dru (2004), *Dislocating China: Muslims, Minorities, and Other Subaltern Subjects*, Chicago: University of Chicago Press.

Gonzalez-Vicente, Ruben (2016), "The Empire Strikes Back? China's New Racial Sovereignty," *Political Geography* 59, pp. 139–41.

Grattan, Michelle (2017), "Chinese Influence Compromises the Integrity of Our Politics," https://theconversation.com/chinese-influence-compromises-the-integrity-of-our-politics-78961, accessed June 7, 2017.

Gries, Peter Hays (2004), *China's New Nationalism. Pride, Politics and Diplomacy*, Berkeley: University of California Press.

Greene, Felix (1964), *A Curtain of Ignorance: How the American Public Has Been Misinformed About China*, Garden City, NY: Doubleday.

Gu Jiegang (1982), 古史辨 (Debates on Ancient History), Shanghai: Shanghai Gujie Chubanshe.

Gu Jiegang (1998), "编中国历史之中心问题" (The Central Issues in Chinese Historiography), in Gu Jiegang (ed.), 《顾颉刚学术文化随笔》 (Gu Jiegang's Scholarly and Cultural Writings), Beijing: Zhongguo Qingnian Chubanshe, p. 3.

Gu Minkang (2017), "警察被重判冲击香港法治—专访香港城市大学法律学院副院长顾敏康" (Heavy Sentencing the Policy Attacks the Rule of Law in Kong Kong—Special Interview with Associate Dean of the Law School at the City University Gu Minkang), http://paper.people.com.cn/rmrbhwb/html/2017-02/21/content_1751735.htm, accessed September 16, 2017.

Gu Yingqi (2016), "文革期间刘少奇治疗纪实" (A Record of How Liu Shaoqi Was Treated During the Cultual Revolution), http://www.wyzxwk.com/Article/shidai/2016/06/365202.html, accessed June 7, 2016.

Gu Zhang (2016), "文革初期的北大——浅析张承先的《"文革"初期的北大工作组》" (Beijing University at the Beginning of the Cultural Revolution—an Initial Analysis of the Workteam in Beijing University at the Beginning of the Cultural Revolution), http://blog.sina.com.cn/huzsh, accessed September 26, 2016.

Guo Jingrui (2002), *The Features and Significance of Jingju Plays (1790–1911*, PhD thesis, the University of Tasmania.

Guo Songmin (2016), "谈谈中国买办知识分子" (On the Comprador Chinese Intelligentsia), www.wyzxwk.com/Article/shidai/2016/04/361132.html, accessed April 4, 2016.

Gupta, Sourabh (2015), "The Rights and Wrongs of US Overflights in the South China Sea," *East Asia Forum*, www.eastasiaforum.org/2015/05/26/the-rights-and-wrongs-of-us-overflights-in-the-south-china-sea/, accessed August 13, 2017.

Gupta, Sourabh (2016), "Beijing Has Case for 'Historic Rights' at Sea," www.chinausfocus.com/peace-security/beijing-has-case-for-historic-rights-at-sea, accessed August 12, 2017.

Gupta, Sourabh (2017a), "Alternative Facts and the Threat in the South China Sea," *East Asia Forum*, https://tinyurl.com/y9tvkv9m, accessed July 27, 2017.

Gupta, Sourabh (2017b), "Blinkered Justice at the Hague on the South China Sea," www.chinausfocus.com/foreign-policy/blinkered-justice-at-the-hague-on-the-south-china-sea, accessed August 12, 2017.

Hägerdal, Hans (1997), "The Orientalism Debate and the Chinese Wall: An Essay on Said and Sinology," *Itineraio*, 21 (3), pp. 19–40.

Han Gang (2013), "周惠谈话"辨伪: 李锐犯了"欺君之罪" (The Falsehood of Zhou Hui Talk: Has Li Rui Cheated the Emperor), http://news.ifeng.com/history/zhongguoxiandaishi/detail_2013_02/19/22266820_0.shtml, accessed August 18, 2017.

Han Suyin (1994), *Eldest Son: Zhou Enlai and Making of Modern China 1889–1976*, London: Jonathan Cape.

Harari, Yuval Noah (2017), "Globalism versus Nationalism and Localism," Ted Talk, https://tinyurl.com/yca2scpu, accessed September 16, 2017.

Harding, H. (1993), "The Concept of 'Greater China': Themes, Variations and Reservations," *China Quarterly*, 136, pp. 660–86.

Harrell, S. (1996), *Cultural Encounters On China's Ethnic Frontiers*, Seattle: University of Washington Press.

Hayot, Eric, Haun Saussy, and Steven G. Yao (eds.) (2008), *Sinographies: Writing China*, Minneapolis: University of Minnesota Press.

He Weifang (2016), "答王银川" (A Reply to Wang Yinchuan), www.chinaelections.com/article/105/241495.html, accessed September 20, 2017.

He Weifang (2012), "改革访谈录6 —著名法律学者、北大贺卫方教授纵谈司法改革" (Well-known Law Specialist Professor of Beijing University on Legal Reform), http://hsb.hsw.cn/2012-05/19/content_8330003.htm, accessed April 18, 2016.Hechter, Michael (1975), *Internal Colonialism: The Celtic Fringe in British National Development*, Berkeley: University of California Press.

Hechune (2015), "中国各省人血统来源：纯正汉族不多" (The Bloodline Origin of Pure Han Chinese Are Few),www.qulishi.com/news/201512/55832.html, accessed September 17, 2017.

Hensher, Phillip (2005), "Biography of Mao is a Work of Unanswerable Authority," www.seattlepi.com/local/opinion/article/Biography-of-Mao-is-a-work-of-unanswerable-1175383.php, accessed March 8, 2017.

Hermann, E. John (2007), *Amid the Clouds and Mist: China's Colonization of Guizhou, 1200—1700*, Harvard University Press.

Herman, Edward and Noam Chomsky (1988), *Manufacturing Consent*, New York: Pantheon Books.

Hinton, William (1972), *Fanshen: A Documentary of Revolution in a Chinese Village*, Harmondsworth: Penguin.

Hinton, William (1989), *The Great Reversal: The Privatization of China, 1978–1989*, New York: Monthly Review Press.

Ho, Ping-ti (1998), "In Defense of Sinicization: A Rebuttal of Evelyn Rawski's Reenvisioning Qing," *Journal of Asian Studies*, 51 (1), pp. 125–55.

Hoexter, Cornne K. (1976), *From Canton to California: The Epic of Chinese Immigration*, New York: Four Winds Press.

Hoffmann, Robert and See Hoon Chuah (2017), "Hard Work, Not 'Confucian' Mentality, Underpins Chinese Success Overseas," *The Conversation*, https://theconversation.com/hard-work-not-confucian-mentality-underpins-chinese-success-overseas-70705, accessed September 16, 2017.

Hostetler, Laura (2001), *Qing Colonial Enterprise: Ethnography and Cartography in Early Modern China*, Chicago: University of Chicago Press.

Hsu, Madeline Y. (2000), "Migration and Native Place: Qiaokan and the Imagined Community of Taishan Country, Guangdong, 1893–1993," *Journal of Asian Studies*, 59 (2), pp. 307–31.

Hu Luobo (2009), "为何六成青年感觉中国人崇洋媚外" (How Come 60 percent of the Chinese Worship Things Foreign?), www.wyzxsx.com/Article/Class21/200807/44305.html, accessed September 20, 2009.

Hu Qili (1967), "邓小平是镇压师大女附中革命学生的黑司令" (Deng Xiaoping is the Black Commander of Suppressing Students at the Middle School for Girls at Beijing Normal University), 新北大公社02621支队编《彻底清算邓小平在无产阶级文化大革命中的滔天罪行》(To Thoroughly Clear Up the Monstrous Crimes of Deng Xiaoping During the Cultural Revolution Compiled by the New Peking University Commune), April 1967.

Hu Sheng (2010), 中国共产党的七十年 (70 Years of the Chinese Communist Party), Beijing: 中共党史出版社.

Huang Guangxue (1987), "民族识别和更改民族成分工作一基本完成--国家民委副主任黄光学答本刊记者问" (The Deputy Commissioner of the

Chinese National Nationality Commission Huang Guangxue Meets the Press), 中国民族 (*Nationalities in China*) (2), pp. 18–19.

Huang Guangxue and Shi Lianzhu (2005), 中国的民族识56个民族的来 (The Origin of China's 56 Nationalities Identification), Beijing: Minzu Chubanshe.

Huang Zubing (1978), 文字改革文集 (Collected Works of the Language Reform), 人民大学语言文字研究所 (The Language Research Institute of Renmin University).

Hui Haiming (2017), "关于张杰的 '周惠谈李锐与庐山会议一文的声明'" (A Statement on Zhang Jie's "Zhou Hui Talks About Li Rui and the Lushan Conference"), http://blog.sina.com.cn/s/blog_4b35d58901014epz.html, accessed August 18, 2017.

Hung, Ho-Fung (2003), "Orientalist Knowledge and Social Theories: China and the European Conceptions of East–West Differences from 1600 to 1900," *Sociological Theory*, 21 (3), pp. 254–28.

Hutton, William (2005), "Complex Legacy of Chairman Mao," *The Observer*, May 19.

Hyer, Eric (2015), *The Pragmatic Dragon: China's Grant Strategy and Boundary Settlement*, Vancouver: The University of British Columbia Press.

International Labor Comparisons (2011), www.bls.gov/fls/, accessed February 27, 2018.

Israel, Jonathan (2001), *Radical Enlightenment: Philosophy and the Making of Modernity, 1650–1750*, Oxford: Oxford University Press.

Israel, Jonathan (2006), *Enlightenment Contested: Philosophy, Modernity, and the Emancipation of Man, 1670–1752*, Oxford: Oxford University Press.

Israel, Jonathan (2011), *Democratic Enlightenment: Philosophy, Revolution, and Human Rights 1750–1790*, New York : Oxford University Press.

Jackson, Peter (2003), "Space, Theory and Hegemony: The Dual Crisis of Asian Area Studies and the Cultural Studies," *Sojourn: Social Issues in Southeast Asia* 18 (1), pp. 1–41.

Ji Xianlin (1998), 牛棚杂忆 (Random Memories of the Cowshed), *The Cowshed: Memories of the Cultural Revolution Ji Xianlin*, translated by Chenxin Jiang, New York: New York Review of Books.

Jiang Zhenghua and Li Nan (1988), 中国人口动态估计的方法与结果 (The Methods and Results of Assessing China's Population Change), in 中国人口年鉴 (China Population Yearbooks), Beijing: jingji guanli chubanshe, pp. 94–106.

Jin Hui (1993), "三年自然灾害"备忘录" (Memo of "Three Years' Natural Disasters"), 社会 (*Society*), Z2, pp. 13–22.

Johnson, Ian (2016), "A Revolutionary Discovery in China," *New York Times Review of Books,* April 21, www.nybooks.com/articles/2016/04/21/revolutionary-discovery-in-china/, accessed September 16, 2017.

Kagan, Robert (2017), "Backing Into World War III," *Foreign Policy*, February 7.

Kakutani, Michiko (2005), "China's Monster, Second to None," *New York Times*, October 21.

Kang, David C. (2010), *East Asia Before the West: Five Centuries of Trade and Tribute*, New York: Columbia University Press.

Karabell, Zachary (2017), "We've Always Been America First," www.politico.com/magazine/story/2017/06/02/america-first-foreign-policy-history-215219, accessed June 4, 2017.

Kastner, Jens (2011), "Lee Charges Stir Taiwan," *Asian Times*, www.atimes.com/atimes/China/MG13Ad01.html, accessed September 16, 2017.

Kennedy, Paul (2009), "The Dollars' Fate," www.nytimes.com.

Kissinger, Henry (1979), *The White House Years*, New York: Little Brown and Company.

Kissinger, Henry (2014), *On China*, New York: Penguin and Putnam Inc.

Kong Dan (2015a), "红卫兵'西纠'是怎么成立的" (How Was the Xijiu Red Guards Set Up), accessed April 14, 2017.

Kong Dan (2015b), 口述史难得本色任天然, (Oral History, Difficult to Maintain Our Natural Colour), Beijing: Sanlian Chubanshe.

Kong Qingdong (2016), "共产党已成准地下党 上课都不敢公开讲马列讲毛主席" (The CCP Has Become Quasi Underground and One Dares Not to Talk About Marx, Lenin and Chairman Mao in Class), http://washeng.net/HuaShan/BBS/shishi/gbcurrent/225485.shtml, accessed August 16, 2017.

Kraus, Richard (2012), *The Cultural Revolution: A Very Short Introduction*, Oxford: Oxford University Press.

Kuhn, A. Phillip (2008), *Chinese Among Others: Emigration in Modern Times*, Rowman & Littlefield Pub Inc.

Kuhn, Thomas S. (1962), *The Structure of Scientific Revolutions*, Chicago: University of Chicago Press.

Kwong, Peter (2006), "China's Neoliberal Dynasty," *The Nation*, www.thenation.com/doc/20061002/kwong, accessed November 17, 2006.

Lagerkvist, John (2015): "The Ordoliberal Turn? Getting China and Global Economic Governance Right," *Global Affairs*, DOI: 10.1080/23340460.2015.1077610.

Lam, Willy (2015), *Chinese Politics in the Xi Jinping Era: Renaissance, Reform, or Retrogression?* New York and London: Routledge.

Lam, Willy (2016), "Xi Jinping Blocks Party Renewal: He Wants to Be the 21st Century Mao," www.asianews.it/news-en/Xi-Jinping-blocks-Party-renewal:-He-wants-to-be-the-21st-century-Mao--37107.html, accessed February 28, 2018.

Lanza, Fabio (2017), *The End of Concern: Maoist China, Activism, and Asian Studies*, Durham, NC: Duke University Press.

Lao Ji (2017), "从反对"邓剧"造假，看今日民心向背" (From the Opposition to the Fabrication in the Deng Series One Can See the Direction of the Public Opinion), www.szhgh.com/Article/wsds/wenyi/201703/133116.html, accessed September 20, 2017.

Lao Tian (老田 2016), "毛泽东告诫刘邓不要搞"会饿死五千万人的大跃进" (Mao Zedong Warned Liu and Deng Not to Do the GLF that Might Lead to the Death of 50 Million People), washeng.net/HuaShan/BBS/shishi/gbcurrent/226111.shtml, accessed August 27, 2017.

Lao You (2011), "文革纪实：文革中'联动'事件真相" (A Record of the Cultural Revolution: The Truth About Liandong), http://blog.sina.com.cn/s/blog_73767cad0100pcyb.html, accessed April 14, 2017.

Lau, Lisa (2009), "Re-Orientalism: The Perpetration and Development of Orientalism by Orientals," *Modern Asian Studies*, 43 (2), pp. 571–90.

Lau, Lisa and Ana Cristina Mendes (2011), "Introducing Re-Orientalism: A New Manifestation of Orientalism," in *Re-Orientalism, and South Asian Identity Politics, the Oriental Other Within*, London: Routledge, pp. 3–20.

Lee Teng-hui (2016), 余生: 我的生命之旅与台湾民主之路 (Remaining Life: My Life Journey and the Road of Taiwan's Democracy), Taipei: Daduhui Wenhua.

Lei Shen (2009), "大跃进不是毛泽东同志头脑发热，而是刘少奇邓小平等人头脑发热" (It Was Not Mao Who Was Hot-headed During the GLF, but Liu Shao, Deng Xiaoping and Others), bbs.creaders.net/politics/bbsviewer.php?trd_id=379112, accessed July 3, 2009.

Leibold, J. (2006), "Competing Narratives of Racial Unity in Republican China: From the Yellow Emperor to Peking Man," *Modern China*, 32 (2), pp. 181–220.

Leibold, J. (2017), "The Australia–China Relations Institute Doesn't Belong at UTS," *The Conversation*, https://theconversation.com/the-australia-china-relations-institute-doesnt-belong-at-uts-78743, accessed June 5, 2017.

Lenin, V. I. (1913), "The Awakening of Asia" and "Backward Europe and Advanced China," *Collected Works*, vol. 19, Moscow: Progress Publisher.

Leys, Simon (1977), *The Chairman's New Clothes*, London: Allison and Busby.

Li, Channa (2010), "A Nobel Peace Prize for Cultural Self-hatred," *New American Media*, http://newamericamedia.org/2010/10/a-nobel-peace-prize-for-cultural-self-hatred.php, accessed February 4, 2010.

Li, Eric (2017), "Xi Jinping's Guide to China's Globalization," *Financial Times*, www.ft.com/content/9a451b08-de36-11e6-86ac-f253db7791c6, accessed September 16, 2017.

Li Changping (李昌平2011), "话说水利" (Talking About Irrigation), https://tinyurl.com/yb7h6383, accessed October 5, 2016.

Li Chao (2010), "刘少奇是被迫害致死的" (Liu Shaoqi Was Prosecuted to Death), *Yanhuang Chuinqiu*, 1, pp. 80–1.

Li Cheng (2016), *The Xi Jinping Era: Reassessing Collective Leadership*, Washington, DC: Brookings Institution Press.

Li Chengrui (2015), "李成瑞先生为孙经先专著《还历史以真相》写的序言" (Preface to Sun Jingxian's Monograph to Restore Truth to History by L. Chengrui), www.360doc.com/content/17/0217/18/30288565_629774477.shtml, accessed August 28, 2017.

Li Jianshu (2016), "难以鼓劲：七千人大会与曾希圣调离安徽" (Difficult to Rouse Enthusiasm: The Seven Thousand Participants Conference and the Departure of Zeng Xisheng from Anhui), 《江淮文史》 (Jianghui History), 4, pp. 28–36.

Li Rui (1957), 毛泽东同志的初期革命活动 (Revolutionary Activities of the Early Comrade Mao Zedong), Beijing: Zhongguo Qingnian Chubanshe.

Li Rui (1994), 庐山会议实录：毛泽东秘书手记 (An Actual Record of the Lushan Conference: On the Spot Notes From Mao's Secretary), Changsha: Hunan Renmin Chubanshe.

Li Rui (1999), 毛泽东的晚年悲剧 (Mao Zedong's Tragic Late Years), Guangzhou: Nanfang Chubanshe.

Li Shenzhi (2000), 風雨蒼黃五十年 (50 Years of Ups and Downs), Hong Kong: Mingpao chubanshe.

Li Xiaopeng (2016), "Dispel the Rumour and Give Back Mao Zedong a Clear Name" (澄清谣诼，还清白于毛泽东), washeng.net/HuaShan/BBS/shishi/gbcurrent/226076.shtml, accessed August 17, 2017.

Li Xuan (2016), "形式相似，内容不同：在中国的民族分类和美国在比较视角下的种族分类" (Similar in Form, Different in Content: Ethnic Classification in the PRC and Racial Classification in the USA Under Comparative Perspective), *Chinese Tibetan Studies*, pp. 92–110.

Li Xuzhi (2017), "周有光是 '汉语拼音之父' 吗？" (Is Zhou Youguang the Father of Latinization of Chinese?), http://bbs.m4.cn/forum.php?mod=viewthread&tid=3941018&extra=page%3D1%26filter%3Dtypeid%26typeid%3D32&_dsign=c566201c, accessed August 30, 2017.

Li Yang (2011), "孔子像给庆祝建党出了个难题" (The Confucius Statue Presents a Conundrum to the CCP Anniversary), http://washeng.net/HuaShan/BBS/shishi/gbcurrent/ 173459.shtmi accessed February 7, 2011.

Li Yining (2009), "厉以宁语录学习" (Learn from Li Yining's Quotation), http://qun.51.com/zhwq/topic.php?pid=397, accessed September 22, 2009.

Li Zhisui (1994), *The Private Life of Chairman Mao, the Memoirs of Mao's Personal Physician*, London: Chatto & Windus.

Lin, Justine Yifu (1990), "Collectivization and China's Agricultural Crisis in 1959–1961," *Journal of Political Economy*, 98 (6), pp. 1228–52.

Lin Chun (2013), *China and Global Capitalism: Reflections On Marxism, History, and Contemporary Politics*, New York: Palgrave.

Lin Chun (2015), "Rethinking Land Reform: Comparative Lessons from China and India," in Mahmood Mamdani (ed.), *The Land Question: Socialism, Capitalism, and the Market*, Makerere Institute of Social Research, Kampala, Uganda, pp. 95–157. Online LSE version (2016): http://eprints.lse.ac.uk/59697/1/Lin_Rethinking%20land%20reform_2016.pdf, accessed September 21, 2017.

Lindblom, Charles (1977), *Politics and Markets: The World's Political-Economic Systems*, New York: Basic Books.

Lippmann, W (1922), *Public Opinion*, New York: Harcourt.

Liu Guozhong (2016), *Introduction to the Tsinghua Bamboo-Strip Manuscripts*, 清华竹笺手稿介绍, translated by Christopher J. Foster and William N. French, Leiden: Brill.

Liu Shaoqi (1939), 论共产党员的修养 (On the Cultivation of CCP Members), first a lecture given in Yan'an and published in 1949 as a booklet by Renmin Chubanshe.

Liu Shaoqi (1985), *Selected Works, Vol. 2*, Beijing: Renmin Chubanshe.

Liu Xiaobo (2002), "联合国——萨达姆的救命稻草" (The UN—Saddam's Life-Saving Straw), http://bbs.creaders.net/military/bbsviewer.php?trd_id=31138, accessed September 20, 2017.

Liu Yingqiu (ed.) (2005), 干旱灾害对我国社会经济影响研究 (On the Impact of Droughts and Floods on China's Social Economy), Beijing: Zhongguo Shuidain Chubanshe.

Liu Zaifu (1985–6), "论文学的主体性" and "论文学的主体性" (On the Subjectivity in Literature I and II), 文学评论 (Commentaries on Literature), 1985, No. 6 and 1986, No. 1.

Liu Zaifu and Li Zehou (1997), 告别革命 (Farewell Revolution), Hong Kong: Tiandi Tushu Youxian Gongsi.

Los Angeles Times (2006), "Premier's Accusation Prompts China's Outcry," (总理的指责提示中国的抗议), March 29, http://articles.latimes.com/2006/dec/19/world/fg-briefs19.1, accessed April 6, 2016.

Lovell, Julia (2016), "The Cultural Revolution and its Legacies in International Perspective," *China Quarterly*, 227, pp. 632–52.

Lü Xinyu (2009), "鲁迅之'罪', 反启蒙与中国的现代性--对刘小枫先生'基督神学'的批判" (The "Guilt" Fo Lu Xuan, Anti-enlightenment and China's Modernity—a Critique of Liu Xiaofeng's Christian Theology), conference paper presented held at Hangzhou titled 文化与社会转型：理论框架与中国语境国际学术研讨会 (International Conference on Culture and Societal Transformation: Theoretical Framework and the Chinese Discursive Environment), Hangzhou, July 21–4.

Luo Pinghan (2003), 大迁徙: 1961-1963年的城镇人口精简 (Great Migration: An Outline of Urban Population Between 1961 and 1963), Guizhou: Guangxi Renmin Chubanshe.

Lv Yongyan (2016), "起底转基因骗子集团农官李家洋" (Exposure of Agricultural Official Li Jiayang As Part of Genetic Engineering Scam Corporate), http://blog.sina.com.cn /s/blog 4b7683ce0102enjl.html, accessed September 17, 2017.

Ma Qibing (1991), 中国共产党执政四十年: 1949–1989 (40 Years of the CCP in Power—1949–1989), Beijing: Zhonggong Dangshi Zilaio Chubanshe.

Ma Quanshan (1998), 新中国工业经济史 (1966–1978 a History of Industry of the PRC), Beijing: Jingji Guanli Chubanshe.

Ma Rong (2012), "中国的民族问题与20世纪50年代的'民族识别" (China's Nationality Issue and the 1950s Nationality Identification), *Northwest Ethno-national Studies*, 3, pp. 12–28.

Ma Ronjie (2016), "张志新被判死刑的真正原因" (The Real Reasons Why Zhang Zhixin Was Sentenced to Death), https://tieba.baidu.com/p/4327907499, accessed September 17, 2017.

Ma Shexiang (2012), 中国农业合作化运动口述史 (An Oral History of China Agricultural Coops), 北京：中央文献出版社, Beijing: Zhongyang Wenxian Chubanshe.

Ma Ying-jeou (2017), "中国大陆亦为我'中华民国'领土" (Mainland China is Also the Territory of the Republic of China), Huanqi shibao, news.qq.com/a/20081009/001587.htm, accessed September 16, 2017.

MacFarquhar, Roderick (1974), *The Origins of the Cultural Revolution*, Oxford: Oxford University Press.

MacFarquhar, Roderick (2016), "Preface: The Once and Future Tragedy of the Cultural Revolution," *China Quarterly*, 227, pp. 599–603.

MacFarquhar, Roderick and Michael Schoenhals (2006), *Mao's Last Revolution*, Cambridge, MA and London: Belknap Press.

Mackerras, Colin (1989), *Western Images of China*, Oxford: Oxford University Press.

Macpherson, C. B. (1966), *The Real World of Democracy*, Oxford: Oxford University Press.

Malik, Kenan (2017), "Are Soas Students Right to 'Decolonise' their Minds from Western Philosophers?," *The Guardian*, February 19, www.theguardian.com/education/2017/feb/19/soas-philosopy-decolonise-our-minds-enlightenment-white-european-kenan-malik?CMP=sharebtntw, accessed February 23, 2017.

Mallory, Walter, H. (1926), *China Land of Famine*, New York: American Geographical Society.

Mao Zedong (1939), "Zhongguo Geming He Zhongguo Gongchandang" (The Chinese Revolution and the Chinese Communist Party), in *Selected Works of Mao Zedong*, vol 2, Beijing: Renmin Chubanshe.

Mao Zedong (1942), "整顿党的作风" (Rectification of the Style of the CCP Party), a speech made in Yanan on the 27 April.

Mao Zedong (1968), 建国以来毛泽东文稿：战无不胜的毛泽东思想万岁 (Mao Zedong Manuscripts Since the Establishment of the PRC), vol. 3, Beijing: Zhongyang Wenxian Chubanshe, pp. 209–214.

Mao Zedong (1976), "On Ten Major Relationships" (论十大关系), *Peoples' Daily*, December 26.

Mao Zedong (1977), "党内指示" (Internal Instruction for the CCP), in *Selected Works of Mao Zedong*, vol. 5, Beijing: Renmin Chubanshe, pp. 75–76.

Martínez-Robles, David (2008), "The Western Representation of Modern China: Orientalism, Culturalism and Historiographical Criticism," *Digithum*, 10, DOI: dx.doi.org/10.7238/d.v0i10.511.

Maxwell, Neville (2014), *China's Borders: Settlements and Conflicts*, Newcastle: Cambridge Scholars Publishing.

May, Ernest, R. (1962), "The Nature of Foreign Policy: The Calculated Versus the Axiomatic," *Daedalus*, 91 4, pp. 653–67.

McDevitt, Michael (2017), "The South China Sea Seven Years on," *East Asia Forum*, https://tinyurl.com/ybqxlbf3, accessed July 20, 2017.

McGregor, James (2017), "The Art of a China Deal Reciprocity and the Trump Pacific Partnership," *ChinaFile*, www.chinafile.com/viewpoint/art-of-china-deal, accessed June 7, 2017.

McKenzie, Nick and Chris Ulhmann (2017), "Chinese Donations Could Compromise: Billionaires Linked to Communist Party Offered Cash to Our Political Parties But with Strings Attached," *Australian Financial Review*, 6 June, p. 36.

McKewon, Adam (1999), "Conceptualizing Chinese Diasporas, 1842 to 1949," *Journal of Asian Studies*, 58 (2), pp. 306–37.

Mearsheimer, John (2016), "Benign Hegemony," *International Studies Review*, 1–3.

Mei Hua (2009), "高端"学者，一场演讲15万元" (High-Profile Scholar Gets Paid One Hundred and Fifteen Thousand for a Talk), www.wyzxsx.com/Article/Class4/200909/105472.html, accessed September 22, 2009.

Meisner, Maurice (1999), *Mao's China and After: A History of the People's Republic*, New York: Free Press.

Minzner, Carl (2016), "Is China's Authoritarianism Decaying into Personalised Rule?" www.eastasiaforum.org/?p=50351?utm_source=newsletter&utm_

medium=email&utm_campaign=newsletter2016–04–24, accessed September 17, 2017.

Mitchell, A. (2004), "Self Orientalism, Reverse Orientalism and Pan-Asian Pop Cultural Flows in Dick Lee's Transit Lounge," in K. Iwabuchi, S. Muecke, and M. Thomas (eds.), *Rogue Flows: Trans-Asian Cultural Traffic*, Hong Kong: Hong Kong University Press.

Mitchell, Ryan (2015), "Is There a China Model?" *ChinaFile*, www.chinafile. com/conversation/there-china-model, accessed January 13, 2017.

Mo Yuanren (ed.)(1987), 江苏乡镇工业发展史 (A History of the Development of Tves in Jiangsu), Nanjing: 南京工学院出版社.

Mullaney, Thomas S. (2011), *Coming to Terms With the Nation: Ethnic Classification in Modern China*, Berkeley: University of California Press.

Natacha, Michel (1975), *La Chine Européenne*, Paris: Gallimard.

Nathan, Andrew (2015), "The Problem with the China Model," *ChinaFile*, www.chinafile.com/reporting-opinion/viewpoint/problem-china-model, accessed September 16, 2017.

Nathan, Andrew (2016), "Who is Xi?" *New York Times Review of Books*, May 12, www.nybooks.com/articles/2016/05/12/who-is-xi/, accessed June 7, 2017.

Nathan, Andrew (2017), "Struggle on the Top," *New York Review of Books*, www. nybooks.com/articles/2017/02/09/china-struggle-at-the-top/, accessed August 7, 2017.

National Prevention of Flood and Drought and Nanjing Hydrological Institute (1997), 四十年水利建设成就——水利统计资料 *1949–1988* (Achievements of 40 Years of Water Resources Infrastructure-water Resources Statistics), 水利水电出版社.

Naughton, B. (1991), "Industrial Policy During the Cultural Revolution: Military Preparation, Decentralization, and Leaps Forward," in Joseph, W. et al. (eds.), *New Perspectives On the Cultural Revolution*, Cambridge, MA: Harvard University Press.

Navarro, Peter (2016), "The Crouching Tiger Interviews: David Lampton From A to Xi," https://www.realcleardefense.com/articles/2016/04/08/the_crouching_tiger_interviews_david_lampton_from_a_to_xi_109236.html, accessed September 17, 2017.

Needham, Joseph (1954–), *Science and Civilization in China*, Cambridge: Cambridge University Press, 25 volumes to date.

Niccolai, Roberto (1998), *Cuando La Cina Era Vicina*, Collana: Biblioteca di Cultura Storica.

NIDS (National Institute for Defense Studies) (2017), *China Security Report 2017: Change in Continuity—the Dynamics of the China-Taiwan Relationship*, 2017.

Nie Yuanzi (2005), 聂元梓回憶錄 (Memoirs of Nie Yuanzi), Hong Kong: Shidai Guoji Chuban Youxian Gongsi.

Nolan, Peter (2014), *Re-balancing China: Essays on the Global Financial Crisis, Industrial Policy, and International Relations*, London: Anthem Press.

Nolan, Peter (2017), "资本主义全球化的双刃剑" (Double-edged Sword of Global Capitalism),http://strongwindhk.Com/Pdfs/Hkfax/No_HK2017-26. pdf, accessed August 30, 2017.

Oliver, Alex (2016), "The Lowy Institute Poll 2016," www.lowyinstitute.org/publications/lowy-institute-poll-2016.

Ong, A. (2004), "The Chinese Axis: Zoning Technologies and Variegated Sovereignty," *Journal of East Asian Studies*, 4 (1), pp. 69–96.

Orlins, Stephen (2017), "The Shanghai Communique: An American Foreign Policy Success, 45 Years Later," *The Diplomat*, thediplomat.com/2017/02/the-shanghai-communique-an-american-foreign-policy-success-45-years-later/, accessed March 2, 2017.

Overholt, William H. (2017), "Cartoonish Sketches of China as a Villain," *Global Asia*, 12 (1), pp. 126–8.

Pan, Z. and G. M. Kosicki (1993), "Framing Analysis: An Approach to News Discourse," *Political Communication*, 10, pp. 55–75.

Pascoe, Michael (2016), "Australia Shouldn't Pay Price for 'Pivot'," *Canberra Times*, www.canberratimes.com.au/business/world-business/australia-shouldnt-pay-price-for-pivot-20160418-go8rat.html, accessed July 27, 2016.

Patnaik, Utsa (2002), "On Famine and Measuring 'Famine Deaths'," in S. Patel, J. Bagchi and K. Raj (eds.), *Thinking Social Science in India: Essays in Honor of Alice Thorner*, London: Sage.

Patnaik, Utsa (2011), "Revisiting Alleged 30 Million Famine Deaths During China's Great Leap,"http://mrzine.monthlyreview.org/2011/patnaik260611p.html, accessed September 17, 2017.

Pei Minxin (2016), *China's Crony Capitalism: The Dynamics of Regime Decay*, Cambridge, MA: Harvard University Press.

Pei Minxin (2017), "China Needs a New Grand Strategy," *Project and Syndicate*, February 9, www.project-syndicate.org/commentary/china-post-cold-war-strategy-trump-by-minxin-pei-2017–02#comments, accessed February 15, 2017.

Peng Shicheng (2017), "毛主席与中国妇女" (Mao and the Chinese Women), www.kunlunce.cn, accessed August 3, 2017.

Peng, X. (1987), "Demographic Consequences of the Great Leap Forward in China's Provinces," *Population and Development Review*, 13 (4), pp. 639–70.

Pepper, Suzanne (1996), *Radicalism and Education Reform in 20th-Century China: The Search for an Ideal Development*, Cambridge: Cambridge University Press.

Pepper, Suzanne (2000), *Radicalism and Education Reform in 20th-Century China: The Search for an Ideal Development*, 2nd edition, Cambridge: Cambridge University Press.

Perdu, Peter (2005), *China Marches West: The Qing Conquest of Central Eurasia*, Cambridge, MA: Harvard University Press.

Perry, Elizabeth (2003), "'To Rebel is Justified': Cultural Revolution Influences on Contemporary Chinese Protest," in Law Kam-yi (ed.), *The Chinese Cultural Revolution Re-considered: Beyond Purge and Holocaust*, New York: Palgrave Macmillan, pp. 262–81.

Perry, Elizabeth (2016), "The Promise of PRC History," *Journal of Modern Chinese History*, 10 (1), pp. 113–17.

Perry, Elizabeth and Li Xun (1996), *Proletarian Power: Shanghai in the Cultural Revolution*, Boulder, CO: Westview Press.

Pilger, John (2016), "The Coming War with China," www.counterpunch.org/2016/12/02b/the-coming-war-on-china/, accessed July 17, 2017.

Qi Benyu (2016), 戚本禹回憶錄 (Memoirs of Qi Benyu), Hong Kong: Zhongugo Wenge Lishi Chubanshe.

Qin Hui and Su Wen (1996), 田园诗与狂想曲——关中模式与前近代社会的再认识 (Pastoral Poem and Rhapsody—the Guanzhong Model and a New Understanding of Pre-modern China), Beijing: Zhongyang Bianyi Chubanshe.

Quan Yanchi and Huang Lina (1997), 天道-周惠与庐山会议 (The Dao of Heaven, Zhou Hui and the Lushan Conference), Guangzhou: Guangdong Luyou Chuebanshe.

Ratner, Ely (2017), "Tillerson Bumbles Around Asia: the Secretary of State's First Big Trip Abroad Did Not Go Well," *Politico Magazine*, March 20, www.politico.com/magazine/story/2017/03/tillerson-bumbles-around-asia-214936, accessed July 27, 2017.

Rawski, Evelyn S. (1996), "Presidential Address: Reenvisioning the Qing: The Significance of the Qing Period in Chinese History," *Journal of Asian Studies*, 55 (4), p. 831.

Rawski, Evelyn S. (1998), *The Last Emperors: A Social History of Qing Imperial Institutions*, Berkeley: University of California Press.

Reid, A. (ed.) (1996), "Sojourners and Settlers: Histories of Southeast Asia and the Chinese," Asian Studies Association of Australia in Association with Allen & Unwin, Sydney: Southeast Asia Publications Series No. 28.

Renmin Wang (2016), "为什么选刘少奇当第二个主席？毛泽东说出真相" (Why Was Liu Shaoqi Selected to Be the Second Chairman of the PRC), www.taiwan.cn/tsh/shzh/201604/t20160418_11435512.htm, accessed March 1, 2017.

Rhoads, Edward (2000), *Manchus and Han: Ethnic Relations and Political Power in Late Qing and Early Republican China, 1861–1928*, Seattle: University of Washington Press.

Rigger, Shelley (1996), "The History of Ethnic Identity: The Process of Peoples," in Steven Harrell (ed.), *Cultural Encounters On China's Ethnic Frontiers*, Seattle: University of Washington Press, pp. 215–25.

Ringen, Stein (2016a), "Xi Jinping Flirts with Danger in His Turn to Ideology," www.scmp.com/comment/insight-opinion/article/1935114/xi-jinping-flirts-danger-his-turn-ideology, accessed August 30, 2017.

Ringen, Stein (2016b), *The Perfect Dictatorship: China in the 21st Century*, Hong Kong: Hong Kong University Press.

Riskin C. (1998), "Seven Questions about the Chinese Famine of 1959–61," *Chinese Economic Review*, 9, pp. 2111–24.

ROC Central News Agency (2016), "Presidential Office Reaffirms ROC Sovereignty Over Diaoyutai," www.globalsecurity.org/military/library/news/2016/02/mil-160217-cnao4.htm, accessed September 17, 2017.

ROC Central News Agency (2017), "Taiwan Reaffirms Sovereignty Over Diaoyutai Islands," http://focustaiwan.tw/news/aIPL/201702110017.aspx, accessed September 17, 2017.

Roche, Gerald (2017), "The Vitality of Tibet's Minority Languages in the Twenty-first Century," https://tinyurl.com/ycofmlur, accessed September 17, 2017.

Rothwell, Nicolas (2005), "Books of the Year," *The Australian*, December 3–4, p. R5.

Roy, Arundhati (2011), *Walking With Comrades*, Harmondsworth: Penguin Books.

Saches, Jeffrey D. (2017), "Donald Trump's Dangerous China Illusions," *Boston Globe*, February 5, www.bostonglobe.com/opinion/2017/02/05/trump-dangerous-china-illusions/51H7yrI9vTE3PSmXDJDl3M/story.html, February 7, 2017.

Said, Edward, W. (1978), *Orientalism*, New York: Pantheon Books.

Sartori, Giovanni (1987), *The Theory of Democracy Revisited*, Chatham, NJ: Chatham House Publishers.

Sautman, Barry (2001), "Is Tibet China's Colony? The Claim of Demographic Catastrophe," *Columbia Journal of Asian Law*, 15 (1), https://cjal.columbia.edu/article/is-tibet-chinas-colony-the-claim-of-demographic-catastrophe/, accessed September 17, 2017.

Sautman, Barry (2006), "Tibet and the (Mis)Representation of Cultural Genocide," in *Cultural Genocide and Asian State Peripheries*, Gordonsville, VA: Palgrave Macmillan.

Sautman, Barry (2012), "Paved with Good Intentions: Proposals to Curb Minority Rights and Their Consequences for China," *Modern China*, 38 (1), pp. 11–39.Sautman, Barry and Hairong Yan (2010), "Liu Xiaobo Stands for War Not Peace," *The Guardian*, October 25, www.mg.co.za/article/2010-10-25-liu-xiaobo-stands-for-war-not-peace, accessed February 4, 2011.

Schein, Louisa (1996), "Cultural Encounters on China's Ethnic Frontiers (Review)," *China Review International*, 3 (1), pp. 138–41.

Schell, Orville (1984), *To Get Rich is Glorious: China in the '80s*, New York: Pantheon Books.

Schell, Orville, Susan L. Shirk, et al. (2017), *Report: U.S. Policy Toward China: Recommendations for a New Administration, Task Force On U.S.-China Policy*, February 8, http://asiasociety.org/center-us-china-relations/us-policy-toward-china-recommendations-new-administration, accessed Septermber 17, 2017.

Schrader, Matt (2017), "Surprise Findings: China's Youth Are Getting Less Nationalistic, Not More: Harvard and Peking University Researchers Just Upended Conventional Wisdom," http://foreignpolicy.com/2017/02/07/surprise-findings-chinas-youth-are-getting-less-nationalistic-not-more/, accessed September 17, 2017.

Seth, Sanjay (2006), "From Maoism to Postcolonialism? The Indian 'Sixties,' and beyond." *Inter-Asia Cultural Studies*, 7 (4), pp. 589–605.

Shambaugh, David (2015), "The Coming Chinese Crackup," www.wsj.com/articles/the-coming-chinese-crack-up-1425659198, accessed September 18, 2017.

Shi Lianzhu (1989), "中国民族识别研究工作的特色" (Characteristics of China's Research and Work on Nationality Identification), 中央民族学院学报 (*The Central Nationality University Journal*), 5, pp. 17–23.

Shijie Huaren Zhoukan (2017), "两个德国人，甩了中国教育一记响亮的耳光" (Two German Slaps in the Face of Chinese Education), www.sohu.com/a/132784267_616577, accessed September 15, 2017.

Sisci, Francesco (2016), "What the Underwater Drone Incident Brought to the Surface," *Heartland Eurasian Review of Geopolitics*, http://temi.repubblica.it/limes-heartland/what-the-underwater-drone-incident-brought-to-the-surface/2111, accessed December 31, 2016.

Skinner, William G. (1959), "The Overseas Chinese in Southeast Asia," *Annals of the American Academy of Political and Social Sciences*, 132.

Snelder, Julian (2014), "Why Do So Many Chinese Expect War?' *National Interest*, http://nationalinterest.org/blog/the-buzz/why-do-so-many-chinese-expect-war-11440, accessed February 9, 2017.

Snow, Edgar (1937), *Red Star Over China*, London: Victor Gollancz.

Snow, Edgar (1971), *Red China Today: The Other Side of the River*, New York: Random House.

Somin, Ilya (2016), "Remembering the Biggest Mass Murder in the History of the World," *Washington Post*, August 3, https://tinyurl.com/y9jop9lc, accessed March 22, 2017.

Song Qiang, et al. (1996), 中国可以说不——冷战后时代的政治与情感抉择 (China Can Say No—Post-Cold War Politics and Sentimental Choice), Beijing: Zhonghua Gongshang Lianhe Chubanshe.

Song Rufen (2012), "我所了解的"畅观楼事件"" (What I Know of the Changguan Lou Incident), in 红色往事 ——党史人物忆党史 (第二册) (CCP Personalities Remember CCP History), Jinan: Jinan Chubanshe.

Song Xiaoju, et al. (2009), 中国不高兴 (China is Not Happy), Nanjing: Jiansu Renmne Chuban She.

South China Morning Post (2015), "Ex-Taiwan President Lee Teng-hui Under Fire for Calling Japan the 'Motherland'," www.scmp.com/news/china/policies-politics/article/1851501/ex-taiwan-president-lee-under-fire-calling-japan, accessed September 17, 2017.

Sow, K. T. (2013), *Managing China's Sovereignty in Hong Kong and Taiwan*, New York: Palgrave Macmillan.

Spivak, Gayatri Chakravorty (1999), *A Critique of Postcolonial Reason: Towards a History of the Vanishing Present*, Cambridge, MA: Harvard University Press.

Stalin, Joseph (1934), *Marxism and the National Question*, New York: International Publishers.

Su Tieshan (2015), "在历史大背景下张志新案真相是这样," mp.weixin.qq.com/s?__biz=MzA4NDU4ODEwMQ==&mid=203626220&idx-=7&sn=28fe8ce81bf55f72a9c1c70b5c33994a&scene=2&srcid=0412Wm-L6tfE3nM17K65JRUsP&from=timeline&isappinstalled=0#wechat_redirect, accessed April 15, 2017.

Sun, Warren (2013), "Did Mao Have a Smoking Gun? Academic Fraud of Frank Dikötter," International Conference on Contemporary Chinese History, Beijing, June 25–7, 2013.

Sun Jingxian (2011), "关于我国20世纪60年代人口变动问题的研究" (A Study on the Demographic Change During the 1960s), *Journal of Marxism Studies*, 6, pp. 62–75.

Sun Jingxian (2013), "饿死三千万"谣言是怎样形成的" (How Did the Rumor of 30 Million Famine Death Come into Being), in 中国社会科学报 (*Journal of Chinese Social Sciences*), 499, www.cssn.cn/zt/zt_zh/fdlsxwzy/fdlsxwzypp/201509/t20150916_2344056.shtml?bsh_bid=1817794612, accessed September 17, 2017.

Sun Jingxian (2014), "驳洪振快有关大饥荒的新谬说" (Repudiate a New Fallacy on the Great Famine by Hong Zhengkuai), 中国社会科学网 (The Chinese Social Sciences Website), www.cssn.cn/index/index_focus/201412/t20141205_1430365.shtml, accessed April 8, 2017.

Sun Jingxian (2016), "Population Change during China's 'Three Years of Hardship (1959–1961)'," *Contemporary Chinese Political Economy and Strategic Relations*, 2 (1), pp. 453–500.

Sun Xingsheng (2010), "把历史的真相告诉人民--采访王光美及其子女的回忆," (Tell the People Historical Truth: Recollections of Interviews with Wang Guangmei and Her Children) http://news.qq.com/a/20100827/000415.htm, accessed July 9, 2017.

Suny, Ronald Grigor and Terry Martin (eds.) (2001), *A State of Nations: Empire and Nation-Making in the Age of Lenin and Stalin*, Oxford: Oxford University Press.

Tan Keng Tat (2016), "South China Sea: Did the Ruling Sink the Rule of Law?," *Straits Times*, www.straitstimes.com/opinion/did-the-ruling-sink-the-rule-of-law, accessed March 1, 2018.

Taylor, Jean Gelman (2005), "The Chinese and the Early Centuries of Conversion to Islam in Indonesia," in Tim Lindsey and Helen Pausacker (eds.), *Chinese Indonesians: Remembering, Distorting, Forgetting*, Singapore: Institute of Southeast Asian Studies.

Teiwes, Frederick C. (1984), *Leadership, Legitimacy and Conflict in China: From a Charismatic Mao to the Politics of Succession*, London: Macmillan.

Thayer, Carlyle A. (1987), "Security Issues in Southeast Asia: The Third Indochina War," Conference on Security and Arms Control in the North Pacific, Australian National University, Canberra, August.

Tian, Shaohui (2016), "China Adheres to the Position of Settling Through Negotiation the Relevant Disputes Between China and the Philippines in the South China Sea," *Xinhuawang*, www.xinhuanet.com/english/china/2016–07/13/c_135509153_4.htm, accessed March 1, 2018.

Timperlake, Ed and Robbin Laird (2016), "Taiwan, Trump, and the Pacific Defense Grid: Towards Deterrence," *Breaking Defence*, https://tinyurl.com/y986bghk, accessed December 30, 2016.

Tønneson, Stein (2006), "The South China Sea in the Age of European Decline," *Modern Asian Studies*, 40 (1), pp. 1–57.

Valencia, J. Mark (2017), "(Mis)construing China's Threat to the South China Sea," NISCSS Asian Forum, https://tinyurl.com/y9gkskl5, accessed May 9, 2017.

Van Praag, Michael C. van Walt (1987), *The Status of Tibet: History, Rights, and Prospects in International Law*, Boulder, CO: Westview Press.

Vietnamnet (2011), "Diplomatic Note in 1958 with Vietnam's Sovereignty over Pracel, Spratly Islands," http://english.vietnamnet.vn/fms/special-reports/10673/diplomatic-note-1958-with-vietnam-s-sovereignty-over-paracel--spratly-islands.html, accessed February 28, 2018.

Vogel, F. Ezra (2011), *Deng Xiaoping and the Transformation of China*, Cambridge, MA: Belknap Press.

Von Richthofen, Ferdinand (1877–1912), *China, Ergebnisse eigner Reisen und darauf gegründeter Studien* (*China: the Results of My Travels and the Studies Based Thereon*), 1877–1912, 5 vols. and atlas, Berlin: Verlag von Dietrich Reimer.

Vukovich, D. (2013), *China and Orientalism: Western Knowledge Production and the PRC*, London: Routledge.

Walder, Andrew (2016), "Bending the Arc of Chinese History: The Cultural Revolution's Paradoxical Legacy," *China Quarterly*, 227, pp. 613–31.

Wang, G. (1999), "A Single Chinese Diaspora? Some Historical Reflections," in G. Wang and A. Shun Wah (eds.), *Imagining the Chinese Diaspora: Two Australian Perspectives*, Canberra: Centre for the Study of Chinese Southern Diaspora.

Wang, G. (2003), *Don't Leave Home: Migration and Chinese*, Singapore: Eastern University Press.

Wang Guangmei, Liu Yuan, et al. (2000), 你所不知道的刘少奇 (The Liu Shaoqi that You Don't Know), Zhengzhou: Henan Renmin Chubanshe.

Wang Gungwu (1991), *China and the Chinese Overseas*, Singapore: Times Academic Press.

Wang Hui (2003), *China's New Order, Society, Politics, and Economy in Transition*, edited by Theodore Huters, Cambridge, MA: Harvard University Press.

Wang Hui (2006), "Depoliticized Politics: From East to West," *New Left Review* 41, pp. 29–45.

Wang Hui (2009), *The End of the Revolution: China and the Limits of Modernity*, London: Verso.

Wang Hui (2011a), 东西间的 "西藏问题 (The Tibetan Question Between the East and West), Beijing: Sanlian Shudian.

Wang Hui (2011b), *The Politics of Imagining Asia*, edited by Theodore Huters, Cambridge MA: Harvard University Press.

Wang Hui (2014), *China From Empire to Nation-State*, translated by Michael Gibbs Hill, Cambridge, MA: Harvard University Press.

Wang Hui (2015a), "毛主义运动"的幽灵" (The Spectre of the Maoist Movement), 人文与社会 (Humanities and Societies), wen.org.cn/modules/article/view.article.php?4252/c18, accessed October 1, 2016.

Wang Hui (2015b), *The Rise of Modern Chinese Thought*, 3rd edition, Beijing: SDX Joint Publishing Company.

Wang Hui (2016), "中央民族大学讲座与讨论纪要: 如何诠释中国及其现代" (Minutes of the Seminar at the Contral Nationality University), http://wen.org.cn/modules/article/ view.article php/c8/82/p1, accessed April 20, 2016.

Wang Jiangyu (2017), "Legitimacy, Jurisdiction and Merits in the South China Sea Arbitration: Chinese Perspectives and International Law," *Journal of Chinese Political Science*, 22, pp. 185–210.

Wang Jiawei and Nyima Gyaincain (1997), *The Historical Status of China's Tibet*, Beijing: China Intercontinental Press.

Wang Jun (1995), 当代中国的文字改革 (Language Reform in Contemporary China), Beijing: Dangdai Zhongguo Chubanshe.

Wang Ke (2012), "多重的帝国和多元的帝国－－唐、辽、元的国家和民族" (Multi-layer Empire and Multi-empire—the Country and Nationalities in Tang, Liao and Yuan), www.aisixiang.com/data/56819.html, accessed September 2, 2017.

Wang Li (2008), 王力反思録: 王力遺稿 (Wang Li's Reflective Memoirs: A Posthumous Manuscript), Hong Kong: Beixing Chubanshe.

Wang Lixiong, (2002), "Reflections on Tibet," *New Left Review*, 14, pp. 79–111.

Wang Ning (2015), "Introduction: Global Maoism and Cultural Revolutions in the Global Context." *Comparative Literature Studies*, 52 (1), pp. 1–11.

Wang Shaoguang (2014), "正常'与'非正常死亡" (Normal and Abnormal Death), www.guancha.cn/WangShaoGuang/2014_02_17_203031.shtml, accessed September 17, 2017.

Wang Yi (2013), "季羡林之子诉北大要求其返还市值亿元文物字画" (The Son of Ji Xianlin Took the Peking University to Court Wanting to Recover Antiques and Historical Art Products Worth of Hundreds of Millions of RMB), news.163.com/13/0320/01/8QCGUQM200014AED.html, accessed April 18, 2017.

Wang Zheng (2014), *Never Forget National Humiliation: Historical Memory in Chinese Politics and Foreign Relations*, New York: Columbia University Press.

Webster, Norman, (2013), "Reflections of a China Correspondent," *Journal of American-East Asian Relations*, 20, pp. 301–6, https://tinyurl.com/ybqhg8va, accessed March 25, 2015.

Wei Se (2006), *Xizang Jiyi*: *Ershisan Wei Qilao Koushu Xizang Wenge* (*Tibetan Memories: 23 Venerated Old People Talk About the Cultural Revolution in Tibet*), Taipei: Dakui Wenhua.

Wen Bei (2015), "文革中疯狂一时的'西纠'" (The Once Crazy Xijiu During the Cultrual Revolution), www.mzfxw.com/e/action/ShowInfo.php?classid=18&id=43818, accessed April 14, 2017.

Wen Tiejun (2005), 三农问题与世纪反思 (Rural Issues and Reflection on the Past Centuries), Beijing: Sanlian Shudian.

White, Hugh (2016), "South China Sea: After the Hague Ruling, What's Next?" *East Asian Forum*, https://tinyurl.com/y7843jnn, accessed July 27, 2016.

Wieringa, Saskia (2016), "How Should Indonesia Resolve Atrocities of the 1965–66 Anti-communist Purge?" *The Conversation* https://theconversation.com/how-should-indonesia-resolve-atrocities-of-the-1965–66-anti-communist-purge-57885, accessed February 28, 2018.

Williams, Michael (1999), "Chinese Settlement in NSW: A Thematic History," A Report for the NSW Heritage Office of NSW.

Wolin, Richard (2010), *The Wind From the East: French Intellectuals, the Cultural Revolution, and the Legacy of the 1960s.* Princeton, NJ: Princeton University Press.

Womack, Brantly (1991), "In Search of Democracy: Public Authority and Popular Power in China," in *Contemporary Chinese Politics in Historical Perspective*, Cambridge: Cambridge University Press, pp. 53–89.

Wong, Edward (2009), "Report Says Valid Grievances at Root of Tibet Unrest," *New York Times*, July 5.

Wong, P. Christine (2003), "Legacies of the Maoist Development Strategy: Rural Industrialization in China from the 1970s to the 1990s," in Law Kam-yi (ed.), *The Chinese Cultural Revolution Re-considered: Beyond Purge and Holocaust*, New York: Palgrave Macmillan, pp. 203–17.

Woods, Jackson S. and Bruce J. Dickson (2017), "Victims and Patriots: Disaggregating Nationalism in Urban China," *Journal of Contemporary China*, 26 (104), pp. 167–82.

Worsley, Peter (1982), "Non-Western Medical Systems," *Annual Review of Anthropology*, 11, pp. 349–75.

Wu, X. and Song, X. (2014), "中国经济转型中的民族分层: 新疆维吾尔自治区的证据" (Ethnic Stratification Amid China's Economic Transition: Evidence from the Xinjiang Uyghur Autonomous Region), *Social Science Research*, 44, pp. 158–72.

Wu Lengxi (1995), 忆毛主席：我亲身经历的若干重大历史事件片断 (Remember Chairman Mao: Several Important Historical Events and Episodes that I Was Personally Involved in), Beijing: Xinhua Chubanshe.

Wu Si (2009), 潜规则: 中国历史中的真实游戏 (Qian Guize the Real Games in Chinese History), Shanghai: Fudan Daxue Chubanshe.

Wu Yiching (2014), *The Cultural Revolution at the Margins: Chinese Socialism in Crisis*, Cambridge, MA: Harvard University Press.

Xi Jinping (2014), *The Governance of China*, Beijing: Foreign Languages Press.

Xi Jinping (2016), "Speech at the 95th Anniversary of the Establishment of the CCP," news.sohu.com/20160702/n457421465.shtml, accessed August 16, 2017.

Xie Baohui (2014), *Media Transparency in China: Rethinking Rhetoric and Reality*, London: Lexington Books.

Xie Chesheng (2013), "内地近20年文物破坏程度比文革时严重" (The Destruction of Chinese Cultural Relics is Worse in the Past 20 Years than the Cultural Revolution), news.ifeng.com/mainland/detail_2013_10/23/30564217_0.shtml, accessed April 18, 2017.

Xie Chuntao (1990), 大跃进的狂澜 (The Raging Years of the Great Leap Forward), Zhengzhou: Henan Renmiin Chubanshe.

Xin Hutuchong (2014), "纳闷，季羡林凭什么登上如此高的地位" (Puzzling for Why Ji Xianlin Has Ascended to Such a High Position), Qiangguo Luntan http://bbs1.people.com.cn/post/2/0/0/141603202.html, accessed April 18, 2017.

Xinhua Wang (2013), "揭秘1954年毛泽东为何要请辞国家主席" (Revealed, Why Mao Wanted Step Down from the Position of the President of the PRC), http://news.xinhuanet.com/book/2013-01/07/c_124195446.htm, accessed February 7, 2017.

Xinhua Wang (2017), "李白究竟何许人也？汉人, 胡人, 还是混血儿?" (Who is Li Bai? Chinese, Foreigner or Mixed Blood?), news.xinhuanet.com/world/2015-10/18/c_128330628_3.htm, accessed September 17, 2017.

Xu Hailiang (2000), "'三五''五五'期间水利建设的经济效益," (The Economic Effects of Irrigation Constructions During the Third and Fifth Five-year Plan Periods), wenku.baidu.com/view/fdc9d305cc17552707220833.html?from=search, accessed October 5, 2016.

Xu Zhuoyun (1984), 西周史 (History of the Western Zhou), Taipei: Lianjing Chuban Shiye Gongsi.

Xu Zhuoyun (2009), 我者与他者：中国历史上的内外分际 (Us and Them: An Analysis of the Boundary Between the Inside and Outside in Chinese History), Hong Kong: Zhongwen Daxue Chubanshe.

Xuan Wen (2017), "孙经先与杨继绳直接对话:'饿死三千万'弥天大谎被当场戳穿" (Dialogue Between Sun Jingxian and Yang Jisheng: The Monstrous Lies of 30 Million Famine Death Was Punctured on the Spot), mzd.szhgh. com/maoshidai/2014–07–11/56759.html, accessed April 8, 2017.

Yahuda, Michael (2005), "Bad Elements," *The Guardian*, June 4, p. 4.

Yan Changgui (2015), "康生的秘书谈康生" (Kang Sheng's Secretary Talks About Kang Sheng), http://blog.sina.com.cn/s/blog_a2a6f7000102vt76. html, accessed April 20, 2017.

Yan Hairong (2015), "Interviews with Zhou Zhe and Liang Zhe (周哲 梁哲), Global Protest Against Monsanto, Whither China's Agriculture?" www. szhgh.com/Article/health/zjy/201505/84820.html, accessed August 15, 2017.

Yang Dali (1996), *Calamity and Reform in China: State, Rural Society, and Institutional Change Since the Great Leap Famine*, Stanford, CA: Stanford University Press.

Yang Jisheng (2008), 墓碑 -中國六十年代大饑荒紀實 (Tombstone: A Chronicle of the Great Famine in China in the 1960s), Hong Kong: Tiandi Tushu.

Yang Jisheng (2012), *Tombstone: The Great Chinese Famine, 1958–1962*, introduction by Edward Friedman and Roderick MacFarquhar, translated by Stacy Mosher and Guo Jian, New York: Farrar, Straus and Giroux.

Yang Liangxu (2009), "曝光揭秘"大跃进"档案" (Revealing the Secret of the Great Leap Forward Archives), http://bbs.creaders.net/politics/bbsviewer. php?trd_id=357868, accessed July 3, 2009.

Yang Shangkun (2001), 杨尚昆日记 (The Yang Shangkun Diaries), vols. 1 and 2, Beijing: Zhongyang Wenxian Chubanshe.

Yang, Songlin (2013), 总要有人说出真相—关于"饿死三千 (Guanyu E Si San Qian Wan—Someone Will Have to Tell the Truth—on the Famine Death of 30 Million), Hainan: Nanhai Chubanshe.

Yang Zihui (ed.) (1995), 中国历代人口统计资料研究 (Zhongguo Lidai Renkou Statistic Information on China's Population Throughout Its History), Beijing: Gaige Chubanshe.

Yao Yang and Wuyue You (2016), "China's Unfinished Gender Revolution," *East Asia Forum*, https://tinyurl.com/ybcs2tpc, accessed September 14, 2017.

Yi Guoming (2017), "拷问双重标准的香港司法审判" (Question the Double Standard of Hong Kong's Judicial Sentencing), www.m4.cn/opinion/2017– 02/1323346.shtml, accessed February 20, 2017.

Yu Jiaxue (2017), "李锐终于走到了末路" (At Last Li Rui Has Reached His Dead End), www.szhgh.com/Article/wsds/history/184.html, accessed September 16, 2017.

Yuan Ritian (2009), "李锐和胡耀邦同流合污之谜" (The Secret of How Li Rui Connived with Hu Yaobang), bbs.creaders.net/politics/bbsviewer.php?trd_ id=378691, accessed September 22, 2009.

Zagoria, Donald (1973), *The Sino-Soviet Conflict, 1956–61*, Princeton, NJ: Princeton University Press.

Zhang Deqin (2006), '催人惊醒的改革大教训' (Wake Up to the Lesson of Reform), *Tianxia Luntan*, www4.bbsland.com/forums/polotics/messages/1523163.html, accessed September 5, 2006.

Zhang Guangtian (2016), "Cong Jingju Geming Kan Xin Zhongguo De Wenhua Baofu" (The Culture Ambition of New China: From the Perspective of the Peking Opera Revolution), www.360doc.com/content/10/0919/23/3472983_54990790.shtml, accessed September 15, 2016.

Zhang Guoliang, Shao Guosong, and Nicholas David Bowman (2012), "What is Most Important for My Country is Not Most Important for Me: Agenda-setting Effects in China," *Communication Research*, 39 (5), pp. 662–78.

Zhang Jie (2009), "原中顾委委员周惠谈李锐与庐山会议" (The Former Member of the Chinese National Consultative Commission Talks About Li Rui and the Lushan Conference), bbs.tianya.cn/post-no05-147664–1.shtml, accessed August 18, 2017.

Zhang Jie (2017), "致李锐的一封信: 请和历史对质" (A Letter to Li Rui: Please Confront the History), http://bbs.sogou.com/481362/U6ZPjmr7OCIKBAAAA.html?p=40030400&dp=1&w=04000000&dr=1, accessed September 17, 2017.

Zhang Shuguang (1995), "腐败与贿赂的经济学分析" (An Economic Analysis of Corruption and Bribery), in Zhang Shuguagn (ed.), 中国经济学: 1994 (Chinese Economics: 1994), Shanghai: Shanghai Renmin Chubanshe, pp. 166–83.

Zhang Weiying (1997), "有些腐败的存在，不是最好的也属次优" (The Existence of Some Corruption, Even Not the Best it is Suboptimum), in Zhang Wenming, et al. (eds.), 中国经济大论战 第二辑 (Big Debates on China's Economy, vol. 2), Beijing: Jingji Guanli Chubanshe, pp. 260–70.

Zhang Wuchang (1997), "以资产换特权，促进私有化" (Use Property in Exchange for Privilege, So As to Promote Privatization), in Zhang Wenmin, Song Guangmou, Zheng Hongliang et al. (eds.), 中国经济大论战 第二辑 (Big Debates on China's Economy, vol. 2), Beijing: Jingji Guanli Chubanshe, pp. 268–9.

Zhao Gang (2006), "Reinventing China Imperial Qing Ideology and the Rise of Modern Chinese National Identity in the Early Twentieth Century," *Modern China*, 32 (1), pp. 3–30.

Zhao Jie (2011), "少数民族对中华文化的重要贡献" (Important Contributions Made by the National Minorities to the Chinese Culture), http://theory.people.com.cn/GB/49157/49165/15794525.html, accessed September 17, 2017.

Zhao Suisheng (2004), *A Nation-State By Construction: Dynamics of Modern Chinese Nationalism*, Stanford, CA: Stanford University Press.

Zhao Tingyang (2011), "Rethinking Empire from the Chinese Concept 'All-Under-Heaven'," in W. A. Callahan and E. Barabantseva (eds.), *China Orders the World: Normative Soft Power and Foreign Policy*, Washington, DC: Woodrow Wilson Center Press, pp. 21–36.

Zhao Tingyang (2016), 惠此中国: 内含中国的天下 (Benefitting China: All Under Heaven Including China), Beijing: Zhongxin Chubanshe.

Zhao Yuezhi (2008), *Communication in China: Political Economy, Power and the Conflict*, New York: Rowman & Littlefield.

Zhao Ziyang (2007), 赵紫阳软禁中的谈话 (宗凤鸣 记述) (The Zhao Ziyang Talk When Under House Arrest (Recorded by Zong Fengming)), Hong Kong: Kaifang Chubanshe.

Zheng Yongnian (2017), "郑永年：'占中'判决于香港前途，IPP 独家专访" (An Exclusive Interview with Zheng Yongnian on the Sentence Related to Occupying the Central and the Future of Hong Kong), IPP Official Weichat, www.kaoder.com/?m=thread&a=view&fid=1005&tid=445709, accessed September 17, 2017.

Zhongguo Nongtian Shuili (1987), "中国农田水利" (Chinese Irrigation Resources), in 中国统计年鉴 1 (China Statistics 1), Beijing: Shuili Dianli Chubanshe, pp. 25–43.

Zhou Suzi (2012), "百岁学者周有光谈政治" (The Hundred-Year-Old Scholar Zhou Youguang Talks About Politics), blog.sina.com.cn/s/blog_8dcf2398 0102x4pi.html, accessed January 16, 2017.

Zhu Jianguo (1998), "张志新案还有秘密" (There Are Still Secrets About Zhang Zhixin), https://tinyurl.com/yasvybas, accessed September 17, 2017.

Index